THAT'S RUFUS

THAT'S RUFUS

A Memoir of Tar Heel Politics, Watergate and Public Life

RUFUS L. EDMISTEN

McFarland & Company, Inc., Publishers
Jefferson, North Carolina

All photographs are from the author's collection
unless otherwise noted.

Library of Congress Cataloguing-in-Publication Data

Names: Edmisten, Rufus, 1941– author.
Title: That's Rufus : A Memoir of Tar Heel Politics, Watergate and
Public Life / Rufus L. Edmisten.
Other titles: That is Rufus | Memoir of Tar Heel Politics,
Watergate and public life
Description: Jefferson, North Carolina : McFarland & Company, Inc.,
Publishers, 2019 | Includes index.
Identifiers: LCCN 2019015321 | ISBN 9781476677972
(paperback : acid free paper) ∞
Subjects: LCSH: Edmisten, Rufus, 1941– author. | Politicians—North
Carolina—Biography. | Watergate Affair, 1972–1974. | United States. Congress.
Senate. Select Committee on Presidential Campaign Activities—Officials and
employees—Biography. | Lawyers—United States—Biography. | North Carolina.
Department of the Secretary of State—Biography. | North Carolina. Department
of Justice—Biography. | Lawyers—North Carolina—Biography. | North
Carolina—Politics and government—20th century. | United States—
Politics and government—20th century.
Classification: LCC F260.42.E36 A3 2019 | DDC 324.2092 [B] —dc23
LC record available at https://lccn.loc.gov/2019015321

British Library cataloguing data are available

ISBN (print) 978-1-4766-7797-2
ISBN (ebook) 978-1-4766-3676-4

Front cover image: Rufus Edmisten at the Watergate hearings,
with Senator Sam Ervin in the background (author's collection);
U.S. Capitol © 2019 Shutterstock

Printed in the United States of America

McFarland & Company, Inc., Publishers
Box 611, Jefferson, North Carolina 28640
www.mcfarlandpub.com

Table of Contents

Acknowledgments

My list of thank-yous will be long, because it is the plethora of remarkable people I have known in my life that have made it, and this book, possible.

I want to begin by thanking the extraordinary Linda Harris Edmisten. As people who know me well have said so many times, she deserves the highest medal for love, patience, refusing to dwell on the dark side, and in my case, pardoning me for multiple stupid acts. She often says to me, "When I make a promise it is for life." I can attest that she is as good as her word. Linda Harris Edmisten keeps her promises, and I am a lucky man that she does.

In the early stages of formulating what this book would be, I asked a vivacious young lady I met at the stable where Linda rides if she might help me get some of my stories down. Tammy Biondi made a good start in putting some things together for me before unforeseen circumstance took her out of state. I can't say enough good things about Catherine Oliva, who also worked on the first draft of the book. I remember well the smoky night at Havana Cigar Bar in Raleigh when Representative Suzi Hamilton recommended Catherine, her childhood friend. Catherine is so bright, and so well-read in North Carolina history and politics. Thank you, Catherine!

When I needed someone to take the transcripts Catherine and Tammy produced and create a book from them, Fran Tracy-Walls of the North Carolina Archives and History Office's Special Collections branch recommended a friend and former colleague of hers for the job. It was in this way that I met Nancy Carter Moore, historical researcher and wordsmith extraordinaire. Nancy has an infectious laugh and a wicked sense of humor that brightens my days. Nancy worked closely with me to create the book you're reading now. Thank you, Nancy! Thanks, too, to Nancy's husband Mark Anderson Moore, who recommended McFarland & Company, an Appalachian publishing house that did a wonderful job and made the process easy for us.

So many people in my early life have been so good to me. My mama and daddy, to whom I owe everything I am. My teachers and coaches were important. Jack Gross was my high school football coach and once told me, "You're not really that big of a boy but you have a lot of heart and determination." I never forgot that. Mrs. Elizabeth Elliott, my high school English teacher, who gave me encouragement throughout high school and when I was at the University of North Carolina at Chapel Hill. Dr. Hadley Wilson, our physician in Boone, encouraged me to work hard and succeed; Professor Ray Dawson, my political science teacher at the university, taught me so much and later worked with me when I was attorney general and Secretary of State, advocating for our beloved university before the General Assembly.

Dr. Bernard Boyd, my Old Testament literature professor, had a huge impact on my life. I took his class because I thought it would be a crib course and it turned out to be one of the most difficult and inspiring courses that I had ever taken. Dr. Boyd walked in every day and told us that "everything makes a difference." He was right, and I never forgot it. Thanks to Danny Edwards, my roommate at Carolina, whom everyone called Remus because they liked to call us "Rufus and Remus." We fought like banty roosters but we were very close. Later he became Lt. Daniel Edwards, United States Green Beret.

The staff members of Senator Sam J. Ervin, Jr.'s office helped a young mountain boy learn the ropes of the Capitol in so many ways. I'm grateful for Pat Shore, May Davidson, Judge Bill Creech, and a host of other people from my Washington days with Senator Ervin.

My Watergate colleagues are legion and most of them, like Mike Carpenter, Gene Boyce, John Elmore, James Stewart and Walker Nolan, have earned accolades in their chosen fields. Many of my Watergate buddies have played significant roles in my professional and personal life since those heady days of Watergate in the early 1970s and I thank them. I would be remiss if I forgot to mention Barbara Kennedy, who was one of Senator Inouye's staff people loaned to the Watergate Committee. Bob Landreville, a Capitol Hill police officer who looked out for me and later visited me when I was Attorney General, was another great help. He could fix anything.

I also want to thank all of my George Washington University law professors—except the one who gave me that D. In all seriousness, our professors knew that we night students had to work harder and "hang in there," but they didn't cut us any slack, and I now know that they were preparing us for the tough times in life. Many thanks to the "Lion of the Senate," the late Senator Edward "Ted" Kennedy, who served on all of the Ervin judiciary subcommittees and showed up without fail, always well prepared. We later became cigar buddies. Senator Kennedy's cigars were considerably classier than my usual cherry-flavored Rum River Crooks. (God, they were awful.) He never told me where his cigars came from but I suspect they came from an island off the coast of Florida. Senator Kennedy was the epitome of courtesy and bipartisanship, and was well-respected by his colleagues—traits we could use a lot more of today, in and out of government.

I am grateful to all those volunteers who helped me win the Democratic nomination for the North Carolina Attorney General's office in 1974, especially Dr. John Dees, whose son Fred Dees was my first driver. Fred later became a top-notch State Bureau of Investigation agent. Thanks to all of my wonderful staff members during my ten years as Attorney General, including Andy Vanore, my chief deputy, who never feared to tell me things I should not do. I wish I had listened to him more often. Had I won the governorship I intended to appoint Andy to the North Carolina Supreme Court. Edwin Marion "Eddie" Speas, Jr., who is a brilliant lawyer and who was the best at handling crises; Grayson Kelly, who started his state legal career with me and as of this writing just left his job as the chief deputy attorney general under North Carolina Attorney General Josh Stein; Grayson's dear mother, Rosa, told me that her son would make a great member of my legal team and she was right.

Many thanks to all those SBI agents who accompanied me on my travels throughout the state and to different parts of the country: Harry Knight, who became a good friend. His stories were hilarious and his laughter was contagious. He loved to come home with me to the mountains of Boone where he amply partook of Mama's bountiful feast. Mama often said he was like another son to her, and he returned her affection. Rod Knowles and his wife, June, were wonderful, refreshing people. Rod was always calm under pressure. During my ten years as attorney general there were so many smart, kind, and gracious public servants. I wish I could name them all and give them thanks personally.

The race for governor brought together an eclectic group of hundreds of outstanding people, each distinct from the other and from all corners of the state. To name them all would fill at least a third of this book. Here are a few: Johnsie Setzer, the co-chair of my campaign. If I ever had a second mother it was Johnsie. She was so generous with her time, money, and encouragement. Garland Garrett from Wilmington, the other co-chair, who traveled back and forth to Raleigh so many times he wore out two sets of tires and put fifty thousand miles on his car. When "Governor for Life" Jim Hunt came back from political death for his encore terms as governor he named Garland his department of transportation secretary. George McCotter from Lillington, a southern gentleman who was politically astute and well connected, did a great job. Phil Stanley, the "Mountain Man" from Ashe County, who, along with Tim Smith, a successful local developer, flew me across the length and breadth of this state so many times I lost count. Had I become governor I would have asked Phil to be my Secretary of the Department of Transportation, and I would have asked Tim to be Commerce Secretary.

How could I ever forget when my loving brother David essentially moved to Raleigh in 1984 to help me with the campaign? All my staff loved him because he was so kind and generous. David forgave me for my human frailties and mistakes but was tough on me when he had to be. I was crushed when he died in the summer of 2000.

My friend Michael Carmichael is indeed unique, with his political brilliance and sophisticated approach to solving problems. Michael was a member of my Attorney General staff. In my race for governor in 1984 he changed our approach from the usual country bumpkin campaign to one that featured nationally known advisors, pollsters and fund-raisers. Michael was responsible for recruiting both Joe Napolitan and strategist and advisor Ray Strother, who was known as the best television advertisement producer in the nation. I liked Ray because he never tried to force me to say or do anything I did not believe in.

Sharon Rose is my country girl from Harnett County who was my loyal campaign assistant in 1984. She later worked at Duke University and recently retired. W.W. Billy Yeargin from Oxford, North Carolina, was a valuable campaign aide who knew the ins and outs of the agribusiness world. He later taught at Duke University. Dick Carlton, my chief of staff during my secretary of state years, and a brilliant homegrown political strategist, recently observed that our 1984 gubernatorial campaign altered the way such campaigns were run North Carolina. I remember he said, "You really weren't supposed to win the primary, but you did." Dick has remained a devoted friend all these years. Also unforgettable: Naomi Henry from Winnabow, North Carolina, who was another "second mama" to me. She checked to make sure I looked okay and had nice looking suits for the campaign. Naomi is in her nineties now and still clear as a bell.

Many thanks to Galen Newsom, whom I first met when I was Attorney General, and to Otis Jones, the legendary sheriff of Cumberland County, who convinced me to make Galen an SBI agent. Galen had a keen investigative mind and scared me with his loyalty. He was bad about wrecking state law enforcement cars, and he loved the thrill of the chase. He was my chief enforcement officer at the Secretary of State's office. Tragically, he died of pancreatic cancer. His wonderful wife, Penny, has been an invaluable help with the Super Kids program for so many years. Keith "K.W." Whitfield, who has been with me for many years, beginning in my secretary of state years, is a true friend. Keith possesses a special brand of law enforcement excellence and is exceptionally cool under pressure. During his time with me Keith defused many tension-ridden moments with a calmness that amazed me. He has shown tremendous dedication to the Super Kids Foundation and the Jim Valvano Kids Klassic, which was founded over thirty years ago by the late Jim Valvano, Don Shea,

Crockett Long, Tommy Baker and me. K.W. Still takes care of "old man Rufus," and I love him. Thanks, too, to Lash "The Whip" Wrightenberry, who hails from Burlington and has been a faithful friend and supporter since my political career began, through the good and the bad alike. He is a true Masonic brother.

Thanks to my friend Rosemary Parker, a fine young lady with two wonderful boys, Danny and Nate. David "Crockett" Long, who may be short in stature but has the biggest heart of any human being I have ever met. He has been my supporter and buddy since my early days as attorney general. He has faced head-on many tragic events with tremendous grace and dignity. Crockett will always have a special place in my heart for his unwavering support for and kindness to those less fortunate than he—like the children who fight for their lives at the Duke Hospital for Children. His staunch commitment to the Super Kids has made it possible for more than thirty-five young people to earn college degrees.

Thanks to Trey Garrett, the character of all characters, who is like a son to me. Trey is the son of my dear friend Garland B. Garrett, Jr., whom I got to know when he was the campaign manager for then-incumbent United States Senator C. Everett Jordan. I came to know Trey when he was a young boy and found him bright, articulate, and full of life. When I became secretary of state Garland suggested I look at hiring Trey. I traveled often and Trey accompanied me on many trips. He learned that there was more to the job than just driving me. Everywhere I went, in any venue, people invariably had problems with some government agency and many were desperate for some kind of help. To them at that moment their plea for help was urgent because they had been ignored and turned away from some faceless bureaucrat. Trey is a great problem solver. Each evening after a trip Trey got busy solving problems that had that day been brought to my attention by con- stituents who saw me as their last chance. He was doggone good at finding help for these people and became the voice they needed to effect real change in their lives.

Jerry McLaurin is one of those princely guys who came to my aid after my loss in the governor's race. Jerry not only befriended me, he also asked me to do legal work for him when I really needed it. He was an early supporter of the Super Kids Foundation, giving generously of his time and fortune. Jerry is a successful businessman who I call "Mr. Dependable."

Thanks with all my heart to Tara Britt, who never stops doing good things for people, especially the unfortunate. Also, she never stops talking. I first met Tara during my guber- natorial campaign in 1984 when she was a volunteer for the campaign. I could always count on Tara! During the primary we had campaign events at the Velvet Cloak Inn. I asked Tara to take her Rufus sticker off and go upstairs to my competitor Eddie Knox's suite and see what kind of food they had. I wanted to make sure we had better food. She came down a while later and said, "Oh my gosh, they have huge shrimps up there. Your food is better, but their shrimps are much larger." I made a call to Earp's Seafood Market and within thirty minutes, we had the largest shrimp. Remember, I won that primary! Maybe the way to the voter's heart is through his stomach!

Tara's work on the Rare Disease Council has been nothing short of amazing and so is she. Along with the work we do together, we have a lot of fun. We have a running joke that if I die first, she's in charge of the herd of professional mourners. I told her I want a pack of exquisitely beautiful women in black cocktail dresses and stiletto heels tearing their hair, gnashing their teeth, beating their breasts and screaming in unison, "Rufus! What are we going to do without you?" Tara will do a great job at that. She is a brand of her own. Once you've met her you'll never forget her.

Many thanks to Dr. Bruce Cairns, one of my heroes. Bruce is the head of the Jaycee

Burn Center at the University of North Carolina Medical Center where he has been responsible for many miracles. I met Bruce shortly after I engaged in a fund-raising effort for the burn center. Knowing of my reputation as "The Singing Attorney General," the Jaycees insisted I cut a record that they could sell to raise money for the center. The "ham" in me was absolutely delighted. I recorded "Honkytonk Angel" and believe it or not it sold about two thousand copies. It was a 45 rpm record—that should tell you how long ago that was. Dr. Cairns has been a trusted friend and advisor and serves as the chairman of the Rare Disease Council. He is a great man.

I can't talk about the beginning of my prosperous, post-political-office career without mentioning Cheryl Mattingly, who has been my loyal Executive Assistant for over twenty years. Her winning personality, huge heart, and capable ways have always inspired confidence in me. Cheryl and I have always had a good relationship. She knows me well enough to know by the time I come up the stairs what kind of mood I am in. She has always been a lovely host and greets everyone with warmth and sincerity. She feels less like an employee and more like an extension of me by now. I am very grateful for Cheryl's loyalty to me all these years.

Thanks to all the wonderful Super Kids Foundation volunteers who believe that we have better lives when our young people are adequately equipped with a good education regardless of their station in life. Bill Carl, a longtime friend and co-founder of the Golden Corral, was my finance director in the 1984 campaign, and was invaluable. My wife, Linda, successfully played matchmaker by introducing Bill to Caroline MacNair. I also owe a lot to John Thompson, a bright, no-nonsense guy who knows how to have a good time. My only regret is that I did not meet John sooner than I did. He and I make a great team on our many projects.

Sincerest thanks to Henry Turner, the vice president of Altria (formerly Phillip Morris), who is my lifeline to a company that has kept me as a consultant since my first days in private practice. Along with Henry Turner, I want to thank Regional Director John Rainey, a fellow North Carolinian who worked with the attorneys general and who has generously campaigned for me as a volunteer. Anna Smith Felts is among my best friends. I have known Anna since her father was a legislator in the late '70s. Anna has been so helpful to me in so many ways, and is boundlessly generous with her time and talent, especially with the cause that is closest to my heart—the Super Kids Foundation.

Steve Gillooly deserves many thanks simply for being the giving soul he is. He is also a strong supporter of the Super Kids Foundation, and my good friend and companion. Kim Tucker, one of the sharpest lawyers I know, has been a wonderful co-consultant with me for ALTRIA. She is a constant source of joy and a darned good lobbyist. Wayne Hurder, former director of the Driver's License Division of the North Carolina Department of Transportation, has graced me with his friendship and companionship on trips nobody wants to take. Wayne is a fascinating person, a natural intellectual who is as down-to-earth as he is brilliant and artistic.

Next to Senator Ervin I probably admired United States Congressman Walter B. Jones, Jr., more than any political figure I have known because he didn't test which way the political wind was blowing and then act like a paper airplane on that wind. Despite great efforts and huge expenditures his detractors have failed to knock him out of office. Sadly, Walter passed away in early 2019.

My heartfelt thanks to Justin Williams, who has been a loyal companion and gardening buddy, and whose refinement gives him a keen appreciation for the good things of life. Thanks for your help, Justin. State Representative Duane Hall, a stellar member of the

North Carolina House of Representatives, has been a staunch supporter of mine in all my runs for public office since his days at the University of North Carolina at Chapel Hill. Duane has my sincere admiration because he can truly reach across the aisle and work with his Republican colleagues to get things done. I so appreciate all his help over the years.

I would be remiss if I didn't thank Jim Jenkins, reporter and writer extraordinaire, who has known me as long as some of my oldest friends and became my friend not long after I met him. Jim has poked fun at me a lot in his columns but has never been malicious or mean-spirited. In addition, his insight into politics is nothing short of astounding. This is the man who told me, long before the election, that I was going to lose the 1984 North Carolina governor's race to Jim Martin. He said "Jim Martin is going to win this. He's going to sneak up on you." I have always been able to trust Jim to tell me the truth without pulling any punches. I wish there were more men in the news business like Jim Jenkins.

Lastly, I want to say that I agonized over this section because I just knew I would have to leave some people out. There have simply been so many people who have given me so much over so many years. If you're not mentioned here, it is not because I don't remember you, or that our stories are not important to me. I'm afraid I will have to once again trust in the kindness my friends have shown me so often and so well and hope that you can forgive me if I left you out.

Preface

For over fifty years I have had numerous people say to me, "You should write a book!" I've always responded, "I might just do that someday." However, since I left government in 1996 and began my private law practice, I have worked full time with no intention of slowing down and have stayed busy with a number of social, political, and charitable activities. With my hectic schedule, I asked myself, "How in the world will I ever find time to write a book?" My wife and dear friends said, "Just do it."

In 2016 I decided to get on with it. I certainly would not have to rely solely upon memory, since my dear daddy had saved virtually every scrap of paper related to my life. It's a good thing he was so interested in what I was up to, because I'm sure I would not have remembered it all. Over the years after his death, people sent me newspaper articles and other materials, many covering events in my life that I had largely forgotten. These discoveries only heightened my desire to get it down on paper. The fact that I had made it to age seventy-five definitely motivated me, too.

I resolved to set aside a few hours here and there to get my many stories down on paper. As time went on, I began to realize there was a lot to this process, and I do want to say that without the professional help of Tammy Biondi, Catherine Oliva and Nancy Carter Moore the book might not have been written. Having them listen to my stories, record them, and put them to paper motivated me to keep going. I probably would not have finished this book by sitting in a room, typing alone, or talking into a recording device. It would have been like talking to a blank wall. I've spent most of my life engaging others, listening, talking, conversing, bantering, and debating. With their attentive listening and thoughtful suggestions Tammy, Catherine, and Nancy enabled me to turn my many stories into this book.

I lay no claim to being a wordsmith. I have always tried to use simple words to express myself. I have never forgotten the admonition of my Appalachian High School English teacher, Mr. Bill Ross, who spoke with a dramatic flair and often said in class, "I don't expect you to speak with the eloquence of Franklin Delano Roosevelt or write a sentence worthy of the praise of Harper Lee, but I do expect you to stop mumbling and write a sentence with a subject and a verb in it."

I have tried for accuracy. We all know that over time accounts of people and events can take fanciful turns due to frailties of the human memory and the richness of the human imagination. Who among us has not embellished a story a bit for dramatic impact? I am no exception, but I have made an honest effort to be accurate. I take full responsibility for any mistakes. Having said all of this, I feel like I had all I could do to get my story down while I still possess some wit and maybe even a little wisdom. I sincerely hope nobody is disappointed.

Introduction

Little did I know when I graduated from the University of North Carolina at Chapel Hill in 1963 and headed to Washington, D.C., the following fall that I would end up playing a visible role in the investigation of the scalding drama of the Watergate conspiracy.

When I went to work for Senator Ervin in early 1964 the awe and splendor of the Capitol nearly overwhelmed me. There at close quarters was the entire governmental process and there, right there in the flesh, were many of the famous officials I had read about or seen on television. To a country boy who had grown up on a farm in the mountains of North Carolina milking cows at 5:30 every morning, the experience hardly seemed real. Each day was loaded with surprises and opportunities I never could have imagined. Heck, I could walk right up and say hello to the likes of Senator Everett Dirksen and yes, even Teddy Kennedy.

Still, none of these luminaries could compare with my boss, Senator Sam J. Ervin, Jr. Mind you, Watergate did not burst upon the political scene until about eight years later. Our years on the Subcommittee on Constitutional Rights and the Subcommittee on the Separation of Powers served as a kind of training ground for handling the Watergate investigation. No human being could have been more superbly prepared to chair the Watergate Committee than Senator Sam J. Ervin, Jr. When faced with the decision, Senator Mike Mansfield didn't have to think twice about who should lead this deeply sensitive investigation that snared so many people who should have known better. Among them was our president, Richard Milhous Nixon, who should have kicked those sycophants out of the White House when they began talking about all those juvenile antics to run up big election numbers. As Senator Ervin wisely said in *The Senate Watergate Report*:

> Watergate was not invented by enemies of the Nixon administration or even by the news media. On the contrary, Watergate was perpetrated upon America by White House and political aides, whom President Nixon himself had entrusted with his management of his campaign for re-election to the Presidency, a campaign which was divorced to a marked degree from the campaigns of other Republicans who sought election to public office in 1972. I note at this point without elaboration, that these White House and political aides were virtually without experience in either government or politics apart from their association with President Nixon.

Most of the key players in the conspiracy came from privileged background, relative to most Americans. They had extraordinary educational opportunities and most came from affluent, well-connected families, so need or disadvantage cannot be cited as the cause of their straying so far from the law. Examining how those who had climbed so high still fell so far from grace makes an interesting study.

The contrast between my mountain upbringing and North Carolina youth and the cosmopolitan, sometimes erudite, always fast-paced days in Washington, D.C., had great impact on me, deeply informed my life, and shaped the man I became. Experiencing such diverse places and people carved a new perspective into me. I have thoroughly enjoyed recalling and relating the events of those days.

It was also deeply satisfying for me to write about a childhood that simply seems magical to me now, all these years later. I loved the simplicity of the time, the scents, sights, and sounds of the farm—the wonderful aroma of newly mown hay, the sun-warmed, clear blue sky, and the absence of constant noise. Sure, the farm work was hard. But memories of those bucolic afternoons spent roaming the woods pretending to be Daniel Boone or Davy Crockett are the ones that return again and again. Having spent countless hours sitting behind Old Bill and Dinah as they pulled the horse-drawn mowing machine, I can attest that there is no greater perfume, no scent that is sweeter or more wondrous than freshly mown hay. To this day I can remember the smell of that hay as it dried on a warm summer day.

I look back at those years when a trip to Boone to Belk's department store was an adventure, and getting a new shirt and a pair of shoes for school or church was downright exciting, and I realize that there is a good side to having *fewer* choices. Today we seem to be under siege by all the choices life offers, and it can be overwhelming.

I also want to pass on some of my harder-won lessons, and what I think of as some good principles for living that have emerged in my life. These principles certainly had their start in my days at the Three Forks Baptist Church, and deepened as I grew older. No doubt my family and wonderful friends were instrumental in my learning the following:

- Choose carefully the friends *you* want to hold dear—real ones, not those thrust upon you.
- Practice empathy. *Listen* to others, and try to understand their point of view.
- Don't forget to thank those who have helped you—the ones who didn't desert you during the hardest times. Then thank them again.
- Avoid the most poisonous trap of all, which I call hubris. Never get drunk on whatever power or advantage you may possess. It will blind you and might just ruin your life.
- Develop and maintain your spiritual side, whatever that may mean to you.

These are the tools that have helped me navigate a life that has been, mildly put, full of ups and downs. It is my sincere hope that they might help others, as well.

1

Issuing the Watergate Subpoena

On the afternoon of July 23, 1973, the City of Washington, D.C., broiled in the summer sun and buzzed with anticipation. I'll never forget how hot and humid it was. The events of this day would come to test the United States Constitution, and the subpoenas in my hand would set this process in motion. I knew this event was making history.

A current of tension ran through the city. Television cameras and microphones flooded the Senate Office Building as photographers and journalists from around the country and the world gathered to witness our emergence and procession to the White House. It was so insufferably hot that day my suit actually changed colors. I was soaked.

Earlier that afternoon a staff of fine attorneys drew up the subpoenas and related documents and when they were finished I simply decided that I would deliver them to the President. I knew that I had worked hard, and I decided that this would be my Andy Warhol moment—my "fifteen minutes of fame." Although nobody had asked me to deliver the documents, nobody objected. I admit, my ego was in high gear. I didn't view this as a simple messenger service, I knew this would be an important event in the history of the nation. Our fine administrative staffer Lydia Gregg was typing up the subpoena so we could deliver it. I got a little antsy as I waited, just from pure adrenaline. The day, after all, was wearing on. I kept checking with her because I couldn't help myself. When she finally handed it to me, I noticed that there was correction fluid over the first three letters of former Attorney General John Mitchell's name. I said, "Don't you think we should retype it?" Lydia said, "Hell, no ... I've done it twice and I'm not doing it again. Take it. They can read." I took it. You didn't argue with Lydia.

It was late in the day but there was still much light left. The air was thick and still, and we all felt a little wilted. I asked the loyal and faithful Polly Dement, who had always been so helpful, to go down there with me. Terry Lenzner said he was coming too, and that was fine with me. I notified Pete Blackston, who was deputy chief of police for the Senate, that we would need a car. When it arrived Capitol Police Officer Bill Kennedy had the wheel. The side of the car said "US Capitol Police," and it was the only police car in the procession of what seemed like hundreds of news people. Every news media person in the Watergate press corps seemed to be there when I emerged from the basement exit of the Old Senate Building.

We walked in a phalanx of Capital Police officers, I with the worn folder in my hand. My heart was pounding. This was hefty stuff for a boy from the outskirts of Boone, a small town in the mountains of North Carolina. As I climbed into the smelly police car, I reminded myself that it was a good thing I was there for such a respectable reason. We proceeded down Constitution Avenue at a creep. There were large clusters of reporters bristling with cameras and microphones. Traffic was unusually light that day, and the biblical image of the parting of the Red Sea came to mind as the car cut through the crowd. Traffic progressively became heavier as we moved along and more press joined us. We spoke in hushed tones as we turned onto Pennsylvania Avenue, and I resolved that I would not let the original copies of the subpoenas go until President Nixon's staff handed me signed copies. As we passed the White House I imagined it hung with funeral bunting, so weighty was the occasion.

It's funny, the things that go through your mind at times like these. I had on a suit that the manager of the Belk's department store in Boone gave me. He had said, "I want to give you a suit to wear on TV." It was just a coincidence that I was wearing that suit, but I remember thinking, "I hope he notices." Renowned law school Professor Charles Allen Wright and Mr. Leonard Garment waited to receive us at the front door of the Executive Office Building. Wright was an advisor to President Nixon and Garment was Counsel to the President and a close confidant. I was just wondering if the President would join us when Leonard Garment said we had just missed him.

After the usual pleasantries, I read the entire exhortation of the subpoena to President Nixon's attorneys. Afterward I marked the subpoenas to show that they received them.

Delivering the subpoena to President Nixon's office on a sweltering summer day in Washington.

"Take this one," I said, "and you gentlemen please sign it. Make a copy and bring it back to me." In a mischievous impulse, I handed the pocket-sized copy of the constitution that I always carried to Garment and said, "You might need a copy of this down here too." Garment took it with a smile. My job finished, the next move was up to President Nixon. We bade his staff a civil goodbye and waded through the throng of newspaper and television reporters. At that time I did not know that this was the first time Congress had issued a subpoena to a sitting president.

We got back into the car, dripping with sweat and lightheaded from the heat and the import of the day. When I got back to the Hill I put away the copy of the subpoena somewhere and forgot about it. Some years later, my wife, Linda, was looking through boxes in the attic and came to me and said, "Are these things important?" I said, "Good Lord, that's the original subpoena."

I moved it to my office where I kept it until I began to fear it might become stolen, lost, or damaged. Then I called my friend President Tom Ross of the University of North Carolina at Chapel Hill and he sent Southern Historical Collection personnel to come view the subpoena. They were overjoyed to have it for the collection, judging from the chorus of "wows" that went up. I knew the subpoena belonged to the public and not to me. I do have a very good copy of one displayed in my office. You can even see Lydia's Wite-Out on it.

2

My Mountain Home

I was born in in the summer of 1941, just a few months before the bombs fell on Pearl Harbor. I was born in Watauga Hospital, a solid 1930s building that was three stories tall and almost as new as I was. It still stands today as Founders Hall on the Appalachian State University campus. I was named Rufus Lige Edmisten because I had a grandfather named Rufus Farthing Edmisten and another grandfather named Lige Holler. Still, I can't fully fathom how Mama could take an innocent little baby boy with a cute pumpkin moon face and give him a name like Rufus Lige. Though I must admit, the name has served me very well in politics. In politics you want to be remembered, and it's hard to forget a name like Rufus. I've often joked that my first name, spelled backwards, comes uncomfortably close to a phonetic spelling of "suffer."

My memories begin about 1945 because I was not one of those prodigies who can recall things from when they are tiny babies. I don't remember anything from before I was about four years old. I remember that Mama told us that she had hung out a big load of wash to dry on the day before I was born. She was used to having kids, so being "with child" didn't slow her down much. She had already given birth to four children before she had me.

Now, I'm not trying to compare myself to Abraham Lincoln, but the house that I grew up in really did start out as a log cabin. My family updated and added to it over the years, but the wood framing and the tin roof on the house were built around the original log cabin. You could see that a thick paper was applied to the logs on the inside to cover them up. Downstairs was a big living room with creaky wooden floors, the room where Mama and Daddy slept, and the kitchen. Central to that level was a big wood stove. We needed to keep the embers going all the time during harsh winters, which occur with some regularity in Boone, North Carolina.

The kitchen had a Good Hearth cook stove that my mama told me was the sensation of the neighborhood when a team of horses rolled it up to our house in the early 1930s. She was proud of it. It had all the fancy gadgets: a water tank, warming ovens and everything. All of us boys had to chop stove wood for it, which is an art unto itself. You had to start with the right wood and cut it to just the right length, not too long and not too short. We stayed busy, among other chores, chopping stove wood and carrying it into the house. That stove was a beautiful thing, and it is a family heirloom, now residing in my brother Joe's summer farm house in Avery County, North Carolina. Every time I look at it I can see my mama cooking and canning.

Upstairs the boys' large bedroom had three beds for five of us boys. It might seem that we would have wanted our own beds, but in the winter time we all wanted to sleep a couple-three to a bed because it was warmer. My younger brother, Baker, and I used to fight over which one of us got to sleep with the bigger boys because they gave off so much warmth.

In the winter the only heat we had was from the wood stove downstairs, and it was always down to embers by the time we got to bed. It was so cold in that house in the wintertime when the wind howled and the snow fell furiously that it was like living in a Jack London story. *White Fang* comes to mind. We even had a picture of a wolf up on the wall above the bed. As I watched the snow filtering through the cracks in the walls of our poorly insulated house, I thought about that wolf and cringed. When I was little that picture scared the daylights out of me.

On snowy nights my brothers and I watched in wonderment as the tiniest, barely visible line of snow came into our room through the wall, crawled down to the floor, skipped a beat, and proceeded across the floor and up the side of our bed. Sometimes it blew right across us. Some-times the line of snow blew back and forth

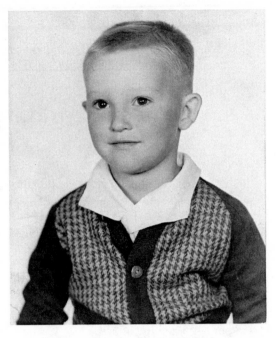

At age 4, a punkin-headed little boy.

across the bed in a thin, delicate zigzag. It was a great form of entertainment to us and we made a game out of seeing how long the line of snow could get without one of us breaking it by accident. We would say that whichever one of us broke the line brought bad luck. Of course, Baker was very young then, and that little squirt was always wiggling around. He was frequently the unlucky brother who broke the line of snow. When he did, we would tease him and threaten to him that we were going to throw him into the river off of the spot we called "The Big Rock" at our regular swimming hole.

Our only sister Betty had a smaller room upstairs. She had to go through the boys' bedroom to get to her door. But right around puberty I kind of liked it when Betty used to bring friends home from school and they would all trot through our room on the way to her hers. It was the highlight of my day when I got to see Ruby Hartley glide through our room on the way to Betty's. She was just heavenly. She had a blonde halo of hair and looked like she had just come out of a Breck Shampoo ad. She inspired in me a decades-long infatuation with Breck Girls. Years later when I was a student at Carolina, when other boys had racy pinups, I had some of those glossy Good Housekeeping headshots of lovely girls up in my dorm room. Shampoo ads!

Down the hill from the house was a spring house and I can remember when I was six or seven years old, going down to carry water back to the house. The spring house was built of wood, and a sparkling little spring ran down the hill and through a cement trough (called a "race") inside. There, cooling in the springhouse, would be our milk, butter, cheese, and anything else we needed to keep cold. People have asked me how we made do, growing up without a refrigerator. Well, in the wintertime, it was cold enough in Boone that you could just set stuff right outside the door and it would stay cold. Sometimes, the house itself was cold enough that you could just put items in a corner of the house and they'd stay cold. The springhouse mainly got used in the spring, summer and fall because the whole world seemed to work as a refrigerator during the winter.

I'm about seven years old in this photo taken in front of our ancestral home place with my brother Baker on the right and a distant cousin on the left; on the porch, my mysterious Uncle John and other relatives from out west.

When you grow up on a farm there is something new and exciting happening every single day. Every day! For example, when the fierce little banty hens were broody and sitting on their eggs (no one dared try to steal an egg!), I jumped out of bed as soon as the sun came up, so excited to see if they had hatched yet! What joy when I saw the first babies peck their way out! They were about the size of a golf ball, their mamas about the size of my fist. I worried myself sick at the thought of foxes and possums getting those little chickens. And they did get them sometimes—out of a half a dozen or so chicks, only one or two would usually survive. When the babies started following their mama around that's when the fun really began.

We were not impoverished in any sense of the word, but by today's standards we would be considered poor. We didn't feel poor because there was always an abundance of food on our table and just about everybody around us was in the same boat except for a few wealthier people who lived uptown.

My mama was a human food processing machine who began with a seed and by her loving touch took that seed all the way from the packet through the planting all the way to the bounty of the table. My mother also canned everything that would hold still. She could have won the McCall's Magazine canner of the year award just about every year. Oh my goodness, could she can. Everything known to mankind, everything Mama could put in a jar, got canned. We had a root cellar with row after row of green beans, beef, and sausage, and jar after jar of pure lard, which is what made our biscuits and fried chicken taste so good. Nobody ever went hungry at our house.

When Mama canned or put up tomatoes, pickles, jelly, green beans or anything she would say, "Well, you know, Aunt Lena might get low on some of these," and she would can some extra. She always thought of others, and didn't waste a thing. My daddy did the same with the produce he grew. He'd drive around the neighborhood with a load of fruits and vegetables, giving the extra stuff away to those who could use it.

We also had some luxuries, which included our wonderful cathedral radio. We would listen to that radio most nights, and it was always on during one of the most memorable

rituals of my childhood: the Saturday night bath. Every Saturday, we'd
have that radio on, and it might be
tuned to WBT, a station out of
Charlotte. Sometimes, and this was
strange for a mountain family, we
could get the Philadelphia Philhar-
monic on it and at other times, we
listened to a program called *The
Firestone Hour*.

As the radio played Mama
heated the water on the stove to fill
the large washtub we used for our
baths. She put cold water in and
then added three or four pots of hot
water, just enough to heat it up to
a tolerably warm temperature. We
did not linger in the tub, we hurried
up! No horseplay or splashing
around was allowed, either. My
older brothers told me that when
they started horseplaying around
in the tub, they got taken to the
woodshed to get a strapping, so I
didn't press my luck during bath
time. Nowadays, it's common to
bathe or shower every day, sometimes several times a day, but when
I grew up in Boone in the mid–
1940s, that Saturday night bath was
it. We bathed on Saturday night to
be sure we were clean for church on

With Mama (Nell Holler Edmisten), Daddy (Walter F. Edmisten), Grandma Nan (Nancy Ray Edmisten), little brother Baker, and our dogs in yard on a Sunday afternoon.

Sunday morning, and just washed up a little all the other days.

My daddy worked two or three jobs to hold things together—just one reason I admired him so very much. Once we boys were old enough to go to the bottomland to do the hard farm work, we left at about 8:00 a.m., usually accompanied by an Ichabod Crane–like figure named Dillard Idol. Dillard wore Jack Rabbit or Pointer brand bib overalls, had one gold tooth, sparking blue eyes and ears big enough to hang a sack of cabbage on. He was always chatting and telling jokes in a rough kind of language. Dillard had never gone past the third grade. His mama would say, "Dillard never had no sense because he never got no learning." To me, Dillard Idol was a fascinating example of one type of true mountain man.

Dillard married Mae Dollar. He liked to joke that he had married money. Mae used to get embarrassed about Dillard sometimes because if he started drinking he would wind up hollering and buck dancing. Silly as he got when he was into the moonshine, Dillard took his responsibilities to the animals on the farm seriously. One time we went to Charlotte to visit someone who was in the hospital, and Daddy carried Dillard with us. It took longer than expected. Well, the later it got, the more Dillard fretted. "I need to get home," he kept saying. Finally, about three o'clock, he just started to bawl like a newborn calf. No matter

With Grandma Nan, Daddy, Mama and Baker in the new house.

what anybody said, Dillard just kept crying and say he needed to get home. As it turned out, the reason he was so distraught is because he needed to milk his cow before dark. Dillard was a creature of the seasons and of nature. He knew the cow would be uncomfortable, and that it was his job to milk her. Until Daddy got him home, Dillard was inconsolable. I can still remember how that cow would come thundering down the hill to Dillard when he called her, she was so happy to see him.

When he worked Dillard did not take many breaks. He said he might just as well "get on with it." When I got big enough to work in the fields it was usually me, my three older brothers, Dillard, and one other hand. The wages for the hands were fifty cents an hour. Five dollars was a big day's pay. Of course we Edmisten boys didn't get paid since it was our daddy's farm.

Dillard had a pocket watch, but I don't think he really knew how to tell time. He always knew when it was lunch time, though, because that's when the wail of the Tweetsie train cut sounded. Starting in 1882 this train ran on a narrow-gauge track from eastern Tennessee through the wilds of the Appalachian Mountains to western North Carolina. Boone was the last stop on the line, added in 1919. My mother told about sneaking rides to Boone on the train when she was a girl. After the line shut down in the 1940s, the Robbins brothers bought the train from country singer Gene Autry. The long, moaning whistle for which the train was named was a distinctive blast that could be heard for miles around.

When we heard that whistle we all stopped work and trudged up the rocky, rutted road to our house where Mama had laid out a midday meal that was something to behold.

She usually had at least three meats, five to six vegetables and, of course, the best biscuits that ever touched the lips of a human being. She made them the old-fashioned way, using lard, which was much maligned during the "low saturated fat" years but is now the top choice of the best chefs for baking. Even though they bake with lard, these celebrity chefs could still use a lesson or two from my mama on how to make a real biscuit.

There were always at least two desserts, and my favorite was blackberry cobbler in season. The season, of course, dictated our options. Dillard always asked for and fully expected a jar of sourwood honey with his biscuits. You would have to watch him for sticking his knife or spoon into the honey jar. That was a no-no. You didn't put your personal utensil into a jar and if Mama caught him she would quickly give him a separate spoon.

Dillard loved Mama's cooking. He got a little bit of everything on his plate and furiously mixed it up into one great big huge pile and cut it up in a kind of hit-or-miss way. It would look like a hay mound on his

Good old Dillard Idol in his Sunday best overalls engaged in a considerably one-sided hug with brother David's wife, Claudine, who we call Deanie.

plate. Now as I mentioned, Dillard only had a tooth or two, and as he laughed and talked while he ate, the spit and food would fly. When I later read some scenes from Chaucer in college I thought of Dillard at dinner. I want to be clear, though, that even though Dillard seemed like a clown much of the time, he still possessed a cunning and timeless capability that is a hallmark of what I think of as a true mountain man.

We all marveled how much Dillard could eat, especially with his lack of teeth (he had a gold one right in the front). If we snickered Mama would look at us in a stern way that meant, "Don't make fun. He's part of the family." We loved Dillard because he was like Daddy's adopted brother. One day, I asked, "Dillard, why do you mix up all your food that way?" He said, "Well, it goes in the same way and goes out the same way." That seemed logical to me.

Another fascinating character from my childhood was Craig Austin. We knew Craig's family because we all attended the Three Forks Baptist Church together. Craig's daddy was James Austin. James was the one who, at Christmas time, would remind everyone "Don't forget to pick up your Christmas pokes." The pokes were little brown paper bags full of treats for us. They would typically have an orange, an apple and a peppermint stick in them. We always hoped that they would have more candy in them than fruit. I think the Austins were some kind of distant cousins of ours. Everybody seemed to be related somehow.

Craig was a brilliant young man, a great scholar and writer, somewhat unusual for our area. Craig had some sort of disorder that had stunted his growth so that he was only about five feet tall, and of odd proportions. I remember he had a little squeaky voice. People made fun of Craig, not realizing they had a genius in their midst. In everyday conversation, you wouldn't think that he had enough sense to get out of the rain, yet you could bring up Voltaire and Craig would give you a dissertation on the French Enlightenment, or eighteenth-century French history, literature and philosophy. He could go on for hours. To me he was like a miniature Sam Ervin, because of his love of reading and breadth of knowledge in terms of history and literature. He had an infectious, gnomelike laugh. And he could write! Craig became a published author and really captured the flavor of Boone in his writing. He was really a star, though he was often very lonely because he was so different. Many days Craig used to walk down to the house to get Mama Nell's cooking. Around twelve noon Mama would say, "It's about time for Craig to be coming down the road here, because he comes about dinner time."

My mama's brother Uncle John Holler was one hell of an athlete. He lettered in several sports. Uncle John was the youngest of Mama's brothers. The earliest I remember him was after he returned to Watauga County after being a first string player for the Washington Redskins in the National Football League. By that time he had attained mythical proportions in my mind. From all I've heard from my relatives and others, Uncle John had been a standout fullback for the Appalachian State Mountaineers at Appalachian State Teachers College. In 1948 he was drafted by the Chicago Cardinals. After that he had played for the Washington Redskins and the Detroit Lions. The Washington Redskins were it! You could hear all of their games on the radio, even in Boone. He played for three different teams. Pretty astounding! It was rumored that Charlie "Choo Choo" Justice, who gained his nickname when a coach said he ran "like a runaway train," once said that being hit by John Hollar was like being hit by a freight train.

After playing professional foot-

My Uncle John Hollar, multidiciplined athlete and professional football player, was bought from the Chicago Cardinals by the Washington Redskins in 1948. The *Redskin Review* of that year says he was 6'2", ran intercepted passes 103 and 105 yards for touchdowns, and won 14 letters in high school and 11 in college in football, basketball, and track. We were mighty proud of him.

ball, Uncle John came back to Boone and worked with the Federal Land Bank Association. For years he invited me to come address the members in one of my public capacities. Those gatherings always drew quite a crowd of people from surrounding counties because they gave away good prizes, toasters and such. (Used to be banks were always giving people stuff for opening accounts. Blenders, irons, all sorts of things. There's not much that folks like better than winning a prize.) Uncle John remained quite a famous figure in North Carolina because he was such an outstanding athlete. I was very proud of him.

I'm really proud of all my siblings. My brother David had an illustrious career in law enforcement. He was with the Bureau of Alcohol, Tobacco and Firearms division of the United States Treasury Department and rose up through the ranks to become the national director of the BATF. Because I knew the city, with its steaming heat and sizzling political intrigue, I said to David, "You'll last one summer. Being an old mountain boy like me, your thermostat was set at 72 degrees when you were born. Once the temperature exceeds that for any length of time you feel like you might blow to pieces." Later on I was up there visiting and I said, "How do you like it?" He said, "I can't stand it." Sure enough, David only lasted one summer in Washington then returned to Boone, where he retired. My brother David (along with his wife, Deanie) was one of the most civic-minded persons I have ever known. We lost him to cancer in 2000, and I miss him dearly.

Tragically, some years after he retired, David was out playing golf and thought he had sprained his arm, so he went to the doctor. In that visit they diagnosed him with cancer that had invaded most of his body. He went through all the horrible things that people with this savage disease must go through.

My next brother was Paul, who appointed himself the black sheep of the family. I told him, "No, I'm going to try to achieve that rank myself through my conduct in life." Some might say I achieved my goal. Still, Paul reigned supreme as the black sheep of the family for years—and I say that with great affection. As a youth Paul was a rowdy fellow who often got into scrapes. Mama used to say he fought like a banty rooster. He held various supervisory positions all over the country and finally settled in Concord, North Carolina, working at the Philip Morris tobacco plant from which he and his wife both retired with good strong pensions.

Paul married a lady named Alice McIntire, who I always secretly referred to as Silas, because of the Bible stories about Paul and Silas. Once, one of the NASCAR drivers of whom I was a fan visited Paul's farm and home with me. We were admiring the miniature donkeys that Paul raised and the driver, who had heard me refer to Alice so many times as Silas, asked for her by that name. "Hey Paul, where's Silas?" It was both funny and embarrassing. Paul didn't bat an eye and said, "She'll be around shortly."

And then there is Joe, the third of the stair-step boys. Joe is the crazy one of the family, which he readily admits. Mama liked to say he was overeducated. Joe and his wife, Patricia, have advanced degrees in things I can barely pronounce. Joe has a doctorate in plant biology from the University of Georgia and for years taught Environmental Diversity at the University of West Florida at Pensacola. Joe lives in Pensacola during the winter and has a little farmhouse in the Montezuma area in the mountains of Avery County. Joe has been a successful academic and has worked for years as an environmental consultant. He has never lost the hallmarks of his mountain upbringing, and is an avid gardener. Joe is a fine man with a generous heart.

And then there is my sweet sister Betty, who was a teacher's aide for years. This program is one I adore because it helps teachers tremendously and benefits students in more ways than we can really know. Now aides are called teaching assistants, and there has been talk of doing away with them, which is just a terrible idea. Betty was always such a good friend and a wonderful sister. Her late husband Dick Church ran an auto repair shop called Dick's Garage where everybody knew you could get your old rattletrap fixed at a good price. Betty was a doggone good mechanic herself. They had three children they adored. Betty passed away in late 2018 and I miss her so. I talked with her so often, and I miss her sweet voice.

My little brother Baker is four years younger than I am. He has had an illustrious career in law enforcement. As brothers will, we fought a lot when we were growing up. We also had a lot of fun. Back in those days Boone got a lot of snow, and when it snowed we didn't have to do so much work around the farm. We had plenty of good tracks leading up to the old cow barn, as we called it. We'd pack it down with that sweet little tractor, then ride the tractor up the hill dragging the sled behind it, and then we'd sled down the slick hill, and use the little tractor to pull it back up. One day I kept yapping at Baker that he wasn't packing the snow right. I guess I had somehow missed the fact that Baker had grown almost as big as I was. All of a sudden he slid the tractor to a halt, jumped off, and beat the hell out of me, whacking me severely about the head, neck, and shoulders. He fought like a crazy man, finally releasing what had to be years of pent-up rage from

Sister Betty Edmisten Church and her cat Frisky in the 1940s near Boone, North Carolina.

receiving the same treatment from me that I had received from my older brothers. I left him alone after that. I didn't taunt him anymore.

Like all my brothers, he went to Appalachian State University and graduated from there. He first worked for the Bureau of Alcohol, Tobacco and Firearms, then came to the U.S. Forest Service, and was appointed United States Marshal for Western North Carolina by then-President Bill Clinton. Baker is retired and living in Boone. He's very nostalgic, as I like to say, "Lost in the '50s and '60s," and I love it. He now cans everything like Mama used to.

We called my mama's daddy Paw Lige and called her mother Maw Lige. Daddy's parents we called MaMaw (Grandma Nan) and PaPaw. Paw Lige lived just outside of town. He was a big landowner for the area. He owned a meat market and butcher shop in Boone City Market. The market's slogan was, "Fresh from the Stall to Y'all," which I always thought was very clever. When my parents were newlyweds, in the early 1930s, my daddy worked for Mama's daddy as a meat cutter.

Although I heard a lot about Paw Lige when I was growing up, I only have a faint memory of him because I was still young when he died. He was ruddy-faced and looked as if he had stepped out of a Vermeer painting. He had a 1947 International Harvester truck with gears that would grind. He'd pull up in the yard and say, "Come over here, you little turd" and give me a penny or sometimes a nickel. He was famous for saying, "Now don't spend that all in one place." He thought that was the funniest thing ever. He let me climb up in the cab of that truck with him and I was so fascinated because it had so many gears. Attached to the

Around 1957 with my little brother Baker in a rare moment when we were not fighting or playing.

steering column was the doohickey that changed the gear. You'd push it then you'd pull up and it might grind a little and off it went. Paw Lige could put that thing in low or high and double clutch it, and I'd be completely enthralled. I loved the noise it made, that grinding whine that only an old International Harvester truck can make.

I'd walk from our house over to Maw Lige's, which would sometimes make me sing "Over the river and through the woods to grandmother's house we go." Paw and Maw Lige lived in a big house with columns. After Paw Lige died Maw Lige lived all by herself in that huge rambling house where they had raised their kids. I remember that she had a spring house *attached* to the dwelling house! It was fancy, not like the spring house we had down the hill from our house. It was through a door off the kitchen and it had a plumbed race. Although she had a Kelvinator refrigerator in the kitchen, Maw Lige liked to use the spring house, I guess partly because it held more and partly because it reminded her of her youth. She said it made the milk and butter taste better, and maybe it did. I remember she also worried about wasting electricity when she opened the Kelvinator.

This house, with its big clean spaces and fancy springhouse, was quite different from the patched-up log cabin that my daddy took my mama into in the fall of 1929 when they were wed. My mother went from a rather well-off country home into one without running water. It was all for love. That's what Mama used to say about marrying Daddy: "That was love."

Now Betty went over and spent a lot of time with Maw Lige, and Maw Lige loved her a lot, though I personally thought I was Maw Lige's favorite of the Edmisten boys. I loved going to Maw Lige's house when I was little. It had all these nooks and crannies. It was bigger and fancier than most houses out our way. I thought it was so fancy! In the spring and summer I loved the second floor. (In the winter it was too chilly and gray.) There were old pictures and a wind-up Victrola that I would play records on. The second floor had the old bead board ceiling, wide heart pine floorboards, and fancy crown molding. Also on the second floor was Aunt Lou's room, which for some reason was a little scary. I barely remember her, but my sister Betty remembers her and says that nobody was ever allowed to go into Aunt Lou's room. We all still wonder why that was. Even still, Betty must have been in there because she remembers that Aunt Lou sat in her rocking chair a lot and that she had the skull of a cow on the wall. Aunt Lou had been a widow for a long time by the time she came to live with Maw and Paw Lige. It was different then because old people were not kicked to the curb. Family always had a place to stay. I still wonder about Aunt Lou and that cow skull up on her wall.

Maw Lige was a melancholy person. I don't remember many times when I saw her smile about anything. She didn't whine or complain, she was just often quiet and she usually looked sad. She suffered terribly from asthma, and she wheezed as she struggled to breathe. When I stayed at her house, her labored breathing sometimes woke me up and I would sit straight up in bed in the middle of the night scared to death for her. I thought, "Oh my gosh, she's going to die."

I was so afraid she might die. When she finally passed away, my mama said she had an autopsy and the results showed her heart was several times as large as it should have been because it had to work so hard just for her lungs to get enough air. Asthma runs in families. Betty had it too. It is a terrible disease, sneaky and debilitating. It can really wear a person down.

Paw and Maw Lige (Lige Holler and Betty Ethel Hollar.)

The butcher pen (now called a slaughterhouse or an abattoir) was the basis of a large part of Paw Lige's business. The butcher pen provided meat for his markets in Boone and Wilkesboro, and this was the basis for the wealth that distinguished Mama's family from Daddy's family. Of course the butcher pen also supplied meat for the family table. After Paw Lige died Mama's brother, Uncle Jones Holler, became the owner of the Boone meat market. Uncle Jones and Aunt Jenny lived across the road from Maw and Paw Lige's in a tiny, beautiful white house with two bedrooms. Their son Craig and I played together a lot when I spent the weekend with Maw Lige. I don't remember if she had a telephone. Maybe she did but back in those days, you'd go off and your mama and daddy didn't worry about you. Mama and Daddy wouldn't have known if I had been kidnapped or whatever, but things like that rarely happened in those days.

Uncle Jones was really good at pin-hooking, which consisted of bidding on and buying cattle before they weighed in at the auction from the sellers who were lined up waiting in their trucks and then selling them at auction in the hopes of gaining a profit. It's like a stock market with livestock. You could bring a cow in there that weighed 1,360 pounds that went for 18¾ cents a pound and he could eyeball it and tell you what it's price was before you could snap your fingers. Nobody could figure out how he did it. His mind was amazingly sharp for a man who couldn't read or write and was at least a few sheets to the wind most of the time.

When Uncle Jones made an offer he was taking a chance that the steer would bring more at auction than the fellow who brought the animal to sell thought it was worth. Pin-hooking was really a gambling enterprise when you come right down to it. The farmers liked it because they didn't necessarily have to stay until their cattle was weighed in and sold in the usual way, and Uncle Jones liked it because he might turn a bigger profit if he did well. He was a great pin-hooker and made money that way, and of course he owned the butcher pen. He was a brilliant man, but not a talker. He was more of a grunter. And his face was always red, for a number of reasons, not only because he was of Dutch origin and the blood showed through his skin more than it did in other men.

We had a lot of family spread out everywhere and everybody came visiting, many without any notice. Around the same time of year every year Mama would say, "Oh Lord, that crowd's coming from out west." Here was a woman who had to put up food for six young ones, and then on top of that, here comes the "out west crowd." That's how Mama and Daddy referred to them. They would come, and they would stay a while. If it got to be too much, Mama would call up Aunt Lena and say, "Lena, can you take them a couple of days early?" They were delightful people, and they were welcomed, but ours was a small, busy house. The Indiana kin would drive up in an old Studebaker, about a '47 or '48, Aunt Etta Foley and her daughter, Marietta, and her brother Jimmy. Everybody said the daughter was an "old maid" (don't shoot me—that was the term back then for women over twenty-five or so who had never married), and Jimmy never married either. So then, the Foley family would move around from Aunt Lena, to Aunt Lottie, to Aunt Nell.

It so happened that all of Daddy's sisters lived in the same place except for Aunt Lydie, who lived in the Aho community of Watauga County. Her name was Lyda, but we pronounced her name "Lydie." Aunt Lydie's husband, Uncle Marion, was a yeoman farmer. He chewed and dipped and the only little bit of money they made was off a patch of tobacco and a cow or two. I had four girl cousins over there, and though the family was just breaking even, all of them grew up and did so well. They all went to college, every single one of those girls. Cousin Eula May became a great teacher and so did Geneva. They all graduated from Appalachian State Teachers College and taught or had other careers.

Visiting them was one of our Sunday odysseys, a Sunday ride that we took. Most of the roads at that time were gravel, except the road to Blowing Rock. Aho is a settlement near there and my Uncle Marion used to tell a story about how it got its name. He'd say, "You know how this place got called Aho?" and I'd say "No, Uncle Marion, I don't". "Well," he'd say, "there was a traveler fellow one time, they told me his name was DeSoto or something like that. He was marchin' through here and he got real tired, and he sat down and said, 'I'm tired, and sighed 'Aho', and that's how it got its name."

It was fun to visit because there were all kinds of rocks and things to climb on. The house backed up on a steep mountain. No one wanted that land; no one would have it because it was tough to farm. But later on, when Aunt Lydie and Uncle Marion died, the girls inherited it and sold it for a good amount of money to people they refer to as "Floridy People," people from Florida who wanted to build houses on the land.

Another thing I remember about relatives who visited us is that every summer, this ghost-like person named Uncle John would appear from somewhere out west. It was a yearly ritual. He appeared, but then he'd get into the house and just hole up in there. He'd been out west working in the wheat fields or something, but then once the wheat season was done there'd be an announcement from my folks, "Uncle John's coming from out west." And he was The Phantom once he got to us. Where they put him, I don't know, he'd just vanish into the house, and stay for about a week, and then he'd levitate or do whatever he did and get over to Aunt Lena's house and then Aunt Lottie's house, the next house out, and then float over to spend a week with Aunt Nell—these were all Daddy's sisters. And he could get a month's stay out of that rotation, easy. I later thought, "This Uncle John's pretty smart because he gets to eat and sleep like this for a whole month every year without lifting a finger."

Our farm was small, about eighty acres, much of it mountainous—but we raised corn for the animals, cabbage to sell commercially, and we had our little allotment of tobacco. A half an acre allotment was nice Christmas money, maybe a thousand dollars a year. Cabbage farming was hard, messy work. The cart would straddle two rows and you would have sometimes six cabbage cutters, those guys walking along with a sharp knife. They cut the cabbage, throw it in the cart, and you'd have two behind, and probably two on the side and old Bill would just walk along methodically, you didn't have to say "Bill, stop" or "Go." He was a smart devil, but he'd bite you if you weren't careful. We'd load the cart up and then you bring it back to a station in the field where we had the scales. We bagged them up and put the bags on the scale, hoping to get fifty pounds or somewhere around that. And then we'd stack those up ready to go to market, and I would haul them on the tractor over to J.C. Goodnight's produce company. That was a tough job.

I was lucky as a little boy because so many of my aunts and uncles and cousins lived nearby. When my Grandfather Farthing Edmisten and my Grandma Nan both died without a will, the land was divided among all their heirs, my daddy and uncles and aunts. There were about a hundred acres in all there. Over time, Daddy managed to buy this land from his four sisters and one brother, all of the land that comprised the Edmisten farm. Regardless, three of his sisters still lived all in a rough circle within a two-mile radius, and I walked that circle countless times over the years. They lived in the little community of Perkinsville.

So many times as a young boy I set out on a pretty day and stopped first at Aunt Lena's. Aunt Lena was married to a man named Robert Shull who owned a motorcycle shop. Also at Aunt Lena's were my cousin Ruby Michael and her boy, Charles Michael, who was one of my gang of fun guys. My cousin Charles Michael was the marbles champion of the whole community. To play marbles, we would find a patch of dirt with no grass on it and then take a stick and draw a circle. Now if you were allowed to play, you had to be sure that no one was trying to sneak in a big, weighted marble, what we called a "log roller." And Charles had this beautiful, flawless way of putting a marble in his hand, and turning his wrist with a fluid, practiced motion and studying that circle and the marbles in it. It reminded me of someone getting ready to make a painting or achieve some other artistic greatness. So this circle had my marbles in it, Buzzy Baumgardner's marbles and Bobby Wilson's marbles, and there would be Charles, cranking that hand over in his professional manner. He would be semi-drooling because his concentration had overridden some of his social graces, and then he would let that marble fly loose like a cannon shot. That marble would fly loose and it was just marbles scattering like a covey of quail. Somebody would always start shouting: "You've got a log roller! A log roller!" But Charles wasn't cheating. He was just that good at the game.

Nobody ever beat Charles at marbles, but we went through the routine anyway. Everyone had his own little sack of marbles. They were your marbles, and you could take them and go home any time you wanted. And you were responsible for their safekeeping. I'd hide mine: I had a place to hide them in the stockyard right across the street from Aunt Lena's house. Nobody wanted to lose his marbles.

After we'd played marbles, we'd usually go into Aunt Lena's house and get something to eat. Each of my aunts had a signature dish. Aunt Lena usually didn't have anything fancy, no cookies or anything like that. It was usually something left over from a previous meal. Lunchtime was called dinner in those days, and it was the middle of the day. If we had something left over after dinner we'd just put a cloth over it and leave it for supper. We wouldn't put in the refrigerator; we'd just pull that cheesecloth over top and let it sit. Aunt Lena might have some dessert left over or some of her great grape jelly made from the grapes that grew out along her wood house. That jelly was just meant for her sumptuous biscuits. Aunt Lena had a refrigerator and other modern amenities, but everything at her place was still done in a very old fashioned way because those girls had come up hardscrabble. They were born in the same house that I lived in as a little boy, but it was less improved then. All those ladies, my father's sisters, lived to be very old. I think it might be because they worked so hard.

After Aunt Lena's, I'd move on down the road and stop in to visit Aunt Lottie. She was married to Bynum Greene, and he was the proprietor of Greene's Service Station. Uncle Bynum was doing well enough to have almost been one of the town people. He was sort of like Paw Lige, in that he was definitely a cut above an average farmer and could have just about fit into the Boone crowd. Now Aunt Lottie had some of the luxuries neither we nor Aunt Lena had, because of the store. Uncle Bynum was also a county commissioner for a few years. Daddy called him "Swifty" Greene. I don't know why he called him that, but that's what he called him. "Swifty" Greene was a Republican, but Aunt Lottie remained a steadfast Democrat.

Aunt Lottie was Uncle Bynum's second wife. His first marriage was to Aunt Blanche, who was Aunt Lottie's sister. When Aunt Blanche died long before I was born, Uncle Bynum married Aunt Lottie. I suppose Uncle Bynum wanted to stay in the family because of our outstanding gene pool.

As soon as I walked into her house, Aunt Lottie would come up with some cookies for me—usually Oreos because they owned the store—served with ice-cold milk or something equally delicious. I remember the brand new 1950s linoleum floor in her house. It was a pretty fancy house, fancier than Aunt Lena's or Aunt Nell's. While I ate my cookies and drank my milk, Aunt Lottie would talk to me. She was very smart and read *The Charlotte Observer* every day, so she was always up on her current events. Just the same, she often got all of us kids mixed up. She'd see you and she'd go "David Jones, John Paul, Joe Allen? Oh, Rufus Lige!" Aunt Lottie was a lovely, generous person. It was easy to see why she'd get us all mixed up. My older brothers were all close in age, like stair steps, as they used to say, until you got to Betty, and then there was a gap of about nine or ten years, and then came me and Baker. Betty was one of my best buddies. We used to practice dancing together. Boy, could we shag!

The whole process of visiting the aunts and cousins on my route took several hours. So there I was, about six or seven years old, wandering around the neighborhood on my own, but never really alone because there were scads of cousins and aunts and uncles all around me. This was a whole neighborhood full of people who cared about me and looked after me. I wonder how many children have that these days.

After Aunt Lottie's I'd drop by Aunt Nell's house. She usually had leftovers under a cheese-cloth just like Aunt Lena did, but Aunt Nell also made apple pie that was just out of this world. And she almost always had it, no matter when I showed up. In those days it seemed like everybody was ready for a visitor at any time with a glass of cold milk and a piece of pie or something just as nice. Nobody announced when they were coming for a visit, either.

Sometimes when I showed up at my aunts' houses I had something to sell for my school. Most years, I'd have seeds to sell. A nickel pack of Ferry Morse brand flower seeds or bean seeds. After visiting Aunt Lottie, I would continue my route across Highway 421 to get over to Aunt Nell's house. Aunt Nell was always the last house on my habitual visiting loop. Aunt Nell had a mischievous chuckle and she'd always say, "How are you doing Rufus Lige?" Aunt Nell lived in a house at the end of the road, and her financial circumstances were less than the others. Her husband, Uncle Lloyd, was a wonderful, kind gentleman, a great big guy who worked for J.C. Goodnight's fertilizer and cabbage house. He just didn't lay up many worldly treasures in his life, so he and Aunt Nell simply didn't have much. I remember one time I had to sell a cheese cutter. It was a little metal thing with a wire strung across it. In our neck of the woods it was mainly used to cut Velveeta. But I knew Aunt Nell couldn't afford Velveeta, and she probably couldn't afford the cheese cutter because it cost a quarter, so I stuck it in my back pocket.

On the way home from my biweekly visits to my aunts I sometimes ran into my friends Bobby Wilson, Dallas Wilson, and Dean Wilson. Bobby's daddy was Alex Wilson, and Alex was a handsome fellow who had been in World War II. (Alex Wilson had what people then referred to as "shell shock" from being in the war, which is what we now call post-traumatic stress disorder, or PTSD.)

There were plenty of younger kids to play with on the way home, and we skipped rocks in the creek and treasure hunted and got into all kinds of things. By the time I got home it was supper time. Of course this was all before I reached the age when we had to go out and work in the fields. It may have felt like it, but it wasn't like prison labor. Daddy waited until a decent time in the morning to have us go out and work in the fields, and we didn't have to go to work until we were twelve or thirteen, depending on how fast we matured and how strong and healthy we were.

This little odyssey to visit my aunts was something that I haven't thought much about for years, but reflecting on it, I think about how wonderful it was. I can see each of my aunts clearly in my mind. They were always happy to see me coming. They all lived to a very old age and now they live on in my memory.

We had a distant cousin we used to play with from time to time, Kelly Joe Edmisten, but we called him Fat Jack because he went through a husky time when he was a boy. One time Fat Jack lost a finger to a lawn mower, and we tried and tried to find it so they could sew it back on, but we never found it. I loved Fat Jack. He began having terrible health problems in middle age and never fully recovered. I'm sad to say that we lost him recently. When he was in the Veterans Administration Hospital in Durham I went to see him and he was just as funny as he'd always been. His daughter Laney told me one day in a moment of frustration that Fat Jack said to his doctor, "I want to be dead—D-E-D—ASAP." Laney said the doctor had to leave the room to laugh, not because of what he said but how he said it. The day that I visited we were waiting for them to release Fat Jack to go home to his family. It's hard to know what to say at such times, so I did the best I could. Sitting at his bedside I said, "Fat Jack, I have enjoyed you. You're a wonderful man and you have the best daughter in the world. I sure wish we could have found that finger you lost to send along with you." We laughed just like old times. I really miss him.

On Sundays after church we got in the car and went to visit a relative or two, and if we kids knew what was good for us, we had to behave. And we did. What we did not do was run crazy around somebody's house, or pick up or handle their things. We were not to touch anything in somebody else's house. Kids today are different, but back then the rule was that you didn't touch *anything*. Before we got out of the car at anyone's house, Daddy would say, "Now you boys listen to me. Don't touch anything in there! And if they tell you to do something, you do whatever they tell you to do."

Sometimes we went to visit Daddy's only living brother, in Johnson City, Tennessee. (His older brother, my Uncle Will, died in the army during the catastrophic influenza pandemic of 1918.) On the way out there Baker and I would count cows. We always got into fights about who saw the most cows. Gray mares counted too, and if you saw one, you got ten points, but if there was a grave yard on your side you lost all your points and had to start over. Of course we found ourselves watching the other person's side more than our own to see if they slipped an extra cow into the count. Then it would be, "Daddy, he's cheating!" On the way back, the biggest treat was the Dairy Queen in Elizabethton, Tennessee. We had no such thing in Boone! We knew better than to ask about it, though, because the rule was, we only got to stop if we had been reasonably well behaved on the trip and *Daddy* decided that. I still get a wonderful, warm feeling whenever I see a Dairy Queen. Sometimes I stop just for old times' sake.

Aunt Johnsie was the funniest lady, always laughing, and Uncle Wade was a real practical joker with a contagious laugh, so they were lots of fun to be around. Uncle Wade could just look at you and crack up, and you would laugh with him. This was summer vacation for us kids. I especially loved going to Uncle Wade and Aunt Johnsie's because they did not farm. There was no farm work to do around their place! There were always plenty of fun things to do, though, and we got to take care of their goats. Uncle Wade worked as a delivery man and he could build anything. They had a large family with seven children and they lived in a tiny three-room house. Uncle Wade and Aunt Johnsie had a refrigerator and running water in their house but no indoor bathroom. Uncle Wade, being the jokester that he was, decided to build a three-holer outhouse. Now, for the uninitiated, a three-holer is an outhouse that has three holes in it, where three kids could sit at one time if they wanted to. (And who would want to?) For the record, I never shared that outhouse with anybody.

Barbara, John, and Gladys were the older kids. When we went to visit Uncle Wade and Aunt Johnsie, sometimes Cousin John, who was off at college, would come home to visit too. They were an amazing family. Most of them went to college despite being raised in such spartan conditions. Maybe for them it was just like it was for my family—everyone knew they were going to go to college, even if nobody knew how they were going to pay for it.

My Grandma Nan lived with us in a little room at the back of the house right next to my mother and daddy's bedroom. She was my daddy's mama. I thought of her bedroom as "The Mystery Room." You weren't allowed to go back there unless Grandma Nan summoned you. I adored Grandma Nan. Almost every day until I was about nine years old, she used to sit me on her knee, put on her spectacles and read Bible stories to me. She made those stories come alive. She even made boring parts interesting to me—like the books of Leviticus and Numbers, with all those rules and unpronounceable names. She always got those names right. I used to look forward to my times with Grandma Nan and learned a great deal from them. She read four or five pages a day to me, and I think that was why I was so good at Bible school.

Grandma Nan's only known vice was snuff dipping and tobacco chewing. Grandma

Nan dipped and chewed, and her favorite brand of snuff was Dental Sweet, which came in a glass jar. We drank our milk from those glasses. She also mail-ordered snuff that came in a little tin tube with a flower on it—Red Rose, I think it was called—and she also made her own chewing tobacco twists from tobacco grown on our own farm. When we went out to harvest the burley tobacco in the fall, Grandma Nan would tell us, "Now you boys bring me back some of those good pretty leaves." She wanted the bright gold burley leaf to make her twists with. She would have none of the lugs, which are those messed up leaves at the very bottom of the plant. She knew how to make the most beautiful twists. She braided those twists so that they looked like a perfect girl's ponytail. She knew exactly how much twist it would take to get her through the year. We would all try to see which one of us boys could be the one to bring Grandma Nan the prettiest leaves. It became a contest. She would pick this one or that one and the other kids would be jealous of the one whose leaves were chosen most often. Eventually she learned to make sure she chose leaves from each one of us so nobody's feelings got hurt.

Another thing that I remember from my youth was that we had lots of animals on our farm and grew most of our own food. We almost never went to the store, and when we did it was only to get the few items that we could not produce ourselves: flour, coffee for Mama and Daddy, sugar, and occasionally, "light bread." Light bread meant store-bought white bread like Merita or Sunbeam. Most of the time, we ate homemade biscuits or cornbread, so "light bread" was a huge treat, especially during tomato season when Mama would make tomato sandwiches. Nowadays, people swoon over homemade biscuits or cornbread, but in those days, everything was made at home, so store-bought food seemed really special. We were really a typical farm family in that respect. We bought very little at the store, but the meals were sumptuous. I don't know what it was about country folks in those days, especially my mama, but we didn't have just one type of meat on the table at each meal, we had two or three. There would be both a beef dish and a pork dish, or some fish that we had caught. Brother Baker was an avid fisherman, and one of our favorite things to eat on a cold Saturday night was fried trout and gravy. The fish would pop as it fried on that beautiful Good Hearth stove. A wave of goodness still comes over me when I think about those nights.

At about age 9 in 1950 with Grandma Nan. She was not in a costume; this is what she wore. Grandma Nan rarely smiled and had a hard life, but she loved us all.

Of course we got school, church and Easter clothes from Belk's a few times a year, and Mama could even make us shirts if she needed to. Now there were many more country people than town people where we went to school and everybody had hand-me-downs. If they got a little thin, sometimes Mama would take the decorative sacks we got when we bought feed from Perkinsville Grocery and make shirts for us boys. The chicken feed is what came in broadcloth that had patterns on it. I remember one time being made acutely aware of being looked down upon when somebody at school said, "Oh, you've got one of those homemade shirts on." I really felt embarrassed then, and I would try later to find something else to wear. I am now ashamed of being ashamed.

For entertainment, we played Rook. We were a Rook-playing family because Rook was not one of those sinful gambling games. It was good family fun. We'd sit at the big kitchen table and take turns because there were so many of us. Only four people can play a hand of Rook. Of course, a little nonsense or ruckus would threaten to break out occasionally, but to calm us down, all my daddy had to do was snap his fingers and look at us sternly. That was the cue he gave us that we were about to go over the edge and risk getting taken to the wood shed. With that foolproof warning system in place, we hardly ever got into any actual fights over the game. There was always a lot of loud talking and carrying on, though. Mama was a really good Rook player and I would usually try to get her to be my partner. I had lots of reasons for this, not the least of which was that I could tell when she held the Rook, which was the card that trumped everything else in the deck. She would try to keep a straight face, but anytime she got that Rook, her eyes would light up and she would get a cherubic expression on her face. She tried so hard to act like a hardened gambler but she couldn't help the tiny, tiny quirk in her mouth she'd get when she knew she had a good shot at winning. When I saw that hint of smugness, I could tell for sure that she was holding the card. If she was my partner when this happened, so much the better. Mama may have inadvertently taught me the skill of watching people's faces to tell how they really feel and what is coming next.

When we were kids playing on our own, we invented our own forms of recreation. My father didn't require us to work in the fields until we were a decent age, around twelve years old, so we had lots of years full of playtime before we were conscripted to the Walter Edmisten Chain Gang. We never had any trouble coming up with ways to entertain ourselves. Baker and I were close playmates and we invented all kinds of toys and games. We dreamed of having toys like the Roy Rogers gun and holster which we heard advertised on the radio, but in our day-to-day lives, there was no such thing. We had to make our own toys. Instead of the Roy Rogers' gun, we made toy rifles out of old wood from around the house and farm and played cowboys and Indians. Sometimes, if we didn't have a toy in hand, we played Tarzan and truly did swing from the grapevines that draped the trees on our farm. Baker and I had wonderful fun. We hung around with a whole bunch of the neighborhood boys and it was just pure joy. One of our constant playmates was Buzzy Baumgardner. He and a few of the other neighborhood boys were always up for adventures. There were four or five of us who would roam the hillsides like a pack of wild dogs. We looked for treasure or pretended that there were caves full of Indians in the sides of the hills. There was one big cave in the area that took me years to get up the guts to explore. When I finally did I found a bunch of bones piled up in there. When I saw those, I thought that a person must have been skinned and eaten there. I ran like crazy and never had much desire to go into a cave since!

When we felt like knocking the stuffing out of each other, Baker and I would have David, Paul, and Joe help us build some homemade stilts. We would walk around on them some, but mainly, we used them to increase the danger in our pretend sword fighting. Actually, the only pretend about it was that we were beating the snot out of each other with tobacco sticks that we pretended were swords because we didn't have actual swords. We'd be about four feet off the ground on these rickety stilts that our brothers had made by hand, using wooden tobacco drying sticks, not light tobacco stalks, to smack each other while we were up in the air. You could wallop someone really good with those sticks, and make him go crashing down. It's a wonder we weren't breaking bones on a regular basis, but it was great fun. To get on the stilts, we had to stand on a hillside and put the stilts lower down on the hill so that we could step onto them. We'd get knocked off of them over and over. Each time, we'd run back up the hill and mount those stilts and go at it again. We'd play on those stilts for hours, and sometimes it would get so rough that Mama would holler out the window at us, "Boys, stop that! You're going to hurt one another." It's really a wonder that we didn't.

Our imaginations ran wild when we played. We just invented stuff, often inspired by the things that we heard on the radio. (We didn't have television until the 1950s, of course.) I used to love *The Phantom*, with that crazy loud laugh he had. And the radio show *Broken Arrow*, a western, was one of my favorites. It was on *Lux Radio Theatre* and starred Burt Lancaster. I remember saving up my money to order gadgets from those shows, so exciting to get in the mail. To receive something in the mail was an absolutely indescribable pleasure when you were a kid out in the country. What a momentous day it was when you finally got enough money together to order something. You usually needed about a quarter. That was what it took to put together an order and send it off in an envelope. You could do a lot with a quarter! Once, I ordered this little gadget that was featured on *Broken Arrow*, and I was so proud of it. Of course, it got destroyed in a week because of rough play, and we were right back to pummeling each other with tobacco sticks.

Once in a while, one of us would be allowed to go out to the Perkinsville Grocery Store, owned by my Uncle Bynum. While we were there, we would most likely buy a Mallo Cup—gooey marshmallow in a milk chocolate cup. They still have them today. The Mallo Cup packaging contained a card that was labeled with a denomination on it: five, ten, or twenty. If you got enough points worth of those cards, you could order a free box of Mallo Cups. Oh my goodness, it was a joyous occasion when we pooled enough cards to be able to order that box of Mallo Cups. We sometimes traded other things for those Mallo Cup cards just so that we could order that Mallo Cup freebie and get it in the mail. Mail was important to people, so very important. Your mailbox was your line to the outside world.

I have to point out that these were not hardscrabble times for us: we had plenty to eat. It's simply that we were on the country side of town, and it felt like we were really set apart from the world, and maybe lacking some of the niceties that the town folks had. Today, the old home place is within the town limits of Boone, but back then the farm hadn't yet been annexed by the town, and Boone seemed so far away in every sense. The world outside of our home seemed like it was another universe, and the mailbox was our portal into it.

Going to Boone was a special occasion. One such occasion was to go to Belk's department store, something we didn't do very often. However, we were sure to get a trip to Belk's at the start of the school year in order to buy our school clothes. We didn't have any fancy outfits to wear to school. All the country kids wore bib overalls. No one from the Boone crowd would have been caught dead in overalls.

Belk's department store was full of fancy, exotic things. I remember so well, when I was seven or eight years old, going into that store with Mama and Daddy. Daddy would drive us because Mama never drove. She could drive a horse rake and get up hay, but she never did get a driver's license to operate a motor vehicle. We never went to Hunt's, other department store in town, which was right across the street from Belk's. We were a Belk's family. We would get our overalls there, and there were other brands, but I always wanted Jack Rabbits. That's what Dillard wore. So, we would get our overalls and a couple of shirts, maybe a pair of shoes and a couple of other items, and we'd be all set for school clothes.

I distinctly remember Mr. Beryl Greene, the man in charge of the clothing department. He was a rail-thin man with bright blue eyes, and one of his arms was missing below the elbow. He was nice to all us country kids as long as he didn't catch us messing with his magic shoe machine. This fascinating contraption was an X-ray machine into which we could put our feet. It enabled us to see all of the bones in our toes and our feet, and we loved to put our feet in there for as long as we could get away with, wiggling our toes around, and watching our bones move. We couldn't get enough of that thing, never mind that it was probably irradiating the hell out of our feet and other things I don't even want to think about. We didn't know about that kind of stuff then. What we worried about was whose turn it was to run around and distract Beryl Green so that we could get an extra shot at putting our feet in the machine.

After our trip to Belk's, we sometimes took a walk up and down the street for a while to see what was going on downtown. There were only a few restaurants in town at that time and I used to wish I could go in and order a milkshake, a hamburger or a piece of that wonderful looking coconut cake that always made my stomach growl just to look at it on the

Early days of the Appalachian movie theater in Boone, where much magic was produced when I was a boy (courtesy Bill Sams).

counter at the Appalachian Soda Shop. Daddy would say, "We've got plenty of good stuff to eat at home, why would you want to pay somebody for something that's not even as good as your mama makes?" I realized later in life how right he was.

Usually the only other time we kids would get to go to Boone was if we had such horrible weather that we couldn't even do anything minor on the farm, like mend a fence. Days like this were rare because on the farm, there's always something to do, even in a blizzard. But every once in a blue moon, it got so bad out there Daddy just gave up and gave in to our pleas and let us go to the movies. On those days, one of our older brothers would take Baker and me into Boone, and we would go to the Appalachian Theater.

We'd each take a quarter and get the treat of our life with it: we could go to the movie for a dime, and Coca-Cola was a nickel. Now, the food at the Appalachian Theater wasn't of the James Beard award-winning quality of cuisine that some movie theaters must have judging by what they charge nowadays, but we loved it anyhow. Our big decision was: would we go for the hot dog at the Appalachian Soda Shop next door, or the candy bar and the popcorn from right there in the theater? And if it was candy would we have the Milk Duds or the Whoppers? Going to the Appalachian Theater was not only an adventure; it was an early taste of what it might be like to be captain of my own destiny.

In those days the movie theater was a place where you got a lot of your news in addition to entertainment. The theater always played newsreels before the main feature film. I can remember seeing newsreels about the end of World War II and the Marshall Plan being

The Appalachian Theater, circa 1948, when there were live shows on the stage as well as newsreels and movies on the big screen (courtesy Bill Sams.)

Candy counter at the Appalachian Theatre (image by Palmer Blair, 1950, provided courtesy of Appalachian Theater of the High Country, Inc., Boone, NC).

adopted in Europe. Oh, how I admired General Eisenhower. He was a hero. The earliest newsreels that I remember had scary footage of tanks rolling down the streets in Poland and France, and images of burned-out, bombed-out buildings and children standing amidst the rubble. It looked like another world to me.

In addition to the newsreels, there was also a serial that would entice you to come back the next Saturday in order to catch the next installment. I'll never forget the one that had a robot terrorizing a small island. These things were tough on us farm kids because we only got to go to the movies every now and then when we couldn't work on the farm. There was no way our parents would free us from our indentured servitude on a weekly basis so that we could keep up with the serial. Only town kids and Boone folks had enough time on their hands to do that. Because it was such a rare treat, going to the movies was truly a thrill.

Of course, the biggest ritual for our mountain family wasn't movie going. It was church going. We attended the Three Forks Baptist Church, the oldest church in Watauga County. It was established in November 1790 and it used to be on the riverside below where our home was, down the dirt road from the bank of the South Fork of the New River. It was said to be the first church established in North Carolina west of the Blue Ridge Mountains and it was the hub of our community. We went at least twice a week: on Wednesday nights for a prayer meeting (a mild, easygoing service) and on Sunday morning for Sunday school and church service. The church service was led by the Rev. Victor Trivett, subject of some of the most vivid memories of my childhood.

When I was a small child, the Three Forks Baptist Church was housed in an old wooden building that had separate entrances for men and women. For Sunday school the church was sectioned off with burlap curtains hanging from rods on the ceiling, and we used them to divide the room into groups based on age and gender. Children's classes were formed according to age and adults by gender. Men and women, married or single, had different Sunday school classes. When drawn open or closed the curtains screeched on the rods. We used to make our own little peaceful alcoves for Sunday school, grouped with our fellows, but first that great screech as the curtains closed. The interesting thing is that even though the groups could not see one another, of course the curtains did not block sound so we could all hear everything going on in all the groups, although not always clearly because of all the different voices in all the different groups. With so many different kinds of voices and sounds all mixed in, it created a powerful effect that made me think of the Tower of Babel from the Bible. If you tried to listen to all of it simultaneously, it sounded almost like there was a bunch of crickets in one corner, and whippoorwills in another and all kinds of animals in between. Because I was in church and where I was supposed to be, it all came together as a pleasing, reverent sound. I'll never forget that sound.

The curtains were drawn back again when Sunday school was over. People chatted between the events, when we were all together again. In those days, males and females didn't sit together in church. All except for my daddy. He always sat over there with the women. I could never figure out why he wanted to do that. I guess he was a nonconformist or maybe he just wanted to be near his "Nellie Mae," as he called Mama.

After the green burlap was pulled into place, everyone settled in, and once the shifting in the seats and the throat clearing came to an end, the regular church service would begin.

Three Forks Baptist Church the way it looked when we went there, about 1945.

The Rev. Victor Trivett was a powerful speaker and an old-time preacher. He was passionate and full of the Spirit when he led the Sunday service, and I took every word straight to heart, even though he reminded me of a grasshopper standing on his hind legs, wearing suit and tie. The Reverend Trivett was tall and exceedingly slim and he had a hollow, angular face and an astounding capacity for sound. He prepared his sermons from selections of a great variety of texts but no matter where they started, they ended up with hellfire, damnation and the Book of Revelation.

He had the cadence of a poet when he spoke. Later on, when I had studied poetry and literature in high school, some of the rhythms reminded me of the rise and fall of his sermons. As he progressed through the sermon the pitch of his voice rose higher and higher. Those high notes were just about the highest I had ever heard in any kind of oratory. The tone was something between the high notes of my cracking adolescent voice and the soprano singing voice of Sister Gladys Brookshire. The Reverend Trivett worked hard to save souls, and his sermon reached its crescendo at a fevered pitch when he described the hellfire and brimstone awaiting unrepentant sinners.

He yearned to save a soul every Sunday if possible. In those days, if you were a Baptist minister and you didn't get somebody saved every week, a new recruit, a backslider, or at least someone recommitting to the faith, you counted it as a failure. I think the Reverend Trivett was a great man because he never failed to scare the living hell out of everybody in our congregation, including me. I don't think I ever got over it: to this day I can see the Reverend Trivett waving his arms, strumming them up and down like a drummer boy in a Christmas play, with all our eyes riveted on him. Only Dillard Idol could fall asleep during one of those sermons.

The last sentence of the sermon was always, "You have heard today's Word." Then came the altar call. "Can I get me a soul today? You know you're a sinner, can I help God save your soul today?" he asked. I'd look around and wonder who could possibly be next to answer his call, since most of already had at one time or another. It was hard to figure where he would find any new souls to save.

As Sister Cleo Bolick softly played hymns, the Reverend Trivett began the Sunday ritual. "As all heads are bowed and eyes closed, the choir will softly sing 'Just as I Am Without One Plea.'"

> Just as I am, without one plea,
> But that Thy blood was shed for me,
> And that Thou bidst me come to Thee,
> O Lamb of God, I come, I come.
> Just as I am, and waiting not,
> To rid my soul of one dark blot,
> To Thee whose blood can cleanse each spot,
> O Lamb of God, I come, I come.

If there didn't happen to be a soul to save that week, he would move on the next best thing: helping the backsliders. The backsliders are the folks who had done something they know is real naughty. "All you backsliders up in the pews, you know who you are. You need to come up and confess your sins." Then, as the Reverend Trivett waited expectantly, an appropriate hymn, a call hymn, such as "Just as I Am" or "Nearer My God to Thee" was played:

> Nearer, my God, to Thee, nearer to Thee!
> E'en though it be a cross that raiseth me;
> Still all my song shall be nearer, my God, to Thee!
> Nearer, my God, to Thee, nearer to Thee!!

Once a month or so he might get a backslider to respond to the call, and everyone would wonder what exactly they were confessing up there at the altar with the Reverend Trivett. Lots of speculative looks from the crowd. Then, there was a third category of people called to the altar, an easier call for folks to answer: rededication.

"There are those of you out there that need to rededicate your life," the Reverend Trivett admonished. Answering that call was something you could do once a week if you wanted to, and some people were definitely regulars. Whether some of those folks were really backsliders answering a more gentle call, none of us will ever know. The Reverend Trivett lived to be eighty-eight, and though officially retired, preached a sermon the very week he passed away.

During the Reverend Trivett's reign, when I was about six or seven years old, I heard my people have the spirit hit them and cause them to stand up and shout in church. We were a small community and knew each other very well. Aunt Lena, Aunt Nell and many of my other relatives were there. My aunts, of course, sat on the women's side of the church, and I didn't pay too much attention to what was going on over there. One day, right in the middle of the church service, I was sitting quietly, listening to what the Reverend Trivett was sharing about hell, fire and damnation when, all of a sudden, Aunt Lena rose very slowly, almost to her full height, and started talking in a language that I had never heard. She was shouting words that I could not understand, "speaking in tongues," they called it.

The spirit had hit her and it scared the living crap out of me because I was just a little kid and I didn't know what was happening. The Reverend Trivett was pleased as punch and said "Go sing it on the mountain, Sister Lena. Go sing it on the mountain!" When I asked about it my sister Betty told me there used to be a shouting every Sunday back in the older days.

The powerful hymns stuck with me. During the sad times and the happy times alike I have always turned to hymns and Bible verses for inspiration and to connect me to the place where I was born, loved, and raised. When in serious trouble, I may start softly singing a hymn as a way of comforting myself. Whether in the valleys of despair or high up in the mountains of joy, I always come back to hymns. They seem to be embedded in my DNA, along with some verses of the Bible. (One of my favorites is, "Jesus, Savior, Pilot Me.") It makes me sad that religion now is mixed with politics and pol-

The Reverend Raymond Hendrix baptizing a cousin in the New River circa 1945.

itics is often infiltrated by religion. I really believe that if you let politics seep into religion, you destroy religion, and if you let religion seep into the political world, you destroy democracy. This was one of Senator Ervin's reasons for being adamant about the separation of church and state.

Speaking of Senator Ervin, he and his friends gathered once or twice a year at Frank Colvard's mountaintop cabin in Ashe County and he'd say, "Rufus, let's sing some of those old hymns." He was a Presbyterian, and they didn't have the Broadman Hymnal we used at the Three Forks Baptist Church. We'd have somebody play the pump organ up there in that cabin, and we'd sing some hymns. He loved that. I sometimes suspected that he wished they had hymns like these in the Presbyterian Church.

The Three Forks Baptist Church was of course the setting of Edmisten family lore because my parents had so many of their early interactions there. Mama and Daddy grew up on adjoining farms, and Daddy would sometimes sit behind Mama at church back when they were single. Once in a youthful attempt to get Mama's attention, Daddy tied the long ribbon from her hat to the church pew so that when Mama stood up, her hat fell off. Mama turned around and there was Daddy laughing. Then, as Mama used to tell us kids, she slapped him one real good for that little trick. My parents always used to tell that story with such glee. Daddy must have known what he was doing, because that attention had the desired affect: Mama married him when she was just seventeen years old.

For some reason, Daddy never prayed in public. When asked to, he said, "I'm not worthy." When I asked Mama why he did that, my mama would say, "Your daddy's just that way." He gave the same reason for refusing a deacon position at the church, though he supported the church faithfully all his life.

Church was so different. There was so much fellowship among us and my goodness, did we ever look out for each other. If somebody had a barn burn or just a run of bad luck, help was on the way. We would put up hay for people or help them with anything they needed. There was no preaching of hate or calls to hateful things. We may have had a lot of puritanical notions about life, but there were never any politics or divisive issues injected into the message during those days. In the mountains, there wasn't a dime's difference between Democrats and Republicans anyhow. Everybody knew everybody else's political affiliations or beliefs, but none of that mattered as far as our church fellowship was concerned.

My father worked several jobs to support us early in his life. One of them was being a meat cutter for Uncle Jones and Paw Lige at the butcher shop; he carried mail for a while; and he had var-

Daddy and Mama in their Sunday best, one summer not long after their 1929 marriage.

ious other jobs, but later, he got one of those choice state jobs with the North Carolina Wildlife Commission. When you said the words "state job" in our neck of the woods, you were talking about an elevated position—one sought after by many and respected by most. Daddy was a North Carolina Wildlife Resources Commission Enforcement Officer. I remember being taunted at school about it. "Your daddy is a snake warden," the kids would jeer, "Your daddy's the possum sheriff! Your daddy's the rabbit police!" I'd just say, "Maybe, but he is but he sure can outrun your daddy!" He referred to himself as a wildlife protector. I was so proud of him. Of course, I never said, "Daddy, I'm proud of you." Mountain people didn't do that sort of thing. I just sort of stood back in a pool of awe and admiration.

Daddy always wore an official demeanor when he had his uniform on. Though he was never in the military, the uniform itself seemed to bring out a military bearing and an authoritative posture in my father. Mama made sure everything was perfectly pressed and starched. His uniform was a beautiful dark green, his shoes spit-shined. In the summer his hat was a pith helmet and the rest of the year it was similar to that of a North Carolina highway patrolman. That hat stayed on, too, unless he went inside. Daddy also had a badge and a gun, and sported a broad black leather shoulder strap that was more decorative than functional. This is what wildlife protectors wore in those days.

We didn't have a telephone in the old house so early on people would have to drive up or walk up to tell him about infractions. "Walter, they're over there illegally taking deer in Meat Camp." If Daddy was in his farm clothes when people came up to report infractions, he changed into his uniform, got into his state car and off he would go. He was fast getting into that uniform! It amazed me. He was like a magician. Presto, he would appear in his handsome uniform and drive off in his official car. It reminded me of Clark Kent changing into Superman! We worried a little as he made his way down the driveway, because good as he was at so many things, Daddy was not really a great driver. "Now Walter," Mama would say, "you be careful. You need to watch where you're going in that car."

Sometimes when he came back he'd have a fantastic story to share. Sometimes, he'd tell about chasing people through the woods and many times they were people we knew. There just weren't that many people in Watauga County, so if you had grown up in that area, you knew most of them. Daddy would say "Oh, that sly so and so from down on Wildcat Road thought he'd get away from me but I knew he would cross at the hickory tree and go hide in the hen house so I was there waiting for him." A local character named Willard Watson once told me this same story, but from the point of view of the man hiding in the henhouse. Willard was a woodcarver, a musician, a storyteller and more, kind of a county treasure. That day he told me, "I was out there shooting squirrels with my .22. It was out of season, but hell, I needed some squirrel meat. I could put a bead on one before you could say scat. And hell, before I knowed it Walt was right up on me. I commenced running and thought 'I'll outrun Walt 'cause he don't know these woods like I do.' I come to a gap in the road and was headed for the chicken house and there he was! He stepped out into the road and said, 'Whoa there, Willard, I got you.'"

Though this was a funny story, enforcement could be serious business too. There was a reason wildlife protectors carried weapons. My daddy told me there were times when the tension was thick because people were out there in the woods, armed and knowing they were breaking the law. They might be under the influence of alcohol or who knows what. Daddy told me he never had to pull his gun, but he would put his hand on it to send a message to a violator. He said one time a man said to him, "I could shoot you dead and nobody'd ever know." Daddy told him, "Don't try it. I know how to use this thing." Of course to me as a young guy about twelve years old, that was just the most exciting thing in the world.

It was like listening to an episode of *The Lone Ranger* or *Broken Arrow*. Daddy was such a good storyteller. That's sort of a characteristic of mountain country folks. They're storytellers. There are linguists and folklore scholars that study mountain language and storytelling. For us it was entertainment and educational, too. It is a very important aspect of our lives, telling stories the way we tell them.

Everybody got quiet when Daddy talked. He was a quiet man who commanded respect. I can also say that when he was off duty, he didn't walk around with this guns strapped on. When the job was over, my daddy took that gun off, and put it way back in the top of the closet as far up as he could step on a ladder, so nobody who didn't know about it could ever get to it. All of us kids knew about it, but we also knew, "Don't even look at that. Don't even think about touching that gun, don't ever get near it." My father never wore a gun without that full uniform on and he understood the danger of guns and made sure we did too.

I once played Tom Sawyer on a raft I built with some other boys. We gathered every bit of scrap lumber and wood we could, tied them together, and even fashioned poles for navigation. It was a big project for little boys. We set sail on a crisp, clear Sunday afternoon after church when we had earned a little play time. We took the raft out to where the water was deep and gingerly got on board. Next thing we know we hear "gurgle gurgle gurgle" and that raft went to pieces and we went down. We were so young, and this was serious business. Nobody even cracked a smile. Nobody even cussed. We looked around with our faces burning, hoping nobody saw. We were mortified that our raft fell apart.

Daddy never knew about this misadventure. We carried the remains of the raft up to the woods and tried to hide them, and did about as good a job as little boys could do. I remember walking by the spot when I was older, laughing out loud at the memory of Daddy, a few months after our failed expedition, asking, "Any of you boys know anything about that big pile of lumber over in the woods?" Nobody seemed to know where that wood had come from and I didn't seem to know quite where to look as I shook my head "No."

The swimming hole was a big part of summertime. Joe was a daredevil. Winkler's Creek had the best swimming hole. It was perfect. Joe would stand on a rock way up high, maybe thirty feet up and jump off—he was the crazy brother, who later became Dr. Joseph Edmisten, professor of botany and ecology. He'd have to hit it just right if he didn't want to break his neck. When we worked long hot days on the farm, this was sometimes just the nicest thing in the world when we'd be finishing up and Daddy would say, "Let's knock off about five o'clock. Let's go up to Winkler's Creek." Now I didn't swim much because my older brothers once threw me into the South Fork of the New River near the spot where we called Big Rock. They thought this was how to teach me to swim, "sink or swim," I guess. I sank, and to this day I have a pretty bad phobia about water. I dog paddled and such but never became a strong swimmer or enjoyed swimming because they scared the stuffing out of me.

Sometimes after Joe and the rest of us boys went swimming, everybody would be in high spirits just screaming and carrying on, and we would stop off at Luther Wheeler's produce stand and get a watermelon. We didn't eat it right then because we wanted it to be cold. When we got home we would put it in the spring house, just leave it in there in a tub of cold water all night long. We all begged Daddy to cut some off of it that night but it was always "no go." Sunday, after church, was the time to have the watermelon. And sometimes homemade ice cream, if the ice cream maker would work and somebody had remembered to get some rock ice.

Of course, the river was also a source of food. There was fishing, but there was also something we boys did. First, I just want to apologize to frog lovers everywhere. I am reformed now and I know that frogs are our friends. Even still, we used to eat their legs. In fact, plenty of people still do. To get them, you have to gig them, and frog gigging is an art. My cousin Charles Michael was one of the great frog giggers, and he was the leader of our frog gigging crew. We'd go down to the river, and one of us would be the fellow with the flashlight and one of us would be the fellow with the gig—usually Charles. A gig is a pole with these sharp hooks on the end that looks kind of like a trident. You use the gig to get frogs while you walk along the river in the water. The frogs are on the bank and you shine the flashlight on them and they don't move. They sit there while you and your buddies figure out which one of you is going to do the gigging. Then, once the deed is done, the gunnysack guy takes over. The gunny sacker is the most junior member of the crew, and he's the poor little stinker, usually Baker in our case, or me back when I was the youngest, who has the burlap sack and has to separate the frog from his legs. He has to cut them right off the frog's body and put them into the sack, then throw the frog's body back into the water, where it would be immediately devoured by snakes and other creatures that were lurking around, waiting for the spoils.

This would have been terrifying for anyone but it was especially so for me because I really was deathly afraid of the water. And of snakes, for that matter, so it was quite a job for me. Most of the time I was neck deep in water and sometimes, I'd go under. Scared as I was I never refused because if I had my brothers never would have let me hear the end of it and would have mocked me to the end of my days.

Not only was the water deep it was cold, cold, cold. In order to improve the situation the little bit that I could, I developed a trick for making the water feel warmer: I drank a lot of liquid beforehand so that I could pee in my pants to warm myself up while in the water. If I drank enough beforehand, this little trick could keep me relatively toasty for a couple of hours. While crude, the creativity of this solution to the problem of cold water presaged some of my more unorthodox solutions to problems later on in my career. The lesson learned was that you solve a problem with whatever you have on hand and sometimes you can't be too proud.

When you live in the country there are so many ways to have fun, and we often made our own fun. During the weekends, there were no animals penned up in the stockyard across from Aunt Lena's and there would finally be some peace and quiet. Sometimes a bunch of us would get together and play a game that we referred to as stockyard tag. The rules were the same as a normal game of tag, except that you could never touch the ground. We ran atop the rails of the pens. You had to stay on them. If you touched the ground, you were out. We'd all go different ways, and this one was chasing that one, and it took quite a bit of dexterity to keep in the game. Some of the girls were good at it too, it wasn't one of these games boys would say, "Oh, you're a girl, you can't do it," and the girls would sit out. Hell, the girls were the hardest to catch because they were more agile than the boys. One such girl was the lovely olive-skinned Glenda, who had the brightest blue eyes and wore little white sandals on her pretty tanned feet. She had a little pixie haircut and she stole my heart. Those little white sandals with the leather fringe were probably the best you could buy at the local five and dime.

Lots of the cousins would play. We always had summer visits from Uncle Robert Shull and cousin Brian who both brought their whole gang of young'uns with them. There were always bundles of little ones and they loved to play this game because they didn't have a stockyard at home. The construction was crude, but practical, with different sized stalls for different sized livestock. There was a tin roof over the yard, the walkway, and a catwalk, up top. We could walk along that and look down at the animals. It was a comforting place to retreat to when it rained.

During stockyard tag, players were not allowed on the catwalk because it was too dangerous. Only the referee was allowed on the catwalk so he could call out the cheaters. When people got up there during the tag game, they would be bumping each other and cheating, so we made it off-limits. Some of the kids would try to get up on the catwalk and run the whole distance of it and then jump down to avoid getting caught. If you hit the sawdust, it wouldn't kill you, but that fall would hurt.

That was part of the magic of growing up in a farm community. We used our imaginations and made our own fun. None of us had read or heard anything about playing tag on the stockyard stalls and fences, we just invented it, and it was a great game.

Bordering our farm was an unpaved road that separated the Walter Edmisten Farm from Cecil Miller's property. His farm had pasture land, an old stand of timber, a mysterious graveyard and some wonderful chinquapin trees. Wonderful as they are, these trees produce nuts that are encased in thorny husks and the thorns are like needles. They made formidable weapons if you threw them at another person and hurt like heck if you stepped on them barefoot.

Mr. Cecil Miller was a successful and well-regarded person in Watauga County. Even though he didn't live within the Boone city limits, Mr. Miller might as well have been an uptown gentleman. He owned several businesses in Boone, including the Boone Furniture Store, where young couples bought their first furniture just after they were married. Mr. Miller had four children and was married to a woman we called Miss Flossie. The two older boys in the family were contemporaries of my older brothers and sister. One of them became a dentist and the other an entrepreneur, just as his father had been. In the middle was Kate, a gentle, sweet girl who suffered from a developmental disability. The whole family was extremely devoted to Kate, and she was a dear soul who thrived upon their loving care.

The Millers were generous, kind people. My father always admired Cecil Miller, although he did say that his one and only flaw was that he was a Republican. Back then, that statement wasn't as loaded as it might be in our current poisonous political environment because the political parties and their adherents weren't at odds with each other in the often vicious, disturbingly personal way that they are nowadays.

Anyway, Joe Miller, son of Mr. Cecil and Miss Flossie Miller, was just two years older than I was and he was my buddy. I often crossed our dirt road and trudged through the pristine woods and through the Millers' pasture to go play with Joe. One thing we loved to do, possibly the most dangerous acts of tomfoolery that I have ever enjoyed: we took .22 caliber shells, put them on a flat rock and hit them with a hammer to detonate them. Good Lord! We enjoyed the bang of it, the noise they made, and it never occurred to us that we were playing with disaster. Those shells could've turned around and whacked us or hit someone off in the distance, especially since we aimed them towards the Edmisten family home. Fortunately, there were no mishaps, though if my daddy had ever caught wind of what we were up to, there would have been a big mishap in the area of my rear end. I would have gotten hauled off to the woodshed for sure. We hit those shells right on the edge and they would explode and crackle and pop. We thought that was so funny. It's amazing we weren't maimed or killed.

Another thing that Joe and I liked to do was play in the graveyard on the property. The graveyard had over fifty headstones. Most of them were very simple, in some cases just rocks straight from the ground, propped up, with no inscriptions. Most were standing, but some were knocked over. We used to pretend that we were in an ancient Indian burial ground. In reality, no one seemed to know exactly who was buried in that cemetery. I asked Mama and Daddy about those tombstones and they said, "Well, there were some poor folks back there who couldn't afford to have decent burials," but they didn't really seem to know any details. Grandmother Nan warned us not to step on the graves, but she didn't seem to know who was buried there either. The graveyard was mysterious and a bit sobering, especially as I got older.

Joe and I had plenty of ways to have fun but the most fun for me was Joe's train room. The train room was absolutely incredible. The whole room was dominated by a huge train set. It had everything: barns, houses, fueling stations, coal piles. It must have been the fanciest Lionel train set ever assembled. It even had little railroad switches. I didn't want it to seem like the main reason I went over to play at Joe's house was to see his train room, because it certainly wasn't. And yet, I did try to make sure that we made our way over to the train room every time that I visited. After I visited for a little while I would say, "Joe, do you have anything new in your train room?" "Yeah," he would say, ever obliging, "let me show it to you."

Joe even had a little cabin built for him in the side yard that was his very own taxidermy shop. Even before high school, he did his own taxidermy and was an exceedingly good taxidermist. That shop was fascinating to me, because my father's job as a wildlife protector gave me a keen interest in learning everything I could about wildlife. Joe had everything I imagined a kid could want, but I was never resentful of his good fortune because Joe was extremely kind and decent to me. If he thought that the Edmisten kids were poor children, he never let on about it. To this day, I occasionally see Joe Miller on my visits to Boone.

As a boy I liked to make my own money, maybe because I saw how hard my daddy worked. At twelve and thirteen I drove our tractor all over the neighborhood, plowing neighbor's gardens and doing odd jobs. People always wanted their gardens plowed in the springtime. These were small plots behind people's houses, everywhere all over the neighborhood, and some as far away as uptown. I had to drive uptown. That was a mile and a half. I would plow three or four gardens before school, just as soon as it got light, sometimes 5:30, 6:00. Go plow them, come back, get cleaned up, and go to school. It was a two point plow, so I could plow two furrows at a time. I became so expert at it that I could do it with my eyes closed and I knew what garden was what. I knew in Ms. Goodnight's garden I couldn't go over eight inches down or I'd pull that water pipe out. Every year, though, I don't know what it was, the pipe got closer to the surface. I'd get there and she'd start screaming and hollering, calling her son J. C. Goodnight to come fix it. I'd say, "Mrs. Goodnight, something happened. It's higher than it was." So that was just a yearly ritual for me to plow Ms. Goodnight's pipe up.

I'd back up, take a swath going forward, then back that into the trench on the outer side and plow it that way. In a little plot you just couldn't turn around and around and around. That was my little enterprise. I'd go back in the afternoon, if it was a pretty day, and I'd "disc" it. That's cutting up the clods and stirring them up real well. I'd do pretty little jobs, always covering my tracks. Then there was the ritual of collecting the money. Sometimes they would pay me and sometimes they wouldn't. I had this little tablet that fertilizer companies used to give away. I found it the other day, it was my little account book. I'd have in there: Earl Petri, $3.00. John Wilcox, $7.00. That was a big one. On Saturday nights before he went out on his dates, David took me out to collect my wages. I'd clean up and go collect my debt. He had a hot red '55 or '56 Ford Fairlane convertible, and it was the most beautiful car in the world. He'd gotten well-off one summer because cabbage was

I plowed gardens on the side for a little spending money and used this tractor as transportation on some occasions.

so high. Daddy let all the boys sharecrop every summer. I remember the year David bought his car, cabbage was five dollars a bag when it was usually three dollars. So he had enough to get a car.

I always had a little cash around and even had a bank account. That tractor was transportation for me, too. I was Casanova on a tractor! When I was too young to get a license to drive a car, I could still poke along the road in my tractor. Nobody minded, because there were plenty of tractors on the road, and the unspoken rule was, if a boy was on a tractor, it was okay for him to be driving. There I was 14 years old and driving around on the roads. I used to think that there was a law that boys under sixteen could drive a tractor on the roads, but there never was. I used to use it as my mode of transportation before I got my license. I'd dummy up something behind the tractor, put something in the trailer and go uptown to the movie, or go to visit somebody. "There goes Rufus in his tractor." That was just my way of getting around. Everybody knew—"There he goes, be careful."

Another big job was stacking hay. We don't see haystacks now. They roll it. The roller wasn't invented when I was a boy growing up in the late 1940s to the mid-1950s. We would take post-hole diggers and dig a big hole, set up a locust or perhaps an old chestnut pole maybe thirty feet long, just like setting an electric wire pole, and tromp all around it and get it stabilized. The hay was always mowed on a good sunny day. Never mow hay when it's wet. That's where we got the saying "Make hay while the sun shines." There's an exception in the Baptist Church that if you had to get hay on Sunday you were allowed to do it. Just remember that. You got a dispensation from the Lord. To put up hay. And the process was, hook up Old Bill to the shafts and the rake, with these prongs back behind. Mama never did drive, but she often rode the rake. We'd walk along what you call the wind rows beside that rake drawn by Old Bill. Once you got enough, you dumped it and so these long lines of dumped hay are there to be picked up and hauled over to the stack. How we would do that was that, after these wind rows were made by the horse and the rake and we tripped a clutch, we reached back there and pulled up the lever and the tongs on the back came up to dump the load of hay. We had two men starting at one end of the row and two at the other end of the row, depending on how long it was, heading toward making a hay shock, we called it. A hay shock was just a big mound, approximately five feet high and five feet wide. We took two poles, two long poles—I wish I had this at home now—and stuck them under the shock and with one person on one end and the other person on the other end with the poles in each hand, hauled those over to the haystack and dumped the shock of hay there. The worst job in the world that I ever had, though, was the "tromper." The tromper is the poor pitiful person that gets to go around that pole and stomp that stuff and all these pitchforks are coming at you and you just have to learn to avoid them. But you have to tromp that hay down or it wouldn't preserve. Sometimes it would take an hour or more to do a stack of hay. And then there it was for the winter to haul in and either feed outside or take it in the barn. The thing was, the chaff would get down in your clothes. It was not a fun thing.

Then there were the cattle and pigs. We always ran about twenty-five head of cattle, and a bunch of hogs. I hated hog butcher day. It's the funniest thing in the world. I grew up not wanting to kill things. I could hardly stand to see a pig shot, or this and that, and I'll tell you why. Early on, maybe when I was ten or eleven years old, I started going over to see my mother's mother—Maw Lige—who then lived about three miles away. I remember I had to cross over barbed wire fences to get there. My grandparents' house, which was a beautiful wooden frame thing, had a wrap-around porch and a yard with no grass. Ma Lige regularly swept it. You know that was the custom back in those days with some farm families, their yard was a working yard, and they didn't want some old lawn out there to fool with. There would be turkeys, big old gobblers having their plumes all fanned out there, and geese, there were guineas and just a whole menagerie in that yard. Course, they would all have their heads chopped off eventually.

Pa Lige owned what at that time was called a butcher pen and later was called a slaughterhouse and today is called an abattoir. That butcher pen had an outside chute where the cattle for butchering that day were waiting. They ran them up a chute and into the place of massacre, and I witnessed that several times. I hated it because if it was a big cow or a big bull, they always seemed to know what was happening, they knew what was coming, I'm telling you. They got this absolutely crazed look when they heard the moans from the animals ahead of them. It's a wonder I still eat meat. If it was a big cow they use a .22 hollow point rifle. Boom, right in the eye. The cow would hit the floor like that, and of course, there were horrible sounds. And immediately, the butcher would slit the throat, the animal bleeds out and you hook them up to the single tree with hooks there and then the process with the skinning and the "dressing out"—huge wads of guts dropping out.

If it was a pig or a goat or a lamb, or a little calf, it was just slice the throat, no bullet. Paw Lige would say, "Don't waste a bullet." I have nightmares about that to this day, but that is the way it was done. Close by Maw and Paw Lige's home, there was a bluff and down below was what we called "the gut yard." And in those days, remember this is the late '40s and mid-'50s, there was a sled with a horse, and every day they'd drag out all the entrails and stuff and put them down in this thing called the gut yard and run the blood down into the creek. It's just the way things happened. If you took a good strong flashlight down to Paw Lige's at night and shine it down there, you'd see all the varmints in the world. Vultures, possums, everything that could move or crawl was down there in that gut yard. There's a trailer park down there now and I tell some of the people I know over there, "You know, that used to be a gut yard. You might end up with a big ol' cow's head coming out of there one of these days." To this day I don't like to shoot things. Baker thinks I'm a wussy. I don't hunt. I love hunters because they want to preserve wildlife. Hunters are very good because they want to conserve. We do need to keep the deer population in check, but just don't use me to do it. Of course, Baker kills four or five deer a year, and that sort of thing.

In the 1950s Daddy's official state car was a black Ford and it had one of those really primitive radios that crackled a lot. It also had a huge spotlight and an antenna that rose up from the left back top of the fender and featured an enormous spring. That spring would make an eerie, undulating sound when it whipped in the wind or bounced in the brush. As youngsters we used to sneak out and see who could make the weirdest sound with that antenna. When not in use, the antenna was strapped down in a little locket, for when Daddy wanted to do some undercover, incognito wildlife protecting. On the day that this story took place, the car was parked in the driveway at the new house. The new house was a brand new fancy ranch house that was a far cry from the old house on the hilltop, where we carried the groceries halfway up a mountain from the front gate and the only vehicle that could make it up to the house was a tractor because the ruts were so deep and rocky.

Before I get to the main story, I have to tell another story about the trouble I got into over the state car when I was a little one. I know I was small because we still lived in the old house. One night Daddy's boss, Mr. Walter Anderson, the head of the North Carolina Wildlife Commission, came up from Raleigh for dinner. He didn't live in the area, he was just visiting as he liked to do every now and then to check on wildlife enforcement. Mama cooked up some fried mountain trout with gravy and all the fixings that evening. Mr. Anderson ate in the kitchen with us, because we didn't have a dining room, just a big old homemade table in the kitchen. We ate early because it was a fall night and the sun was going down earlier. After our meal we adjourned to the living room. Daddy, Mr. Anderson and I were sitting in the living room shooting the breeze when the subject of Appalachian High's football game came up. The Edmisten clan was planning to attend, and I blurted out "Are we going to take the state car or the other car tonight?" Well, Daddy was sitting so close to me that Mr. Anderson couldn't see when he flicked me with his thumb so hard I swear it seemed like a ten-pound sledge hammer. He got me right in the ear, a good solid PLUNK, and I thought that ear was going to explode right off my head it hurt so bad. I managed to stutter something like "Uh, I meant the other car," and slumped back on the couch in silent, abject misery. Of course Daddy wasn't supposed to take the state car out on anything but state business.

One good thing of many about my daddy was that you could do something bad and though the punishment might be strong and swift, that was the end of it. He didn't ride you for days and days about it, he wouldn't torture you over it. He never revisited the incident in anger and never brought it back up again. When it was done, it was over with and done for good. Now, he might rub it in a little by making an appointment with you at the woodshed so you had something to think about for a while that would be sure to make the point that you had done something wrong. Long were the nights that I dreaded the next morning because Daddy's last words had been "I'll see you out at the woodshed tomorrow morning at eight." Then sometimes when I got out there he wouldn't even give me any licks, maybe because he could see I had suffered enough all night long lying awake and just thinking about getting a whipping.

Back to the main story: one summer night when I was around thirteen years old, Mama and Daddy went off somewhere in our family's personal car. Our personal car was always some kind of old rattletrap because Daddy didn't care about some fancy car. They might have been going to some school event or something, but anyway, I didn't go. Baker must have gone with them, because he wasn't at home. And I said to myself, "Well, they're gone. I think I'm going to go play Wildlife Officer." So I proceeded to the bedroom where his uniform was and I was thinking, "I just know I'm going to catch some wildlife violators tonight. I know there's somebody out there hunting at nighttime or fishing out of season. I'm going to make me some enforcement contacts and catch some violators." I went in there and put the pants on first. They hung half a foot below my big toe so I rolled up the legs. I found the shirt and tried the belt but it didn't fit so I rushed downstairs and got one of my belts. I ran that belt through all those loops, and pretty much tied those pants around me. I put the shirt on, and of course the sleeves were longer than my arms. I found the badge and pinned that into the right place. Then I did a bad, bad thing. I suddenly forgot all I knew about never touching Daddy's gun, and I climbed up and got it from the closet and strapped it on my belt. Then I put on that thick leather strap that went across my back, and of course I put the hat on. It rolled around like a milk bucket on my head, so I filled it in with newspaper to make it fit a little better.

When he wasn't driving it, Daddy left the keys to the state car on the kitchen shelf in a little dish that held odds and ends. Now, I had seen my daddy drive the cars many times, and of course by then I had driven the tractor all over the place and my brothers had let me drive the old 1951 Plymouth from Miss Margie's house, down a quarter-mile stretch of road, though I managed to knock the oil pan out that day. I will always love Joe for taking the blame for me that day. I knew how to start the car because I'd seen it started a million times before. I got in the car, and the seat was huge and too far back for me, but I managed because even though I was in the squeaky-voiced time of puberty, I was big for my age. I must have just been starting puberty, or I wouldn't have spent my time concocting a stunt like this instead of going to find a girl somewhere to talk to or, later on, trying to sneak up onto the roof of her folks' house to get into her room. But at that point, I still hadn't succumbed to those kinds of thoughts, so I cranked that car up and mind you, this thing was not an automatic. It had a clutch and a brake and who knows what else. Off I went, sitting on the edge of the seat so that my feet could reach the car's pedals. I slowly backed it out of the driveway, watching very carefully so I didn't hit the cement blocks that formed the little entry into our driveway. The road that went by our house was gravel and it had a big ditch on the side to capture the storm water runoff from the road. That road and that ditch had been there ever since I could remember. I had ridden horses up and down that road since I was a little kid.

So, I was carefully backing the car out, planning to head off down to the River Bridge, because that's where I was likely to catch a violator. That bridge was about a mile and a half from our driveway as the crow flies. I had to make a sharp turn to the right onto the one-lane road to get there. In the blink of an eye, I ran off the road into the ditch. No matter how hard I tried to get out, the car remained stuck. I heard the crinch-crinch noise of the car as I put it in reverse, then forward again. I panicked as I realized that I had taken so long getting situated in Daddy's uniform, they might be back any minute.

I thought I would rather be dead, lying in a casket than be in the fix that I was in. Humming "Nearer My God to Thee," I thought about Mama and Daddy and all the people coming by to look, saying, "Oh, ain't he pretty?" as they leaned over the casket to say their final goodbyes. I just sat there because I was so wedged into that ditch that I couldn't even open the left side door of the car. I was pretty sure there was no structural damage to the car, but it was just flat stuck. Providence was alive and well, and it shined upon me that night. I heard the familiar sound of Bill Gragg's Dr. Pepper delivery truck coming around the bend! Bill Gragg lived up the road about half a mile from us, across the street from his mother and father. His father was Sylvester Gragg and he was the gum chewiest man I ever met in my life. He always was vigorously chewing gum, often in tandem with his wife's gum chewing. They were quite a sight to behold at the town basketball games, snapping and chewing gum loudly and in unison. They were wonderful neighbors.

The minute I saw his truck, I crawled out of that car through the passenger side window. There I was in full North Carolina Wildlife Commission regalia, gun and all, flagging down Mr. Gragg. He slammed on his brakes and the Dr. Pepper truck lurched into a sudden stop. "What the hell are you doing there? Where'd you get them clothes?" he hollered. I was in no mood to explain anything at that point. The whipping Daddy would give me if he caught me like this! "Bill, l-l-look," I stammered, and couldn't get another word out. He busted out laughing,

"Damnedest thing I've seen in my life. Wait till Walt gets you. He's going to skin you alive!"

I said, "Bill, Bill, I'll make you a deal." Now I had plowed his garden before and had done some other work for him, so he knew that I was a hard worker. At twelve and thirteen I drove that tractor all over the neighborhood, plowing neighbor's gardens and I did a good job. I said, "If you get me out of here, I'll plow your garden for the rest of your life for free." Bill just kept laughing. I pleaded with him. "Bill, Mama and Daddy are coming home soon, it's almost eight o'clock." "All right," he said, still laughing. "Just stay there, you little turd." Then he got back into his truck and put it into low gear. I stood there wringing my hands, praying "Oh God, don't let anybody else come by here. They're going to tell on me. Please, Lord, let nobody be on this road." I knew everyone on that road, and most of their habits. I knew that Bill Gragg's mother and father were home and in bed by eight o'clock. I knew that Uncle Charlie who lived down the road was way in, because he didn't get out much. He drove a motor grader for the state. I knew that Mr. Avery Jackson down the road was one of those very, very early risers so he was in bed by about this time every night. That accounted for about everyone other than the kids who might come driving down the road to park in the place at the end that we called Lover's Lane.

As I waited for Bill I must have run through every hymn and Bible verse I knew, beseeching the Lord to save me from what was the impending doom if Mama and Daddy drove up. Don't forget that Daddy was a *state employee* and this was a *state car*. He would have to answer to the state authorities about what in the name of Sam Hill was his boy out there doing in that uniform with that GUN and the state car in a ditch. I segued along to "Rock of Ages, cleft for me, let me hide myself in thee."

Bill maneuvered the Dr. Pepper truck around in our driveway so that it lined up with the car. "Hang on there, you little shit," Bill yelled out the window over the laboring rumble of the truck's engine. "We got to pull this SOB out front ways. If we pull it out backways, your ass is really going to be in trouble 'cause it's going to scrape that thing." He pulled up in front of the car and pulled out this great big logging chain and started hooking it up to the car's axle. "Hurry, Bill," I begged. "Please, Bill, hurry! Please God, let Bill hurry," I chanted to myself. To my great relief as the truck pulled slowly forward, the car moved out of the ditch little by little, making that crinching sound as it went. It finally cleared the ditch and was back on the road. "I ain't going to tell on you, but you're going to plow my garden for a long time," laughed Bill as he put the chain away. I had to ask him to park it for me because I was still shaking so badly I could not do it.

"What are you going to do about that dirt all over it?" he asked. "Oh, Lord," I pleaded, and the answer came to me like manna from heaven. On the side of that brand new house was a water spigot. Mama used it mostly for watering the flower garden, but that night it was the answer to my prayers. As Bill pulled away in his Dr. Pepper truck I picked up the hose and started washing furiously. Then I realized I still had the uniform on. "Use your head. Use your head," I cautioned myself. My mind was racing. I figured that Daddy was going to see the car before he saw anything else, and he would wonder why it was dripping. So I said to myself, "What will I tell him?"

I figured that by just quickly washing the whole car off, I could tell him, "Oh, I thought I'd just wash your car for you, Daddy." I just needed to get out of that uniform. I rushed into the house, stumbling over everything and nothing worked exactly right because I was shaking so much. The old mountain saying "shaking like a dog pooping peach seeds" came to mind, but I didn't linger on the thought. I was racing against time. Should my parents pull up that very second, I needed to look like I had been washing the car. So, after I changed, I got that hose out and squirted myself over real good. Then, I got back to work washing that car like crazy. I must have set a few world records along the way getting it done. All this activity from the time that Bill Gragg gave his parting, "Goodbye, you little shit," to when I was done washing the car was about seven minutes total elapsed time. I know because I counted.

As soon as I finished, I saw a set of headlights coming around the corner, going past Miss Rhodie Greer's home, a log cabin converted to a modern home. It was Mama and Daddy. I took a deep breath, trying to seem calm and composed. "What are you doing?" called my daddy as they rolled into the driveway. "Well, Daddy, I was just kind of messing around here and figured I would wash your car for you." He looked at me, paused for a beat, then said, "Well, all right. I don't know that it needed it, but all right. Be sure to cut that hose off." I wasn't off the hook yet. Parents have an uncanny way of knowing when their kids have been up to something. Plus, Daddy hadn't seen his uniform yet. I was terrified that I had messed up by forgetting to put one of the items back or in any of a thousand other ways I had not even thought of yet.

As far as Mama was concerned, I don't know if she suspected something or not, but she was always my protector. I had a notion then, and still have to this day, that my mama knew something was up because she never asked any questions about the incident, either at the time of its occurrence or later. Usually, when she had been gone, she asked what I had been up to all that time, but on that night, she didn't ask. And of course, we didn't have a television, so at that point there would have been no easy excuse to give her on the spot if she asked how I had frittered away several hours. I was still nervous. I knew I couldn't let my guard down completely. I feel like I must have held my breath for most of the following week. Nothing happened. I thought Bill Gragg kept his word but later found out that he told Betty about it right back around the time it happened. I found out when I told Betty and she said, "Bill Gragg told me about that. If you had ever been mean to me, I was going to tell on you bigger than life." So Betty knew back in the day, but she kept that secret for years. She didn't tattle.

Time passed, and neither Mama nor Daddy said anything to me about that night. They didn't so much as ask a question. "This shall remain sealed in my bosom until the appropriate time," I vowed to myself. "Only then will I ever tell my daddy about my terrible transgression."

That time finally came, some thirty years later, in 1984 when I was running for Governor of North Carolina. I was speaking at a North Carolina Wildlife Federation meeting in Winston-Salem. I was on the program as the keynote speaker, and I'll never forget that night. I got up to make my speech, and my daddy was up on the podium because he was being honored as the Wildlife Supervisor of the Year for the Seventh District. I got up to give my little address. They all loved my father so much, it was a very friendly crowd. I began to thank the group for all they had done and share with them how much wildlife had always meant to me, and I thought, "This is it. This is the time to tell my daddy what I did that night." I shared the story of that long-ago summer night when I was sure I was going to meet my maker. The crowd roared with laughter and there was a standing ovation. I said, "I have finally confessed," and was met with a sly grin from my father. My pulse still quickens when I recall the night I stole Daddy's car, and it happened over half a century ago.

My favorite horse in the world when I was a boy was an American Quarter Horse named Lady. My daddy had picked her up somewhere or other, and she was just the brightest, smartest horse I'd ever known in my life. We had several horses on the farm, but Lady was special. She was a Western Cutting horse, trained to help herd cattle, and she was so smart that if you had a fence gate with a handle that slid back, she could slide the handle with her nose, swing the gate open, go through the gate, turn around, back up, pull the gate shut with her nose and let me reach down and latch the gate without getting off of her. It was phenomenal.

By the time I was twelve or thirteen years old, I would ride Lady through all the countryside by myself. We had many adventures together. Because there were so many fences in the way, it could be hard to navigate from where we lived to where Maw Lige and Craig lived, about a mile or a mile and a half away. I developed a system for dealing with those obstacles: I carried a set of barbed wire cutters with me and would cut and then patch the fence.

In addition to fences, there were other hazards along our route. Lady and I had to go down a gravel road, and then we'd get to the New River water bridge, which Lady absolutely would not walk over unless you dismounted and negotiated with her until she acquiesced and you could coax her across the bridge, walking along side of her. Once across the bridge, I would remount and go along my way. Then we had to go through here, and go through there, and up past the butcher pen that was near their houses. All told, what with the fence splicing and everything else along the way, it took me about two hours to get to Craig's house, but it was worth the trip.

Once I got there, he'd get on his horse, a small pony-type steed that liked to try to bite us. Once he was on, we'd race all along the mountainside. It was the most exhilarating feeling. We were free, just free. Lady could always beat Craig's little mount in a race, too. That was a given. I didn't go over there as often as I would've liked because it took so much work to get over there, what with having to cut and patch all of those fences. I wanted to put gates in so Lady and I could get over there more easily. Paw Lige wouldn't have cared and Uncle Jones had passed away by the time I was a teen, so there would have been no opposition from the folks on that side of the mountain. "Why don't we just build gates there?" I asked my daddy. I was sure nobody would have minded. My daddy said, "No, we can't because it's not our land. How are you getting there now?" he asked. When he asked that question I had to fib about the route I was taking and then drop the subject. I told him that I went all around the New River bridge and way up the mountain road the long way, but I never did really go that way. I always had my fence cutters with me.

I mentioned the new house. In 1952, when I was in seventh grade we got a brand new house, built it right up from the ground. We had all of this beautiful land by then, most of it the same land that had belonged to my grandfather. So much prime space to

Our new house built right on the road—no more hauling groceries up the rutted, rocky lane—and Daddy's state car in the driveway in 1952. This is the car I drove into a ditch right around the time this photo was taken.

build on! But my mama said, "No, we are going to build this house right alongside the road." You have to understand that over the years, we all got really tired of lugging the groceries and things all the way up the hill from the car at the bottom of that rutted, rocky driveway, to the house.

We had lived way off the beaten path for so long that we were tired of all the mud and grit that went along with being far from a road. Everybody likes to rhapsodize about the wonderful snowy winters in the mountains, but the snowy wonderland didn't last very long, usually only a couple of days unless we had a truly gargantuan snowstorm. After that, there is just mud, muck, ice, and slush.

Still, putting the house right on the road ended up causing no end of trouble, with people constantly knocking down our mailboxes and driving through our yard, backing into our driveway and running over Mama's flower garden in the process. Later, Mama said she wished we had put it up in the field.

A ranch-style with all the modern amenities of 1952, it was a fancy thing! I didn't know until much later that it was my mother's inheritance from her parents that made that house possible. My mother wasn't much into "My, me, mine." She would never have gone around bragging, "You know, I built this house with my inheritance." That would have been way out of character for Mama. I was in my sixties when my sister Betty told me, "Well, you know, Mama had the money to build that house." We dug and poured the footers and laid the foundation—my daddy's dose of Scotch-Irish thrift made sure of that—then we hired out whatever we couldn't do. Bricklaying and electrical work, those sorts of things. I was eleven years old when we moved in there.

We each had our own rooms! Betty had a room of her own and didn't have to traipse through anyone else's room to get to it, and there was even an extra bathroom by her room, so things were really looking up for her. Then there was a bedroom with two beds in it and another one on the end. David and Joe were already gone by the time we built the new

The steep, rocky road to the old house. Mama used to complain when we had to carry groceries over the ice or through the mud. This road is the reason the new house was built right on the side of the highway.

house, so it seemed huge. It even had a rec room, which Daddy hired gum-chewing Sylvester Gragg, a local carpenter and father of Bill Gragg, to build. Mr. Gragg was an excellent carpenter. Like lots of carpenters, he always had his pencil behind his ear, but his ears were big enough that he could also hold a whole ruler, one of those fold-out kinds, behind one of them. We spent a lot of time in the rec room that he built, mostly passing the time at the ping pong table. We became very good at ping pong. Baker and I used to spend hours playing, and sometimes Joe would join us and we would have these ping pong tournaments and just played that game to death.

There was also an old piano in the rec room. No one in my family played the piano, but since my daddy also loved to sing hymns, we'd invite in a relative or a neighbor over to play while we sang. We'd take out the Broadman Hymnal and everyone would sing. Betty was a wonderful singer, and the rest of us held our own, though there was an exception and that was my mama. She sang in the choir for many, many years, but honestly, Mama could hardly carry a tune although she was a faithful choir member of the Three Forks Baptist Church for many years. I'll never forget the time the Reverend Trivett said "everybody sing!" and I overheard one of the usually sweet ladies whisper to another one "except Nell!" I don't think Mama heard her. I sure hope she didn't.

The livestock market was located right across from my Aunt Lena's house. Every Tuesday and Wednesday during the season there were trucks lined up in front of Aunt Lena's house, filled with mother cows and calves bawling like crazy. The calves would cry any time they were separated from their mothers and the mothers would call to them. Bawl, bawl, bawl. It was upsetting to some of us children, but it was a nightmare for Aunt Lena who lived right by the stockyard. Sometimes the trucks lined up along the whole three quarters of a mile down to our house, some parked on the side of the road. The drivers often backed into Mama's garden to turn around. She got so mad about it, Daddy put a cinder block wall around it, and then they knocked that down too.

The atmosphere at the livestock market was electric and I was fascinated with all of the goings-on. The market attracted people from many miles around. I loved the chant of the auctioneer, and delighted in watching my Uncle Jones do the mental math to figure cattle prices. The scents and sounds of that market were just incredible, and they were something that thrilled me inside out. Sawdust, cattle bellowing, people talking, laughing and smoking, the smell of the livestock, manure, and anything else you could imagine and of course, tobacco spit flying every which way. I couldn't get enough of that place!

Speaking of livestock, I was an enthusiastic member of Future Farmers of America as a boy. Growing up on a farm, it was a natural fit, and I really loved farming and farm animals. This is why I first saw myself as a veterinarian and agriculture agent, before I got swept away by my political interests. In high school I became president of the Daniel Boone Chapter of Future Farmers of America.

When I was a teenager, Jim Graham, who would later become the Commissioner of Agriculture, was a judge of the Future Farmers of America Speech Contest the year I made it to the state finals. Mr. Graham knew my father. They met at the Laurel Springs Upper Mountain Research Project in Ashe County, where Mr. Graham worked at that time. After the contest he came to me and said, "Well, you made the best speech, but you didn't have on a Future Farmers of America jacket. The judges thought you didn't care enough to wear the jacket." That really stung. I had never gotten a Future Farmers of American jacket because we couldn't afford it at that time.

I told this story to one of my friends from Little Washington, North Carolina, Keith Hackney. Keith is a lawyer who comes from a long line of well-known Hackneys who have been in the forefront of manufacturing and economic development in North Carolina for

The Daniel Boone chapter of the Future Farmers of America at Appalachian High: John Critcher, sentinel; Jimmy Stewart, reporter; Johnny Bodenheimer, treasurer; me, president; Earl Keller, secretary; R.T. Tait, advisor; and Dale Moretz, vice president.

years. He and I are big buddies and he shares the University of North Carolina season basketball tickets that he inherited from his father with me. This day, when I told the story, we were riding to the ball game with the Clerk of Court of Beaufort County, who had been big in Future Farmers of America.

Little did I know that my story led Keith to do some research with the help of a young man in Watauga County whose father was a family friend and local agent for Farm Bureau Insurance company. Together they figured out what year I had been president and the contests I had won or judged. (Future Farmers of America jackets had patches with emblems from all of our activities and the contests we won.)

To my great surprise and delight, on the opening night of the exhibit commemorating the 40th anniversary of the beginning of the Sam J. Ervin Watergate hearings, Keith called me back to a hidden spot away from the huge crowd at the North Carolina Museum of History and pulled out a beautiful royal blue Future Farmers of America jacket with the big beautiful symbol, my name, my badges, and the name of my chapter on the front. I was so moved that these men would do this for me. I wear that jacket quite often when I make an appearance on WPTF Radio's *Weekend Gardener*, especially when it takes place at my beloved Farmer's Market. It was my great honor to be presented with a Future Farmers of America North Carolina Lifetime Achievement Award a few years back. I will never forget the day my thoughtful friends presented me with that beautiful jacket I so wished I had as a boy.

During my high school years, I became adept at finding ways to skip class so I could do things that I thought were too important to miss out on. I was interested in so many things, sometimes I just had to skip school. On some Tuesdays in the spring and fall I would sneak around the back way from Appalachian High School and walk down the hidden back roads to get to the livestock market. I didn't dare walk down Highway 421 because someone might see me and tell my dad "Walter, I saw Rufus walking down the road during school hours." Even at the market I tried to keep a low profile so that I didn't become noticeable enough that someone would say something to Daddy. I could imagine someone going up to my daddy and telling on me. "Walt," I imagined they would say, "I saw your boy Rufus down at the auction."

There were several auctioneers off and on over the years, but the mainstay was Hyatt Williams from Cove Creek, North Carolina. Hyatt had a dark complexion and thinning jet-black hair that he always wore slicked back. He had piercing brown eyes, and boy, was he ever a good auctioneer. Typically, the auction took place around two o'clock, but on one particular Tuesday when I was about fifteen years old, the start time came and went with no sign of Hyatt. I was sitting in the arena at the livestock yards, waiting for the auction to start. Fifteen and then thirty minutes went by, but still no auctioneer. The crowd started buzzing, wondering what was going to happen if no auctioneer showed up. Then, Wade Tugman, a big, tall man from down around Deep Gap, North Carolina (he reminded me of Matt Dillon on *Gunsmoke*) stood up and waved to me. With that hat on his head, he looked about seven feet tall. Wade knew my Daddy and he knew me, and he knew that on more Tuesdays then I care to admit, I was up there in the back corner, studying the ins and outs of that livestock market, sometimes even walking around chanting like an auctioneer, showing off to people as I delivered my own rendition of an auctioneer's lively, singsong chant: "Forty-five, forty-five and-a-now-fifty. Fifty, fifty, going once, going twice, sold to number twenty-four."

"Hey Rufus!" hollered Wade. "Come on down here. Hyatt's not here today, take 'er over boy." I was both terrified and overjoyed, my heart pounding. I felt the joy of getting the chance to try my hand at something that I had always wanted to do. Wade said, "Well, now, we'll just do the best we can today." I think he was preparing me for failure, just in case. Facing the crowd he asked, "Are y'all okay today if Walter's boy tries the auction?" No one voiced any objections.

They drove that first cow into the pen, and one of the elders in the crowd yelled out a price and the auction was on. I was nervous at first and then I was on fire! The words were rolling off my tongue! I knew most of the people in the crowd and what their secret bid sign was: some would nod, some would wink, others would scratch their noses. No one yelled out or made an obvious sign that they were bidding. That kind of thing was for rubes. My Uncle Jones would cock his head and blink his eyes. Others would tip their hats, or pull on their ears.

I don't know how in the world I did it, but I got through that whole auction. It was a relatively light day, with no pigs or goats to sell, but I was still quite proud of my accomplishment. I knew my cattle, and it had shown. Normally the auction took about two hours. On that particular day, it took a little less, and I learned firsthand why auctioneers need to talk so fast: if they don't, it will take way too long to get through the auction. As far as I know, nobody had a bad word to say about the job that I did. Nobody offered to pay me, either.

The owner of the livestock market, Lester Carroll, was a red-faced man who had a great big belly and no ass, almost as though his back got sucked out his front. Lester carried two wallets. He always had one in his left pocket and one in his right pocket, both of them chained down firmly. *Nobody* was going to pick the pockets of Lester Carroll. That day he said to me "Well, that was good, son" which was pay enough for me. "Don't tell Daddy," I replied. "Well now," said Lester, "you know Walt's going to find out about this." Though I'm sure he did, Daddy must have decided to spare the rod and not say a word to me about what happened that day, which, by the way, was truly one of the highlights of my life. Who knows, maybe he was just a little proud of me for pulling it off.

During my early childhood, we used to refer to the town folks as the Boone Folks. Living in town made all the difference. Looking back on it, maybe the Boone Folks really weren't all that different from us, but there were a very few elite families who lived in town and they did truly live in a different reality than us country kids. They were the well-off children of the professors, the dentist, the doctor, and the lawyers in town. And of course, I can't overlook the enormously fortunate kids of Mr. Klein, the man who owned Boone's Western Auto Store, which was the epicenter of the toy world. Western Auto sold everything from bicycles to toy trucks, and we could only imagine what it would be like to have access to all of those playthings. I always wanted a toy steam shovel, but I never got one.

Town kids wore fancy clothes, got to play in the band at high school and participated in all kinds of activities that the country kids missed out on. They lived in the ritzy part of town, and there was a big division between the town people and those of us who lived out in the country, two distinct zones that neither group would cross into except for clearly defined reasons. My family lived just outside the perimeter of that zone, but we were definitely on the other side of the socioeconomic fence from the town kids. And there were kids who lived much farther out in the country than we did, and we could start a fight in a hot minute if we brought up their locale to them in a derogatory way. People were aware of the class distinction and were sensitive about it. Hog Elk was only about ten miles from the town of Boone, but it may as well have been in another country. Back in the mid–1940s our world was very much confined to the area on the outskirts of town, unless we had a clear purpose for going to Boone.

So where I grew up, as with most other places, there was a definite sense of class or social hierarchy. Early on when we were in the old house on the hill, I'm sure we were considered poor dirt farmers by townspeople and even by other country people of greater means. Though nobody looked down on Walter Edmisten's boys because they were fine boys who were good athletes and could whoop just about anybody around town. We were raised right, worked hard, and most of us did well in school. People uptown in Boone had bathrooms in their homes. We had no indoor bathroom, and no refrigerator into the early 1950s, until we moved into the new house.

Even when we lived at the old house, I never thought we were poor, because we had everything we needed. We had the johnny house, the corn crib, the smoke house, the woodshed, and the barn. We had all kinds of vegetables and fruits and preserves in the pantry, a spring house full of sweet cream butter and milk and cheese. My grandmother churned the cream into butter and took great pride in stamping a rose in the top of each round. We had meat and chicken from the farm, and grains and more from our own fields. The stark memory of the long years of the Great Depression loomed tall in both Mama and Daddy's minds, so they always made sure to plant and harvest plenty and put up plenty for later.

Aside from the town people/country people hierarchy, the country people themselves had a kind of pecking order. There were places in the county that were looked down upon, like Hog Elk (the real name of the town was Triplett). If you said somebody sounded like they were from Hog Elk, those were fighting words. Then there was Upper Meat Camp. If you were from Upper Meat Camp there was supposed to be something wrong with you in the head, certainly not a fair assessment of the people there, but this is what people do. Every place has these hierarchies, and my home was no exception.

People have said that I tend to treat people from all walks of life the same, and if I do, then I'm sure I learned it from my mama. She never did seem to take note of social classes. Here is a story that demonstrates this. When my daddy died, President Clinton called Mama to express his sympathy. That's the president of the United States! And Aunt Ruby Michael comes to the door with a pie and my mama says, "Well Mr. President, I'm sorry, but somebody's at the door. I've got to go." The president!

3

The Foundations
of My Political Leanings

When I was a boy we learned to get along with people of all political persuasions. About half my extended family was Republicans and half were Democrats. Still, they all thought just about alike, and they didn't kill one another over what differences they did have. I remember hearing my daddy say, "The Edmistens are members of the Democratic Party," and that was good enough for me.

Now, back in the hills we took politics seriously, but not to the point where we got mad at somebody. There were furious times during elections, though. Some of the local Democrats would drive me around as a little kid and send me up to knock on the door to charm people into coming out to the campaign car. Now I don't know what their transactions were—I am absolving myself of any knowledge of any sort of undue influence or vote buying. I do know the campaign organizers would do everything they could to get people out to vote. I tried to do my part. I was helping haul people to the polls before I had my driver's license.

The whole process intrigued me. I would listen to things on the radio that had to do with politics—back in those days the radio and the local press covered local political events, speeches, rallies, anything that came up. If a congressman came to town it was a big deal. Now you get very little coverage when a local politician comes to town. It had to be the radio, newspapers, or adults, because nobody my age really talked much about politics. Most kids out in the country were too busy with the hardscrabble of life. Unless they were town people, most folks out in Watauga County were just scratching out a living. Their mothers and fathers either worked "down t'noir" (down in Lenoir) at Broyhill or some other furniture factory, and their kids often followed the same path.

I think there were many other things about my childhood that shaped me for a life of engaging and persuading people. Along about the third grade I had severe atopic eczema, and my poor little old hands would crack wide open. Mama made me these little cotton mittens to wear at night so I couldn't scratch and make it worse. The crook of my elbow was often just one big blister. I was so embarrassed about it. My ears would have these huge cracks. Sensitive souls that they were, my playmates would say things like, "Your ears look like they're going to fall plumb off." It made me feel like such an outcast, and I think it made me crave acceptance. I think I overcompensated by trying to be a friendly person to everyone, to get everyone to like me and accept me in spite of this leprosy-like thing I had. It took me until college to get over it, I know because when I was on the Appalachian High wrestling team, I remember my brother Joe saying, "Tell them you've got leprosy and they'll run from you and you'll win the wrestling match!"

I really think this condition shaped me. There were kind teachers who would stop people from picking on me. I remember one time some boys were going to take me out and whoop me and they got me cornered. One of them said, "Where'd you get that crud? What, did you let a cow lick you?" Miss Gibbs, a little bespectacled woman with her hair in a bun and a lot of lip on her, told them "You boys get away from him." She didn't let them get me. There were other teachers who did the same. I was ready to fight those boys, though, if they'd come at me. I wasn't that big then, but every brother older than me had taught me how to fight. I didn't like to fight, but I could do it. I was skinny, but all that farm work made me strong. You try to hold down a 150-pound pig so you can castrate him. It took four big strapping boys, but we got it done. Milking cows is hard work too. I'm glad Miss Gibbs defended me, but I like to think Miss Gibbs kept that boy who was picking on me from a whipping he'd never have forgotten in his life.

I have always loved to hear people speak. As a boy I loved to watch their mannerisms, and I loved how the cadence of their language went. I would sometimes sit back and mimic the speech of the orators I heard. To get my fill of this I relied upon speakers who came through town—lawyers and politicians and the odd snake oil salesmen. There were two terms of court a year, and I liked to attend the criminal term because I knew that I might get to hear some fiery speeches and arguments. I found some clever and creative ways to skip school to go hear the court proceedings without getting caught.

We had always had some political types in the family here and there. My Uncle Bynum was a county commissioner for years—he was a Republican—and I had a great uncle who was a sheriff and a Democrat. I listened and I learned. When I was in high school Mr. Hugh Alexander often came to speak. He was the congressman for our district, I think then it was the Ninth District. Of course now computers determine the districts and let the candidate choose their voters when it ought to be the voters choosing the candidates. We must find a way to have nonpartisan redistricting if we want to preserve our democratic process—at least as it was envisioned by the founding fathers.

Once Congressman Alexander was giving a speech at the Watauga County Courthouse. Now I had seen the park rangers on the magnificent Blue Ridge Parkway, in their beautiful uniforms with those impressive hats. Those uniforms were the closest thing I had seen to my daddy's handsome wildlife uniform. I knew that they patrolled the most beautiful scenery in North Carolina in the most traveled park in the nation. I thought to myself, how do I get to do this? So I said to Congressman Alexander, "I'd like to work summers on the Blue Ridge Parkway helping the park rangers, can you help me do that?" And he said "Well, why don't you write me a letter about it." So I went to the library and looked up something to do with Congress and how it was set up, and wrote him a letter. He wrote back and told me he was sorry, there weren't any jobs like that available at that time, but we kept writing, corresponding over the years. Later I learned that it was probably a staff member writing those letters. But at the time, to me it was from *him*. It was really something. Here was this important man, and he was writing to *me*. Isn't it funny that I have found myself in this position so many times in my career, answering hundreds of letters from people a lot like I was when I wrote to Hugh Alexander. Sometimes it really means a lot to some people to get a letter from an attorney general or a member of Congress. This is why I almost always attach little personal notes to the bottom of a letter, even if it's just a little scribble. Bill Alexander, an excellent elder law and estate attorney in Raleigh, is Congressman Hugh Alexander's son. I have known him since he was just a boy.

4

High School Days

My political leanings became clear by high school, even though being in politics was not part of my plan. I was the class president freshmen, sophomore and junior year. Senior year I couldn't be class president because I was student body president. I became adept at putting together coalitions to win office.

I liked learning about how politics worked because there was something in me that said *this is a wonderful way to get to be around people in an exciting way.* I had always had this desire to engage with people. I could walk up to an old tree stump and strike up a conversation. The political life seemed like a way to engage with people in a meaningful way. On my senior trip to Washington, D.C., I was proud of myself because I knew more about the city and the political process than anybody else on the trip. For my senior picture, I wore a little trinket that had the Capitol on it that I bought on that trip. You can see it in my senior yearbook. I wish I could find that little souvenir today. Some girl probably has it.

The cheerleaders at Appalachian High School had a favorite chant for the basketball team that went like this: "Jeepers Creepers, jump and jive we're really proud of our first five. They may not boogie and they may not jive, but come on team, let's skin them alive!" The favorite football chant of the cheerleaders who, in those days, were chosen not so much for their agility but for their charm and good looks was, "Push 'em back, push 'em back, way back! A-P-P-A-L-A-C-H-I-A-N. Appalachian, Appalachian, win, win!" At times, later in life, when I was ready for something to move forward faster I caught myself absentmindedly chanting the cheerleader slogans of Appalachian High.

Sadly, no cheerleaders performed at my wrestling matches. How different my wrestling team experience might have been if there were a bunch of pretty cheerleaders providing me with encouragement during my matches. I suppose that since it was not a team effort, no one thought that it warranted a cheering squad. I was out there all alone, for once hoping and praying that I would *not* see the light. I don't mean that in a religious sense—I mean seeing the gym lights the way you do when you're pinned on your back. That meant that you were done for and that match was over! Even though there were no girls in short skirts jumping up and down to cheer me on, I did actually have a very good cheering squad with me most of the time: my brother Baker, sometimes my older brothers, my sister Betty, and of course, Mama and Daddy. In 1963 I became the state lightweight champion. (I weighed one hundred and fifty-four pounds at that time—a far cry from my current weight.)

At Appalachian High, rather than teacher's aides, we had what we called "practice teachers." They were student teachers from Appalachian State Teachers College. During my junior and senior years of high school, there were some good practice teachers and some not-so-good ones. Appalachian High School was known as "the laboratory" for the teachers at Appalachian State Teachers College. Students had to teach in local high schools before graduating. These practice teachers often were only a couple of years older than the high school students. Consequently, mad crushes sometimes developed between practice teachers and students at my high school. I must admit, I had a couple of crushes on my practice teachers.

Other than the practice teachers, Appalachian High had another connection with Appalachian State Teachers College: the schools held their games on the same football field. The schools had different practice fields, but the actual games were all held at the ASTC Stadium.

Appalachian High School's basketball court was in the central auditorium where we gathered for assemblies and student body meetings. The court was actually on the auditorium stage, so when you watched a basketball game at Appalachian High School, you were sitting back in theater-style seats watching the game being played up on stage. This configuration made the action of the game somewhat difficult to see from far left and far right angles, although no one seemed to have any problem seeing me foul out. Basketball really wasn't my sport.

My three older brothers all went to ASTC and they all practice-taught, but not at Appalachian High. They practice-taught at Beaver Creek High School in neighboring Ashe County. Most of the time, they worked as a coach or assistant coach during that time. In fact, one year, my brother David practice-taught at Beaver Creek High and developed a basketball team that went on to win a high rank in the state championship in its division. Playing on the team was a very special experience for many of the players and David made lifelong friends with some of them.

One time, when I was on the football team at Appalachian, we were playing Beaver Creek on a cool October night. Somehow, the Beaver Creek team fumbled the ball and I retrieved it. A loud cheer erupted from the crowd and I started running like hell. "Go, Rufus, Go!" the crowd cried, and cheered even louder as I ran faster. Then, I began to hear yelling that sounded like the crowd was saying, "No, Rufus! No!" I suddenly realized that I was blazing toward the Beaver Creek goal line. It dawned on me that I had better turn around and quick! I wheeled back around amid taunts, cheers and laughter and thankfully managed to get back to where I had picked up the ball before I was tackled.

Although it is funny now, I have never forgotten that miserable, miser-

On the football field.

able night when I was the laughingstock of my own teammates, the entire Beaver Creek team, an assortment of fans on both side, and especially painful, my very own mama and daddy. After all, here was the president of the student body of Appalachian High School, jersey number 47, furiously running the ball the wrong way. It was a rough bus ride home.

I believe this taught me a lesson: if you start going the wrong way, get a hold of yourself, turn around and head back the right way. As former President Bill Clinton liked to say, if you find yourself in a hole the first thing you should do is quit digging. Big thanks to Beaver Creek High School for witnessing my embarrassment on a very chilly October night in front of what I then considered the whole world, including the Good Lord and all of the heavenly hosts, and helping me to learn these guiding principles.

When I wasn't playing football, I was active in school politics and attended local political events, which is where I met Mr. Rob Rivers and his wife, Bonnie Jean Lewis. For many decades, the Rivers family had owned the local newspaper, the *Watauga Democrat*. Growing up, that's where we got just about all of our news. Mr. Rivers' father, Robert Campbell Rivers, had bought the *Watauga Democrat* in 1880 from the paper's founder. Despite the name of the paper, the editor did his best to present fair and balanced coverage of events and to publish news that would be of interest to all residents of the county. Everybody read that paper, and it is still the best paper around there.

Mr. and Mrs. Rivers and I shared an avid interest in politics, so we really hit it off. They invited me over and we had wonderful, spirited discussions in their living room. They had two daughters, and their older daughter went off to journalism school—an unusual thing in and of itself in 1950s Watauga County, North Carolina. Then there was Rachel Rivers. At first, I didn't think too much about Rachel, who might be off riding horses or out with her friends when I visited, because she was a couple of years younger, but I was just thrilled to talk to Mr. and Mrs. Rivers and they encouraged me to be active politically. Well, by her sophomore year, Rachel had become a beautiful, sophisticated young woman, and naturally, I asked her out on a date.

Now, you talk about "uptown," Rachel Rivers was it! Rachel Rivers was the embodiment of an uptown girl: she was a well-read debutante who was a bit edgy for her time and place.

Rachel just looked elegant and aristocratic. She had the fancy clothes, the gorgeous hairdos, everything in the world. She brought to mind that hymn "Heaven is Mine." Best of all, Rachel's family loved to talk politics! All of this appealed to me.

In high school, everybody knew that Rachel was quite different than other kids in Boone—and if she was different from the average town girl, she was *really* different from the average farm kid. From an early age, Rachel had everything that a child in a small mountain town could wish for. As a young girl, she would ride her very own pony through the streets of downtown Boone, and even if the pony did its business right in the street, most people just smiled and said, "Rachel is such a cute little thing."

I was truly impressed by how well-read Rachel was, especially compared to me in those years. She was a fan of Henry Miller's writings and had read *Tropic of Cancer* while she was still in her mid-teens. I realized later that this was significant because this book was extremely controversial and, in fact, it wasn't legally published in the United States until the early 1960s. Rachel must have gotten her hands on a hot copy (either illegally printed or illegally imported) to have read it in the 1950s. Now, at that time I read the *Progressive Farmer* from cover to cover every month, but that was about the extent of my literary forays except for what I had to read for school. When Rachel told me that she had read *Tropic of Cancer* I asked, "Well, did he survive the disease?" Later on, I found out how risqué that book was and thought, "My goodness, Rachel!"

One night, Rachel and I were at the Horn in the West grounds, site of the acclaimed outdoor drama of that name. During the show's off-season, high school kids went to the grounds to talk and possibly do some canoodling. Unfortunately, instead of smooching, that night we got into a spirited argument about horses. Rachel was a splendid equestrian who knew a lot about horses, but I thought I did too. My knowledge of horses was more inclined toward workhorses than the fancy horses Rachel rode in the big horse shows at Blowing Rock. The argument had something to do with Thoroughbred horses and it got very heated. At one point, I made the mistake of saying, "You're crazy. You don't know what you're talking about!" Well to my surprise Rachel flung open the car door, jumped out, and shouted, "To hell with you!" I was shocked. Back in those days, high school girls didn't say things like that. I asked, "Where you going?" "I'm going home," she said. "Well, get back in the

With the enchanting Rachel Rivers.

car! I'll give you a ride!" I insisted. "I'll get myself home." Rachel replied. "Rachel, get back in the car, dadgum it!" I pleaded.

She wouldn't get in the car, even though it was around eleven at night and it was a mile and a half walk from Horn in the West to her home. I drove next to her for a while, pleading with her to accept a ride home, but she simply wouldn't get in the car so after a while, I said, "Okay, suit yourself," and drove off. A couple of days later, I saw Rachel and we got along just fine, as if nothing unpleasant had happened between us. She was quite a mercurial girl, and both she and the world she inhabited held many surprises for me. While they never put on airs and always kept their mountain accents, Mr. and Mrs. Rivers and their children were in social circles far beyond anything that I had ever known. They were a part of a world that I would never have been able to even imagine if they hadn't given me a glimpse into it. It was exciting.

At one point during my senior year of high school, Rachel asked me to be one of her escorts to the Terpsichorean Club's North Carolina Debutante Ball in Raleigh. I had never heard of this event, which is an annual gala where debutantes from around the state are presented to society. It is a "coming of age" event for the daughters of the upper crust of North Carolina. It still exists today, but is less popular perhaps because of its elitist connotations. In my high school days, it was a huge deal. The girls would go to Raleigh and spend days and days of partying, visiting this house and that, and then there was a big weekend gala with even more festivities, including formal balls. Rachel just told me, "It's a big party in Raleigh." Well, I've never been one to miss a party. I accepted her invitation with no idea of what I was in for and how much it was going to cost me.

Now I was used to coming to Raleigh for the State Fair, but had never gone to this kind of high society event. I had taken Rachel to the junior/senior prom and my goodness, was she elegant on that night. She had on a beautiful black dress with a huge, crinoline skirt that she probably got from New York or somewhere like that and she was truly, astoundingly beautiful. Her complexion glowed and her hair was wavy and a gorgeous shade of natural blonde, just like one of the Breck Girls I so loved to admire.

Rachel gave me a punch list as soon as I accepted her invitation. First on the list: "You'll need to rent a tuxedo." Now, I knew about formal wear from my junior/senior prom, but I only had a vague notion of what attire would be appropriate for this big gala. I was baffled by the set up for this ball, especially when she told me, "You'll be one of two. I'm going to have two escorts." I don't remember with one hundred percent certainty who the other escort was, but I seem to recall it was Frank Payne, Jr., one of my classmates. I arranged to rent a tuxedo and get myself and my tuxedo and shiny shoes to Raleigh at the appointed time. I had the money to pay for the trip from all the little jobs I did around the neighborhood, plowing people's gardens and so forth. Still, this was an expensive weekend for me. In addition to the fancy clothes there was the hotel—and this party went on for three days!

I stayed in an old hotel that stood where the Raleigh *News and Observer* building is today. It was called the Park Hotel, if I am not mistaken. I shared a room there with my fellow escort, and we attended different events and had to wear different outfits to each event, so we had a whole wardrobe of clothes in that room with us.

Most of the people whom I met there were from Tarboro, Elizabeth City, or other places "down east." There were not many of us from the mountains.

As escorts, all we had to do was dress up, show up at the events, decorate the arms of our dates, and have our names called out in a beautifully festooned ballroom at Memorial Auditorium (then the original, simple, Greek revival building without the 1990 additions). This trip was my introduction to high society much more so than it was Rachel's, for sure. While I enjoyed spending time with Rachel in Raleigh, I remember being anxious to get back to the hills of Boone and the world I knew.

Then there was the Blowing Rock Horse Show incident, during my senior year in high school. Rachel was not my date for this one, she just knew how much I enjoyed parties, so she had finagled me an invitation. This horse show is a marvelous social event. Rachel invited me to go to the reception at the Blowing Rock Country Club that was associated with the horse show. The night of the event I drove over to the country club in our 1957 Plymouth. At the party, I spoke to Rachel a few times over the course of the evening, but was mostly off by myself. There I was, a simple country boy in this dazzling setting. No one from my neck of the woods had ever been to the Blowing Rock Country Club unless they were making a delivery or worked there as a waiter or service person. I looked around and took it all in, including the unattended bar that was loaded with liquor bottles. It seemed like they had about a thousand bottles of every kind of liquor there was in the world. You know, I didn't know what all that stuff was. I mean, I had swigged some moonshine and bootleg liquor during my high school years, and I had even experienced the discomfort of drinking myself sick a couple of times by then, once under the watchful eye of my brother Paul, who took it upon himself to introduce me to beer. Ditto for the time I drank myself sick under the tutelage of Mr. Tait, my agricultural education teacher at Appalachian High School.

I went over to that bar and said, "Well, I might as well help myself." After all, I didn't have to accompany Rachel home safely, or have any real responsibilities at all. I must have poured myself a tiny bit of everything just to try it out, and just because it was there. As you might expect, in short order, I was drunk as a boiled owl. When I was ready to go, I got into my car, cranked it up, drove it out onto the driveway of the country club and promptly passed plumb out. The car was still running, and I ended up curled up in my car sleeping right there on the driveway. Somebody saw me sleeping there like that and called the Blowing Rock Police, who quickly made his way over. (Bill Greene WAS the Blowing Rock Police Department at that time, the chief, deputy chief, and the whole force too.) Now, Bill knew my family well. He pulled the car off the road, tried to wake me up, and as I came to, he said, "Son, I'm going to have to take you in." Every fear that a human body and mind could dredge up came alive in me all at once. It wasn't just the fear of going to jail for the night. How was I going to face Mama and Daddy when they heard about this? I thought of every hymn I could sing, and every Bible verse I could remember, as I tried to discourage Bill from hauling me down to the station.

"Just let me sleep out here," I pleaded. "No," he said, "I'm going to let Big Walt deal with you." That drive from the Blowing Rock Country Club to the Watauga County Jail was the longest ride that I've ever had in my life. We got over there, and I remember Sheriff Ernie Hodges came in, and Ernie proceeded to call my daddy. It must have been around midnight.

I silently pleaded, "Please put me in jail. Just please, please put me in jail," because nothing could be worse than my daddy coming to get me in this fix. Well, it was to no avail. Walter Edmisten came striding into the building and saw me sitting there in a stupor. "Let's go." That was all he said, but those words hit me like lead. I got up and got in the car with him. As was his way, he didn't say a word, not one word all the way home from the Watauga County Jail building. When we arrived, I staggered into the house. Daddy looked at me. "Okay, we'll tend to this in the morning," he said evenly.

I fell asleep, waking periodically throughout the night to puke my guts out, only to be awakened at five in the morning by my father's voice. "Get up! We're going to go down today and we're going to do some logging. You're going to log this day." Well, logging with the horse is an extremely difficult task, even for someone in peak physical form, much less someone horribly hung over. I had watched Dillard logging with Old Bill a hundred times over the course of my young life, and I appreciated what a demanding task it was. You and the horse need to work as a team. Thankfully, Old Bill knew what he was doing. David and Joe hacked away at the trees with a crosscut saw, taking them down and chopping off all their limbs. I drove Old Bill as he dragged the logs down a steep embankment.

It took a lot of physical energy and coordination as well as mental concentration. If we were not alert we might get tangled up in the logs and chains and get maimed or killed or get somebody else maimed or killed. Old Bill really saved my life that day because he instinctively knew when to turn and how to keep the logs from hitting me. Several times during the day, I stumbled from sheer weakness after having upchucked all night long, and I noticed that my daddy was closely watching. About lunchtime, he said, "All right. We'll let Dillard finish this up this afternoon. You go home and let your Mama fix you something."

When I got home Mama didn't say a word, though of course she knew what had happened. I don't think I had ever had any punishment worse than that one. This was the most incredibly horrible moment of my life, my mama fixing me breakfast without a word. None of us ever mentioned that night again.

Within a few months of this incident, I started a new chapter of my life in college at UNC–Chapel Hill. A couple of years later, Rachel went off to journalism school at the University of Missouri. During that time, we both changed but were still very fond of one another. She once told me, "I'm proud of you," when she had read a write-up of something I had done while part of the student legislature at Carolina. Over the years, Rachel and I ran into each other, and I would visit her when I was in Boone. She married a fine gentleman named Peter Armfield Coffey, who went into the newspaper business with her, eventually becoming executive editor of the *Watauga Democrat*. The paper was sold in the 1990s, but Rachel and I still ran into each other occasionally at various social events. She had kept her good looks and jovial nature and started becoming more and more like her mother, developing even deeper reserves of kindness and graciousness.

At one point, Rachel was the president of the North Carolina Press Association and she invited me to speak to the group. Shortly after that, the executive director of that association called me with some horrible news, "Did you hear about Rachel?" I hadn't, and braced myself. "She was riding horses at their place over in Cove Creek. She went riding by herself and did not come back. The horse came back and then they went out and found Rachel dead." It was crushing news.

To this day, no one knows what caused Rachel to be thrown from her horse and killed. It was a sad and sudden end of a fine lady who was in the prime of her life. There was much speculation as to what could've spooked the horse or what had happened. Many of us have been thrown from horses, and most of us have just walked away from the incident. This may have been one of those falls where a twist of fate caused her to fall in just the wrong way and the fall proved to be fatal. Rachel was a lovable, vibrant, and complicated person. I have nothing but fond memories of her.

In my family, there was no question of whether we were going to go to college. The Edmisten kids were going to college, period. It was a given. My four brothers went to Appalachian State Teachers College and they played football, wrestled and participated in other activities as well. They were high achievers, just like Betty. Even in football, in their high school days, Joe, Paul, and David played on the same football team together for a couple of years and they were stars! I sat back in the stands with great pride throughout the games as the announcer exclaimed about this great play made by Edmisten and that great play made by Edmisten. He was talking about my big brothers!

I don't know how we knew we were going to college, because no one ever said it or laid out a formal plan for us. We just knew somehow that we were expected to go. At Appalachian High School, many students did not go to college, so the school did not have a guidance counselor. The closest thing that we had to one was Mrs. Margaret Gragg. She was a very proper lady who was a full-time English teacher. A couple of afternoons a week, she performed some of the functions that a guidance counselor might.

At first I wanted to go to North Carolina State College for agricultural science and animal husbandry, especially after Mr. Bud Tate, my agricultural education teacher, organized a trip to Raleigh for me and a few of my fellow students. On that visit, we went to the animal science department, the branch of the university that dealt with cattle, my favorite subject. We saw the most amazing thing there: a cow with a window right into her side! It was the most incredible thing that I had ever seen in my life. She had a little glass stopper right there in her side, and she was standing there perfectly quiet, chewing her cud and eating her hay. There was a technician dressed all in white who pointed out the location of her rumen and other digestive organs and we were able to look right into that cow and actually see her insides as the technician pointed them out to us.

"This is absolutely miraculous," I thought to myself. And that cow was just so content. That experience absolutely solidified my desire to find some way to go to NC State and major in animal husbandry. I was convinced that my life would be rounded out by working with horses and cows and pigs and various other beasts of the biblical world. My mind was made up to attend NC State.

Then, about halfway through my senior year, I got a life-changing call from Dr. Gene Reese, a dentist in Boone. He said, "Rufus, I am the Watauga County chair of the Morehead Scholarship Foundation associated with the University of North Carolina at Chapel Hill. I would like to nominate you for that scholarship. There will be other students in the county who will be nominated by other people, but is it okay with you if I nominate you as a candidate for this award?" I was thrilled!

I had no idea what to expect, so I got all geared up and tried to prepare for whatever might come my way during the selection process. The interview was scheduled and there were, just as my English teacher Miss Elizabeth Elliott had warned me, several other nominees from Watauga County. There were, of course, other high schools in our district, among them Cove Creek and Blowing Rock high schools. Appalachian was by far the largest, and there were a couple of nominees from there. The committee met in the old Daniel Boone Hotel, a place that had always seemed mysterious to me. I had helped my family haul table scraps and leftovers away from there for slop for our hogs, but had never been in the place as a guest.

They held the interviews at night, and all of the interviewees got to eat dinner at the hotel. I thought that was probably the most incredible supper I had ever had at any time in my life. There we sat, in a dining room with white tablecloths and silverware embossed with the Daniel Boone Hotel logo. I don't remember what we ate, but I know I was trying my best to remember all the things that Mama said to me during the course of any meal: "Get your elbows off the table! No slouching at the table! Don't belch out loud! Don't talk with your mouth full!" And, most assuredly, "Don't *sing*." I had a lifelong habit of breaking into song wherever I might be when the feeling moved me.

Once the meal was finished, the committee members adjourned to another room and called the candidates in one by one for their interviews. I remember there were about five people on the committee: Dr. Reese was the chairman, and Dr. Devant from Blowing Rock Hospital, and a few people I didn't know who were graduates of UNC-Chapel Hill. We sat together in a separate room as each boy was interviewed. I was among the last. A few weeks later I got a letter from Dr. Reese saying that I was chosen by the Watauga County committee to represent the county at the regional selection competition for the Morehead Scholarship Award. At that time the Morehead Scholarship was the grandest, all-inclusive award that could possibly be given to a college student. It paid for everything, absolutely everything: tuition, room, board, books, and even laundry.

Our regional level competition for the award included students from several counties in Western North Carolina. The interviewers looked over our high school transcripts and asked us about our plans for the future. I remember saying that whatever I did, I wanted to be good at it and that I studied hard. I also said that I had always wanted a career that involved farming, but that I was open to other ideas and I distinctly remember saying that I sort of liked government and politics.

Meanwhile, you could have told me that I was going to be a neurosurgeon when I grew up, and I would have been more likely to believe it than if you had told me that I was going to win that district scholarship competition. But I won it! Throughout this process, I don't remember discussing the goings-on with my mama or daddy. It's not that they didn't care, they just really knew nothing of the college admissions process. I depended on my older brothers and people here and there for advice.

As the winner of the district selection round, I went on to the final competition in Chapel Hill. So, the time came for the state contest. At that time (early 1959) I had never been to Chapel Hill. The interviews were held off of an upper chamber of the Morehead Planetarium. The building reminded me of the painting of Solomon's Temple in my grandmother's picture book of Bible stories. The chamber where the banquet later took place was stately and ornate, a ceremonial room. There was a seat there that looked like a throne. The room was strikingly beautiful.

Candidates from all over the United States were there. Roy Armstrong, the executive director of the John Motley Morehead Scholarship Fund, was the chief inquisitor during our interviews. Mr. Armstrong had been on the University of North Carolina staff in different capacities for thirty or more years and had at one time been director of admissions at Carolina. After my interview, I thought that I had done okay, but I had many doubts about how I measured up to the other candidates. As I left the interview room I had butterflies in my stomach. After all, I had grown up on a farm dehorning cattle, castrating swine, and shoveling horse manure, and here were all of these other young men that were from big cities like Atlanta and New York. Part of the idea of the scholarship is to populate the university with diverse, talented people that the committee thought would contribute to the college community.

When my interview was over, I had some time to wander around the UNC campus and I got to see some of the town of Chapel Hill. I passed under Silent Sam, a statue of a Confederate soldier. Students later told me that he was known as Silent Sam because he was supposed to fire his rifle every time a virgin walked by him, but he never did get to fire that gun. I think that almost every college campus has something comparable in its lore. I always did get a kick out of the myth of Silent Sam and never imagined that this statue and others like it would cause so much controversy.

It's hard not to fall in love with Chapel Hill, especially in the springtime. "Oh my goodness," I thought, "This wouldn't be so bad at all. I love this place." My mind soared far above any thought of the cow with the window into her rumen that once so impressed me at NC State. I wandered the campus reading every plaque. I was entranced. I wanted to be part of this place. I got to have a good long look and to really explore because there were so many candidates that it took a couple of days to interview them, and we all had to stick around in order to attend the banquet at the end of the process.

Mr. John Motley Morehead himself attended that banquet. He was elderly at the time, in his early nineties. It was an honor to be in his presence. Mr. Morehead came from an accomplished, admirable family. His father was a congressman and his grandfather had been governor of North Carolina. Mr. Morehead himself was a distinguished chemist who had invented a process for manufacturing calcium carbide, a process that was the underpinning of success for the Union Carbide Corporation. Mr. Morehead had no children of his own and was a generous philanthropist, giving much of his fortune to his alma mater, the University of North Carolina at Chapel Hill.

I thought my mother would have wholeheartedly approved of my behavior at the banquet. I did not slouch or talk with my mouth full. I did not break into song. I also ate everything they put in front of me, even though there were a couple of weird things on the table, including some kind of squid-like thing which I had never encountered before.

A few days after I got home, I got my letter from the scholarship committee. The original has become lost over the years, but it read something like this:

Dear Rufus Edmisten:

We enjoyed having you in Chapel Hill and it was a pleasure to meet you. Unfortunately, we will not be able to offer you the John Motley Morehead Scholarship because we have determined that, at this time, you are not qualified to enter the University of North Carolina at Chapel Hill due to a deficiency in your high school course work.

Admission criteria include coursework in diverse subject matter including at least two semesters of a foreign language. You are lacking foreign-language credits as well as the required coursework in calculus. Until those academic deficiencies are remedied, you are not eligible to attend the University of North Carolina next fall. Therefore, we must regretfully inform you that you cannot be a recipient of the Morehead Scholarship.

I felt so deflated after reading that letter. I had been one of the top students in my high school class and yet no one had thought to tell me that I should be selecting coursework with an eye towards college admission requirements. I couldn't have been more disappointed. As a kind of consolation prize, the committee offered me $200 a semester if and when I attended UNC. This may seem like a small amount of money nowadays, but in 1959 it was a lot! (While preparing to write this book I found receipts for the costs to attend Carolina for a semester in 1962—for 12 credits, my tuition was $87.50, fees were $52 and laundry was $20, for a total of $159.50 for the semester.)

I couldn't wait to use it to help pay for my freshman year at Carolina. There was only one small problem: I hadn't even applied to Carolina yet, and apparently, I wasn't even qualified to attend. I had to come up with a solution and come up with it quickly. Summer was just around the corner, and I knew that my father was expecting me to work like a dog out in the fields, as I had every summer for the previous five or six years. However, I was determined to show the Carolina admissions committee that I was qualified to attend the university in the fall, so I made some inquiries and found out that I could take a foreign language in summer school and be eligible to matriculate in the fall.

When I spoke to Daddy about it, he gave me permission to spend the summer in Chapel Hill. I enrolled in Spanish courses to meet the foreign language requirements, but I dreaded enrolling in calculus. I wasn't good at math and I disliked math class pretty fiercely. Fate must have been smiling upon me, because as I read through Carolina's course catalog, I noted something strange which pleased me very much. For whatever reason, Latin could be substituted for coursework in calculus! I have no idea where that loophole originated, but I wasn't going to argue with whatever convoluted logic was behind it. I signed up for Latin class before they could change their mind.

I loved Latin class. I used to put my own name through the declension. Some readers might be interested to know that Rufus is a Latin word and, more specifically, is a second declension masculine adjective meaning "reddish or ruddy." I used to amuse my friends in class by running my name through all the cases: "Rufus, Rufi, Rofo, Rufum, Ruforum, Rufis," etc.

In addition to summer school, I worked like crazy at different odd jobs to pay for my summer school tuition. At the end of the summer, I was accepted at Carolina. That's the story of how I got to Carolina. It was through the process of applying for the Morehead Scholarship that I became familiar with the school and fell in love with it. I am so glad that despite my trepidation, I took the opportunity to apply for that scholarship. Many times in my life, I experienced stress and ferocious turmoil due to the demands of political life. I had to fend off verbal barbs and arrows where my character was questioned and I was called every name that anyone could think of. During those times, I sometimes did momentarily wish that I had gone to North Carolina State, become a county agent or a veterinarian, and led a peaceful life out in the country. After all, animals are usually much kinder to human beings then human beings are to each other. Still, when all was said and done, I found myself once again glad that I had attended Carolina.

5

Going to Carolina

The real turning point for me was when I went to Carolina. This is what took me far away from my childhood idea of being a veterinarian or a county agricultural agent. All of a sudden, I was thrown in amidst people from all over the state, the country, even all over the world! I remember there was even a boy from New York City! Douglass Burkhart. We took him out on a hunt for the elusive snipe. I guess he held that bag out in the middle of the woods for a few hours while he thought we were out rounding up this mythical creature. We had gone back to the dorm, of course, leaving him to discover the prank. Attending college at the University of North Carolina in Chapel Hill opened my mind, fired up my imagination, and solidified my political aspirations. Of course I chose political science as a major! Even still, I never dreamed I would become, as one reporter called me, "a footnote in history" because of my role in the Watergate proceedings.

As far as what made me eventually get into politics, a lot of it comes down to something I think plays an enormous role in every life: fate. An enormous amount of what happens comes down to time and circumstance—being in the right or wrong place at the right or wrong time. The question is, are you prepared to handle whatever it brings? It could be good or it could be bad. If you are an optimist like I am, you know that fate has brought you great favor in life. I have many reasons to feel that fortune has smiled upon me. For example, how did I meet my wife who is the most lovable, cool, calm, precious thing in the world? It was fate. A happy accident. The happiest accident of my life.

I had an entrepreneurial streak as a boy, and I had saved up some money over the years from my side business doing yard work and plowing gardens. I had intended to use that as seed money to buy myself a little piece of land where I could start my own farm. Instead, I put that money toward my education. That money, plus additional money I earned from working jobs in Chapel Hill, helped me get through school.

My mama and daddy helped me as much as I would let them. I came across a letter from my mama from my first year in college. In it she shared news from home, and added, "We also sold the little dwarf calf, if you need any more money. Are you eating regular and right? I don't want you coming home poor as a snake. You haven't told me anything about your roommate. Your daddy sold his steers yesterday, and paid most of it on the note. How are you doing with your studies? Are you studying hard and applying your time right? Keep yourself clean. Don't wash your own clothes because they will get dingy and won't look good. Everybody misses you." Daddy also wrote a couple of checks during lean times.

Before I headed off to Chapel Hill for the fall, I helped out with some work on the farm. There was still tobacco that needed to be harvested, and I had to cut and stalk it in the field, just as I had since I was 12 or 13 years old. It was my job to put a stake in the ground, every five stalks of burley or so, and then spear the stalk. You have to do that job just right so that you don't split the stalk, which would prevent the tobacco from hanging the way it needed to when it got put up in the tobacco barn.

The day before I was set to go to Chapel Hill, Ms. Lunette Barber, a longtime friend and co-worker of Daddy's, came to visit our home. She was the wildlife information officer/wildlife education director for the North Carolina Wildlife Resources Commission. She was always a welcome visitor, and we enjoyed her company very much. Ms. Barber was just as eccentric as she could be. She was from Johnston County, North Carolina, in her mid-fifties and never married. Ms. Barber was always dressed like she was about to go off and see a Broadway show in New York City. She wore a fox stole, which did quite a job of accentuating her rather vulpine eyes. She had one of the most pronounced southern accents that I have ever heard. She drove an old state-issued 1950 brake-and-clutch Ford. It lacked the telltale whiplash antenna that the Wildlife Protection officers' vehicles had, but was otherwise the same type of vehicle that they drove. That car was loaded up with all kinds of wildlife brochures and who knows what else. Ms. Barber looked like a travelling Watkins Woman, those ladies who would drive around the countryside selling liniment, cattle drench, vanilla extract and other assorted necessities.

Ms. Barber was very fond of me and she just kept exclaiming how wonderful it was going to be for Walter and Nell Edmisten to have one of their boys attending Carolina. Her words made me feel better about going, because I was very nervous about the move. Ms. Barber volunteered to give me a ride to Chapel Hill for the start of the school year, and I accepted. It was quite a job to shift the clutter of wildlife brochures around enough to fit my luggage into her car. Mama had packed me a big load of clothes that she had carefully labeled, including a vast quantity of labeled underwear because she wanted to be sure that I always had clean underwear. She did not want to fret about me getting into an accident

Our barn, where I fed and milked many cows and hung burley tobacco for curing. It later served as a place for Daddy to hang my campaign posters.

and having to have a doctor or nurse see me in dirty underwear. She also sent me with an enormous trunk full of her homemade canned goods that I relied on all semester long. We managed to cram everything into the car, and I set off very apprehensively, quite aware that I had rarely been away from home for longer than a couple of nights in a row, and a weekend wasn't quite long enough to get homesick. When we got to Chapel Hill, Ms. Barber dropped me off at the dorm. I thanked her for the lift, and I really meant it. She was a nice lady. I saw Ms. Barber later on in life. Once, when I was running for governor, I saw her on a warm spring day wearing a fur coat with "I'm for Rufus" stickers attached to every conceivable spot on it.

The dorm I had been assigned to was Avery dorm, which still stands today. I was given Room 403. It was the fall of 1959, Chapel Hill was still very small-town North Carolina, and the dorm reflected that. I had no roommate assigned yet, so I moved into my room alone. I have no idea how I got that trunk up to the fourth floor of the dorm, but I managed. I picked my half of the room and put my things away. The rooms were arranged in quads, with four rooms sharing a shower and single pay telephone per floor. Long-distance phone calls cost a fortune. The rule was that you had better have either a darn good reason if you called home collect or you had better bring quite a stack of change with you and know that it was going to run out fast. Phone calls home for me were very few and far between. I knew that other guys would get frequent phone calls from home, because their roommates hollered down the hall "Your mother's on the phone!" I knew I wouldn't be getting one of those calls. Due to the cost, long distance was a dreaded scourge in our family and to most country folks and frugal Scotch-Irish folks.

During that first week of school, I was the most pitiful, homesick creature you have ever seen in your life. I was absolutely heartbroken, half aware of things around me, just walking around in my own world. There was orientation at Memorial Auditorium, where they did the old thing that scares the bejesus out of you: some old faculty member at the front of the auditorium saying "Look to your left and to your right. When this is all done and over with, one of you won't be here." I looked around at all the nervous faces and knew my face wore the same expression.

After orientation, I settled in for the week, having a class here and there.

I tried to develop pretty good study habits, but I have to admit that I did deviate from them on occasion. The second week of school, and I am not proud of this, I ventured down from Avery dorm, and I walked what was probably close to a mile down to Franklin Street. Now, for the unini-

Lunette Barber, wildlife educator.

tiated, Franklin Street is the main street running between the main campus and downtown Chapel Hill. On the other side of Franklin Street, opposite campus, were all the dens of iniquity. Until this point I had avoided any sort of stuff that would have bothered Grandma Nan or have had my mother thinking I needed to rededicate my life next time I was at Sunday services at Three Forks Baptist Church.

I got together with a bunch of guys: one of them was from Marion, and one was a big, tall, blond-haired guy from somewhere around Rocky Mount. They said "Let's go down this alley, down in here to the Rathskeller." I was intrigued by this place. It was literally a dive: the establishment was in a cave-like basement, totally underground with several chambers. I had saved up enough money for a roast beef sandwich, a rare treat. From then on, that was the only thing that I ate when I went down there. The food was exquisite to my young and unpracticed palate. (Though I had Mama's care packages and many other opportunities for feeding frenzies, food was and is a major preoccupation for lots of boys my age and I was no exception. A little later in my college career, a very nice young lady recognized a hungry young man when she saw one, took mercy on me, and invited me to have a meal with her every once in a while. Her name was Anne Sexton, and she had beautiful, black hair. We met in class and she instinctively knew that I didn't have a lot of money. I had an adequate amount, but it was just what little I made, and I had to be very careful how I spent it. You could just about blow a week's earnings on a meal if you weren't real careful about it. I still think of Anne and remember her kindness.)

Back to the Rathskeller—in those days, shocking as it seems now, no one paid any attention to how old you were when it came to serving beer. I swigged my first beer down fairly easily. I had already had a little experience with drinking during my high school years, so I thought I had some idea what was in store for me that night and the next morning. So one beer goes down, then another, then another, then "one more is all right." I was crushed with homesickness and the beer seemed to serve as a balm, so I just kept on drinking. It seemed to help me feel better about everything. All told, we probably downed about six beers apiece. Then, we all went our separate ways. I headed toward Avery dorm, stepped across the low rock wall along Franklin Street that marks the campus boundary, and then my world started turning. It was turning and turning.

"Oh, Lord," I thought, "Please don't let me vomit." Well, it commenced. And I didn't just vomit, I puked all the way to Avery dorm. All the while I was thinking, "This too shall pass." I said a couple of Bible verses, thinking "Strong drink is the devil's brew." Then, the dry heaves, "Oh Lord, oh Lord."

Thank goodness there was no one there to see me. Can you imagine, in today's world, with everyone walking around with cameras on their mobile phones, what might have happened? My puking might have gone viral on YouTube. There I was, crying and dry heaving every pitiful step of the way to Avery dorm. I didn't think I could make it the four flights up to my room without passing out, so I ended up flopped on a couch in the basement TV room.

I finally fell asleep there, and woke up the next morning with a cold, shivering chill, feeling deathly ill and praying for the hand of death. But I had classes. And with my farm boy upbringing and all of the wrestling training, and other discipline that I had been raised with, I was not about to miss a class. I got back up to my room, and the thought of eating anything again brought on the dry heaves. Somehow, I made it to class.

I remember very vividly that one of my classes that day was biology. They happened to be cutting up frogs, dissecting them. The smell of the formaldehyde threw my stomach for a loop! I felt that all of the frogs I had ever gigged or de-legged and eaten had exacted their cruel revenge on me that day in class.

It took me until along about three o'clock to decide I was going to live after all, though I still felt bad. This was on a Wednesday, and I made my mind up that I was going to find a way to thumb a ride home that weekend, because I just missed it too much. That hangover lingered into Thursday. I had arranged my schedule so that my Friday classes were over with early on in the day. By the time I got out on the road on Friday afternoon, I was all healed up, and felt so happy to simply be alive that I vowed I would never drink again. I stood by the side of the road, all dressed up in my college boy clothes, and hoped that someone would take mercy on me and give me a ride. All of my guardian angels came together and I got home before dark that day.

After a while, I got over my homesickness, and I was a very good student. I eventually became a member of the Order of the Old Well, a group for students who had achieved excellence and contributed to the university experience in significant ways.

I got my grades reported through an optional postcard system that I thought was very handy: we supplied a postcard to our professors and they used it to communicate with us throughout the semester. By the end of the term, the postcard would have our midterm and final grades on it, as well as any comments or notes that our professor had written to us or we had written to them. I saved many of those postcards. They saved me from having my grades publicly posted on a bulletin board.

I told you about the Morehead Scholarship, my small stipend, and how these things became the determining factor in my enrolling at Carolina. There was still the question of how I was going to supplement that stipend so I could pay for everything. I never considered asking my daddy for money. I thought he had sacrificed enough over the years, even through the Great Depression. Sometimes, he had held three jobs at one time: cutting meat in the meat market, farming and carrying the mail. These were all jobs that he found time to work during the slices of time that he wasn't on a wildlife protection enforcement call. Throughout my life, I've not had much trouble asking for what I want, but I just wasn't prepared to ask my daddy for money for college.

My solution was clear. During my first two weeks of school, I got my first job, working a couple of hours a day at the old Wilson Library, where my archives lay today. My job consisted of going through the card catalog and keeping the cards in order according to the Dewey Decimal System. People would just throw those cards back in there, and I'd put them back in order.

Well, as you might imagine, I couldn't while away my young life just sitting there trying to keep the Dewey Decimal System afloat and have any kind of meaningful new experience, so pretty early on, I got a new job at the Carolina Inn, which had some job openings in their cafeteria. Another job that I remember having during college, and possibly the worst one I held during those years, was busing at the main dining hall cafeteria, Lenoir Hall. For some reason, you got a better deal if you were a bus boy there, instead of working at the slightly more rarefied Carolina Inn cafeteria. The Lenoir Hall Cafeteria was huge: we called it the Slop Shop. Working there was a rough job because there was a vast amount of work busing those tables and just about every student ate there and would sit there and look at you. Sometimes I would wonder if the other students were looking down on me because I was cleaning up after them, but I never let that bother me. I remember helping to scrape plates at the Boone Elementary School because I liked the cafeteria ladies behind the counter. They were always so good to me and gave me extra of whatever it was that I wanted, so I'd volunteer to scrape plates for them. I would scrape them into a big thirty gallon container. Later someone would pick up that big container full of food waste and feed it to their hogs.

Anyway, I liked working at the Carolina Inn better than I liked working at the Lenoir Hall Cafeteria. I bused tables there and I made a vow that someday, I would come back to the Inn and spend the night there and eat in the fancy dining room. (I never graduated to donning a tuxedo and serving in the dining room;, I was relegated to the cafeteria where I bussed tables.) Later on, after I had been on Capitol Hill for a couple of years and had saved up enough money, I drove myself down to Chapel Hill and had the best steak on the menu at the Carolina Inn.

Believe it or not, I was a fraternity boy for a very brief while during my freshman year. I was a member of Kappa Alpha, Upsilon Chapter. Kappa Alpha had the reputation of being one of the wildest fraternities on campus. When I first arrived at college, another young man from Boone, Bob Bingham, invited me to rush Kappa Alpha. Bob was from a very fine family over in the Cove Creek area, near the Tennessee line. Bob said, "We'd like to think about you coming over during rush week." Well, I didn't know what "rush" meant or what rush week was. I didn't know Rush Week from the biblical tale of Moses and the bull rushes. Bob talked me into going.

I don't know what Bob told the brothers about me, but somehow, they accepted me into the fraternity. I don't know how, because my clothes weren't the right way, and I was really country, but they let me join. So I was a member, but I didn't live there because I couldn't afford it. I couldn't afford to eat there either. I was just a member of Kappa Alpha, a fraternity known for being a bunch of hell raisers. They would go to Richmond each year to celebrate the life of Robert E. Lee and throw a raging party. They completely baffled me. I went through their orientation or pledging or whatever it was.

They said "Well, we're going to take you on a little trip." They blindfolded me, dropped me off in the woods somewhere and said, "We'll pick you up in about an hour or so," meanwhile intending to leave me out there all night. Well, to make a long story short, I beat most of them back to campus. I was country boy enough to know signs and directions and find my way through the woods, and thumb a ride back to the frat house. I was sitting around with my feet propped up, smoking a filterless Pall Mall and trying to look cool. "You boys are a little late aren't you?" They just shook their heads and let me be.

I stayed in their little club for about a month, and the last straw was when somebody said to me "You've got to get downtown to Julian's Menswear and get you some khaki pants and madras shirts. You need a decent belt and some Weejuns." At that time, the rage in fashion was a little pink belt, about half an inch wide. I thought, "I'll be damned if I'm going downtown to spend my hard-earned money on a pink belt to strap around my skinny ass." I never showed up to any of their functions again. I just never showed up again. I remember telling Bob Bingham, "Bob, it ain't me."

Later on the Kappa Alpha fraternity house ended up burning down. I am sure that many of my fraternity brothers went on to do great things in life. Still, my brief tenure with Kappa Alpha was a turning point in my life. I learned that when you're in something that you don't enjoy getting up in the morning and going to, just stop doing it. You don't have to feel bad and you don't have to explain. It was just one of those things. I didn't dislike those boys, I just didn't have anything in common with them whatsoever. While they were attending fancy social events and swimming contests in high school, I was probably dehorning cattle and castrating hogs.

Probably the best thing about leaving the fraternity was that I had time to I immerse myself in the Student Party. I was elected chaplain and participated in a lot of debates. I made a lot of good friends at Carolina. One of them was Danny Edwards from Tryon, North Carolina. He was my roommate in Avery dorm, where we lived in 403 for a couple years.

For some reason, somebody started calling us "Rufus and Remus." Remus was so country. Man, was he country: his accent was a combination of western North Carolina hillbilly and a dollop of southern twang. He was a good ol' country boy whose father ran a contract chicken farm where he grew birds for a large poultry processing company. We stayed in touch for a while after college, even after he was Lt. Daniel Edwards, United States Green Beret.

While we were in college Remus invited me to go to Tryon to meet the family. Tryon was just a tiny town, but was well known for its horse farms. Remus' mother was a loving, kind person, and I thought that his home was so idyllic. There was a little standard gauge railroad that wrapped around the hillside behind their home, and the train would go by a couple of times a day. Just a nice little train and, like the Little Engine That Could, that little train made its way up the Saluda Grade, the steepest standard gauge mainline railroad grade in the United States.

I remember that Friday night, we went up to this fancy restaurant up on a hill. On Saturday night, we decided to go over to a big dance in Lake Lure, the town where the movie *Dirty Dancing* was later filmed. We danced in that pavilion, the very one featured in the movie. On that particular night, there was a square dance, and a whole bunch of Remus' buddies from Tryon went over there with us. We had a great time, and didn't imagine that a great tragedy lay ahead that very evening.

These guys had never even thought of a day of college, they were just boys from around town who liked to do a lot of whiskey drinking. One ol' boy who was there, a boy named Possum, was one of Remus' good buddies. On the night we went to the dance in Lake Lure, Possum and Remus were driving in separate cars (I was riding with Remus) with Possum leading, and we were all heading home. There was a long, straight stretch of road with a T-shaped intersection with a country store right at the intersection. We were driving along quite a stretch behind Possum and heard a terrible noise in front of us. It was the sound of something horrible. Remus and I got to where he was, and saw that he had completely failed to turn at the intersection and had driven his car right into that country store.

We had been about a mile behind Possum, so by the time we got to him, he was just lying there, with blood gurgling out of an open wound in his throat. Somebody was holding his head and crying deliriously. We heard an ambulance coming, but we knew it was too late. Remus and I were both shaken. I had never witnessed a person dying before, and Possum was Remus' good friend. There was no crying, just a heavy silence during that long drive back to school. It was so terrible that poor Possum was already gone before he got to the hospital and his family never even got to say goodbye to him. Remus and I remained close after that devastating night.

I got home as often as I could, often by thumbing a ride. In those days, if you wore a coat and tie, and a jacket, some nice people would say, "That's a college boy, he's probably okay," and they would pick you up. The hardest part was getting from Chapel Hill to the main road. The main road was 421 (now Interstate 40), and there was always lot of traffic on it. I sometimes had to wait quite a while before somebody going up that main road would stop, but I could usually make the trip in five or six hours with a little bit of luck. Of course sometimes a driver would go only 20 miles and the let me off, so sometimes I would end up in Wilkesboro on Friday night.

At that time, my oldest brother David was assigned by the Bureau of Alcohol, Tobacco and Firearms to Wilkes County, North Carolina. Now, at one point a national magazine dubbed Wilkes County, which is one county below where I lived in Boone, as the moonshine capital of the world. So David was stationed there, if I happened to get let off near Wilkesboro I'd check in on him. If he and his colleagues had a moonshine raid planned for that night, they would take me with them and I would be part of the raiding party. When they went to raid it had to be a good clear night because they weren't going to be out there working in the rain. First they had to spot the "still place," that's what they called them. Then David and the rest of us would start to surround the place. David would put me in a strategic position and he'd say, "All right, now, if one makes a break for it, you get him." The magic about it, which is so unbelievable to people today, is we didn't have to use guns. We would just let out the most blood curdling war whoop that you've ever heard and just scare the living daylights out of them. The surprised bootleggers would break like a covey of quail going into flight in every which way in the world. David would have an idea who was in there, and he would assign each of us to one or two of them. Because I was so young, I got assigned the younger ones, the ones that looked like they could run.

So if they ran we took off after them, "Stop! Stop!" and it was like playing tag football. We got to them, put a hand on them and that was it. Nobody—and I bet you I went on fifteen of these raids—ever tried to even fight me. They knew what my brother would do. There seemed to be a kind of a symbiotic relationship between the revenuers and the moonshiners. They knew David and his crew were after them, and it was understood—they were just doing their jobs. David wouldn't even wear a weapon most nights. David would know a lot of them and he'd say, "Okay, Press, let's do this the right way. You know what the drill is. I'm not going to take you in tonight. Nine o'clock Monday morning at Judge Johnson Jay Hayes' courthouse, you show up there. You got me?" "Yes, sir, David." Think of that! This would never happen today. I asked David, "Did anybody ever fail to show?" He said, "Only one time." The bootleggers would go in, go before the judge and bail would be set. Then they would wait for the trial.

Unless they had been busted repeatedly, they'd get a little fine. The real problem was that these bootleggers weren't paying taxes. Repeat offenders were arrested on conspiracy, and might get sent to federal prison like Junior Johnson, the famous race car driver. Now David never arrested Junior, but David told me one time that they raided Junior Johnson's mother's house because they had information that there was a huge stash of sugar there. (Moonshine took a lot of sugar.) They got down in the basement and there was just bag after bag of 100- pound bags of sugar. Obviously to make the moonshine—and David asked Mrs. Johnson, "What are you doing with all this sugar?" And she said, "Well, you know it's been a good spring in the garden, I've got a big canning to put up." Oh yeah, right. Junior is my friend and was one of my clients for a while, by the way.

Even if I didn't stop by David's on the way to Boone, thumbing a ride could be quite an adventure. I remember one time during the fall of the year I had gotten all the way up to Wilkes County (this is after David had left Wilkes County to go to another assignment that he hated) and there was a big football game on that night. My old high school, Appalachian High, was playing West Wilkes High School. It was the fall of the year. A car pulled over and I heard vroom, vroom, vroom, vroom, which meant that the engine was souped up to unbelievable heights. And this was probably 1960. There were two boys in this car, these two old country grits, nasty and slobbery, and I know something is not quite right from the way they screeched the wheels. I said, "Boys, I'm going out to a ball game." "Git in here!" they hollered. I got in the back seat and had the most so harrowing ride of my life. They had to be doing eighty miles per hour on that crooked road, and they'd hit a bump and the car would jump through the air—you know, we'd come to a little tiny hill, take flight, and land "WHAM." The more I said, "Please, please, let me out," the more they'd laugh, they'd just laugh maniacally. I thought, they are going to get us killed! These boys were intent on scaring the living daylights out of this college boy, and man did they get it done. They finally stopped the car and said, "You lek that ride there buddy, school boy." They called me school boy. At that point I didn't care what they called me as long as they let me out. When they finally did, I promised myself to be more careful about what rides I took when I thumbed between Boone and Chapel Hill.

For our final year of college, Remus and I decided to move out of the dorm and into a manufactured housing unit, better known as a trailer. It was in a trailer park called Blackwood Junction. The park was owned by the Tapp family and had a few trailers and a country store. One of the Tapps' sons was named Vernon and the other was named Neil. Remus and I rented our trailer from Neil. It was an orange trailer that might have made the cover of *Squalid Living*, if there ever was such a magazine. The sewer ran behind the trailer and the back end of the trailer was about ten feet off the ground, propped up on cinder blocks and all kinds of other things. Thank goodness there was never a strong wind, or that trailer would have sailed away.

Ma and Pa Tapp were just so country. They were wonderful people. This was 1963 in North Carolina and country ways had not changed since I had come to college. So guess what I was doing as a part-time job? I was out there milking cows again, and walking around with that cow smell all over my hands again!

Remus had a car and that's how I usually managed to get to class. When I couldn't get a ride from Remus, I thumbed my way into or out of town. Somebody was always traveling up or down Highway 86. We were about halfway between Chapel Hill and Hillsborough. Hillsborough had cattle auctions I used to go to watch with my good friend Ellen Scouten. One time Ellen was out there with us at the mobile home, and we were having a few drinks and raising Cain. As the night wore on, we were all getting more and more intoxicated. Somehow, Ellen mistakenly opened the back door of the trailer, the one that's ten feet off the ground, and out she goes, rolling down the incline. I commented, "Lookey yonder. She looks just like a damn watermelon rolling down a hill." From there on out, her nickname was Watermelon. All the people who knew her started to call her Watermelon and the name stuck. I never told this story when she was a fancy schmancy Special Deputy Attorney General, or around her legal peers, but I have called her Watermelon for all these years. She is now quite an accomplished bass player in various bluegrass bands. She remains my steadfast friend to this day.

There were some real sketchy types living down there in that trailer park with us, although I'm not sure that Remus and I had much room to judge at that point. There were

With my college roommate, Daniel "Remus" Edwards, left.

some pretty tough ladies, too. One night, one of the ladies had a Tupperware party and Remus and I crashed it. Of course, the hostess' greeting to us was less than friendly. "What are you boys doing here? Look, y'all are in enough trouble because last Sunday at church time y'all were up there playing Hank Williams and all kind of stuff that isn't sacred music." But this lady was known for her good cooking, we had heard and smelled that much, so Remus and I were not easily deterred. I gave her my best hungry college boy look. "Well, would you just let us hang around?" She gave me the stink eye, but didn't kick us out. We hung around until she brought out a delicious looking chili concoction. "Can we have a little bit of that chili?" I pleaded. "Yeah, then get on out of here," she snapped as she filled some paper cups with chili for us. She was beyond exasperation as she handed them over. "Now get out of here!" That was the last time I crashed a Tupperware party at a trailer park.

6

Law School and Washington, D.C.

Sam Ervin, Teacher-in-Chief

I graduated from Carolina in the spring of 1963 and I was married to my first wife, Jane, that summer in Deep Gap, North Carolina. We decided we were going to go to Washington and go to law school. Jane went on ahead of me while I inquired about a position on Senator Ervin's staff. When I learned that there were no openings I followed her up there, determined to take whatever job I could get. I scoured the market for jobs like security guard, store clerk, anything that allowed me to go to law school at night. Then I came upon an opening at Ascension Academy, a private Catholic boy's school in Alexandria, Virginia, and I remember interviewing with the headmaster who had eyes so dark they looked black. He was slender in frame and his speech was staccato and clipped. (I was not long off the farm and Washington area people sounded like Yankees to me.) I seem to have made a favorable impression on him. He did not ask too much about my background and did not seem to care that I did not have a degree in education. I was hired!

I had never taught school a day in my life. The school served the same age groups we would see in elementary school. I believed I could be a good teacher because I had my best teachers as examples. I had some good teachers over the years. My third-grade teacher Miss Buckland was one of them. I learned a lot about the Catholic religion and about teaching during the year I was at Ascension Academy. When Headmaster Victor Summers found out I was in law school he asked angrily, "Why didn't you tell me?" I guess my enrollment in law school let him know that I was going to be moving on, and he didn't like that. I took that to mean that I was doing a passable job.

My job in Washington with Senator Ervin began in 1964 just after I left Ascension Academy. I treasured and fully absorbed every moment I had with the senator, whom I came to think of as my mentor. Every day I could not wait to get to work. The senator was a great teacher for me, the greatest teacher I ever had. I never thought I would put anybody above Mr. Ross, my high school English teacher, but Senator Ervin was the best. I learned so much from him. I was going to law school five nights a week and doing things as a regular staffer and learning all the ropes. There was always a Senate hearing going on. Working with Senator Ervin allowed me to ace my constitutional law course. It was nearly unbelievable. I was learning the law and living it every day in our nation's capital.

Sometimes I went with Senator Ervin when he sat on other committees. One such was the Armed Services Committee. I went with him without even asking and Senator Ervin did not object. He knew I was a headstrong young man but he had a lot of faith in me.

After that, every chance I got, I went with him. It was a thrill to see him on the floor of the Senate. When he made speeches, I sat beside him. It was just amazing for this farm boy from Boone to look around at all the flags and other trappings of power and see all of this real action in Washington. Until that time, even Charlotte, North Carolina, seemed like a foreign place to me. When I began working for Senator Ervin I was abruptly catapulted into this intensely exciting world at a fascinating time in history. I was interacting with the likes of Senator Everett Dirksen, Senator Wayne Morse and many of the notable public figures I had heard of on the national scene. My breath just caught in my throat sometimes. I couldn't believe I was there.

To my great benefit, the excitement of my job eased some of the extreme stress of law school. My former wife helped me get through the rigors of law school, and I want to give her credit for that. We studied together, and during those days, one of us would drive while the other one would read the law. It seemed like to succeed we had to be at the books every minute. It was hard to find time while I was working in the Senate. I was so busy doing everything. I often edited hearings and I had to get those right and put in proper context, because original sources are debated on the floor and committee hearings. This was a big job for a young guy. I was copy-editing transcripts of hearings on things like privacy, separation of powers, the rights of the mentally ill, and the rights of American Indians. I was gaining an understanding about what was going on and getting a feeling about what was about to happen.

To my great joy, as soon as I graduated from law school in 1968, I was named chief counsel and staff director of the Senate Subcommittee on the Separation of Powers. I was twenty-seven years old. Does anybody at that age know enough about anything? I think it is astounding that I passed the District of Columbia and North Carolina bar exams without ever taking a bar or review course. I wasn't being cocky—I simply didn't have time to take the courses. I am still proud of this.

I learned so much more than constitutional law from Senator Ervin. One example of his genius is that he figured out early on where he wanted to be, and he got there. The United States Senate was where he wanted to be, particularly on a committee that addressed the separation of powers, and that was one of the reasons he was so good at what he did. He wasn't serving because he wanted to be president. He wanted to be right where he was.

He had a keen interest in curbing the abuse of power and preserving the checks and balances built into the United States Constitution. When Senator Ervin took the train to Washington in

With Senator Sam J. Ervin in Washington.

1954, he was ready for the challenge of Watergate, though it wouldn't come until almost twenty years later. In the interim he took on Senator Joseph McCarthy —one of his own— to protect and preserve the rights of the American citizen. It was a destination for him. He never even aspired to leadership in the Senate. He just wanted to be able to use what he had learned as a lawyer and judge to protect the law and have the law work in government as it was designed to work. With his brilliant mind he could easily have gone further, but, he did not seem to want the trappings of power.

Senator Ervin did not engage in any yelling matches with people of opposing opinions. He was interested in effecting change by persuasion. He often changed the minds of other senators—like when he was on the floor of the Senate talking about prayer in schools and how important it was to maintain a strict separation of powers. He argued that if we allowed religion to creep into the governmental process we would lose political freedom, and if we allowed the government to interfere with religion we would lose religious freedom. It would be a dangerous precedent to set, because it would be about the diminution of the wall between the church and the state.

I watched in awe as Senator Ervin delivered his impassioned speech on the separation of church and state. Senator Wayne Morse of Oregon—a striking personality, quite the ora- tor and an imposing figure with his flowing white hair—remained on the floor to hear Sen- ator Ervin's speech. When the speech was over, Senator Morse said "Sam, I just heard your speech and after giving it some thought, I am changing my vote. I don't think this is right. We should not have forced prayers in school." This kind of about-face was nearly unheard of and is something I will never forget. Rarely does a speech change a vote. Nowadays, most people make speeches for sound bites to send home. I witnessed this incredible moment. Senator Ervin was not only brilliant as a scholar and interpreter of the law he was effective as a senator and looking out for the rights of the average person.

One time Senator Ervin was asked to give a speech to the National Well Waters Asso- ciation. Although I had written up a bunch of grand stuff, he just went off the cuff. He simply stood up, thanked them for being there, told some jokes, and then commenced with "The Constitution was..." and followed up with an extemporaneous talk. I was a little put off. I had worked on that speech for three days—but of course he pulled off a successful address. All he said to me was, "I got your speech and I don't believe they wanted to hear that. It was boring." It was hard to hear but at least I could count on Senator Ervin to tell me the truth. He probably did my speech writing some good that day.

Jane and I sometimes had the Ervins over for dinner, and the senator seemed to love it, maybe because his wife, Miss Margaret, didn't cook. He would say to Jane, "Rufus is headstrong; you have to calm him down once in a while," and I knew that was advice for me indirectly. He also gave me and other young lawyers direct advice, such as "When it comes time for testing, there is only so much time a person has and their brain can only absorb so much. Make your presentation and your writing short, concise and understand- able to the ordinary everyday person. The judge will know the law. Always come back to basics. There is a precedent and there has to be some good reason to change legal precedent." I've read long boring briefs and followed his advice on law school tests. I gave each question thirty minutes and I divided my answers up in ten minute segments—ten minutes reading question, ten minutes outlining, and ten minutes writing the answer. I kept that habit and it worked well for me. I made the law review and good grades in law school because of Senator Ervin's advice. One fellow in law school, I vividly remember, carried around with him a stack of index cards and he went around saying, "Pick a card." The card would say *McPearson v. Buick* or some such thing. He would cite the case and outcome on the card we picked. He was so intense and over-studied all the time. One time we had an open book exam and he rolled in a shopping cart full of stuff! I don't think he ever made it out of the weeds and I'm not sure he ever graduated from George Washington University. He should have had Senator Ervin's excellent advice.

Senator Ervin often taught by showing rather than telling. He reminded me a lot of my daddy that way. My daddy never lectured either. Mostly I learned by watching him. He led by example and the senator was the same. Sometimes the senator would give advice in the form of a parable. He was giving the nation advice during Watergate. I came to think of him as the "teacher-in-chief." He came from a family of teachers and scholars, so it was a natural approach for him. He could be direct when it was important, such as when he thought someone was violating the United States Constitution.

I was grateful for Senator Ervin's help and advice. I often thanked him for giving me the opportunity to be with him. We never had a heart-to-heart, because mountain men don't do that. I would tell him in indirect ways, such as, when he said, "Well, you had to miss law school tonight to drive me," I might say, "I've learned enough today to make up for missing law school." I often wanted to tell him how much he meant to me, and how I hoped so much that one day I could be just a small percentage of the man he was. But mountain men just don't do that. These things are simply not said.

One way I could show my thanks to Senator Ervin was by helping him in whatever way I could. There were times when his arthritic hands made it hard for him to button his shirt or tie his tie, and I was there to help him—I felt proud that he trusted me with such personal things. I think of those times now when I have trouble buttoning my own shirt due to the aftermath of Guillain-Barré syndrome. There were other personal moments I cherish, too, because I was just in awe of this man, my mentor. His little granddaughter Catherine called me "Rooshus," and every now and then the senator did too, in the course of a work day or trip. It was a little nod to a personal family moment he shared with me. Here is a story he liked to tell about Catherine. The senator had taken her out for a Sunday drive on a beautiful day, and a loaded horse trailer passed by. As soon as Catherine noticed it she said "Grandad! What a nice man to take that horsey on a Sunday afternoon drive!" They had one of the closest families I have ever seen.

Senator Sam Ervin was one of those rare individuals who could talk with people of political beliefs very different from his own and find common ground. By the time he finished, people who may have opposed his ideas admired him without having to give up the ideas that were important to them. He was a man for all seasons, and a man who had respect for his fellow citizens. There has been a lot written about the senator. I had the rare opportunity to be with him often on a personal basis for over ten years, so I have a few things to say, too. When you travel with someone, you get to know them pretty well. Senator Ervin called the trip from Washington, D.C., to Morganton, North Carolina "the long trek," on which we would "spell ourselves." If you "spell," in mountain talk, you take a rest or a break. This probably evolved over the years from "resting a spell." While we traveled we had peace and quiet and a chance to think. I knew when not to disturb him. While Senator Ervin was a figure larger than life to me, he still had to shave in the morning and do all the little things mortal beings do, and then there was the stress of being on the road. Sleeping (or having trouble sleeping) in a different place every night, eating whatever you could get, and trying to stay focused on the job at hand can wear a person down. My larger point is, when you are close to someone in these circumstances for years, among other things, you know if that person has an evil heart. One of the little things I loved about Senator Ervin that tells a lot about his character, is that when we were on the road and he wanted a night cap, he never sent me into the ABC store to buy the booze for him. He'd just walk right on into the liquor store himself. He liked his mixed with what he called "Gin'gail."

This is the part where I need to talk about what one senator said—that he once heard that Senator Ervin use "the N word" when telling offensive jokes in the Senate caucus room. I never once heard the senator use that word, and I know that in all of the times I was with him under all kinds of circumstances, if that word had been part of his lexicon I would have heard it. It really bothered me that this senator made this claim. I recalled that the senator was present at a hearing on the nomination of a candidate for the Supreme Court. This judge had been given a mediocre rating by the American Bar Association. Senator Ervin's accuser commented, "So what if he is mediocre? There are a lot of mediocre judges and people and lawyers. They are entitled to a little representation, aren't they? We can't have all Brandeises, Cardozos, and Frankfurters and stuff like that there." I am happy to say that his argument did not convince anyone. Considering this comment, I do not put much credence in his memory of Senator Sam J. Ervin, Jr.

In the early years Samuel James Ervin, Jr., was a country lawyer in Morganton, North Carolina, who walked to work every day. In fact, he told me he never drove a car back and forth to work. If it rained, he said, he just stopped along the way and sat on porches and talked with people. Combine that down-home "Mayberry" sense of sociability with his Harvard University Law School education (which Senator Ervin described as "sitting at the feet of the greatest legal scholars in the world") and what you had was a fine human being with a wickedly sharp legal mind.

Senator Ervin was more upset about the abuse of power committed by President Nixon than anyone else in Congress. Senator Frank Church had done some work regarding the spying the Army was doing on civilians but for the most part, at that particular time other senators were interested in other things. When it came to the rule of law, or which legal opinion meant what, Sam Ervin was the expert. He could cite case histories without notes, quote an entire paragraph of *Marbury v. Madison* verbatim, and establish the relevance of a case in clear, concise detail. During the Watergate hearings the American people (and the rest of the world for that matter) came to see this. He could also quote entire passages of Shakespeare flawlessly and read the Bible backwards. Inside his jovial country exterior there was a fine intellect and a steel-trap mind.

His country southern demeanor and delivery just made him more effective. It has always been my theory that if we had a dry, professor-like academic sitting in the Senate trying to do what Senator Ervin was doing, the American public would not have paid much attention. When you combined the senator's personable character with his unbending scholarship he was uniquely suited to take on Watergate. He certainly was successful at it, too. There was nobody else like him. When I think of some of the many things I learned from the senator, one stands out. He often told me "Rufus, don't ever forget your old friends. You don't get a chance to see enough of your old friends so why rush out to make new ones?" Wherever we went he always commented that he hoped an old friend might be there, like Clyde Nolan from Shelby or Judge Will Pless from the mountains.

He sometimes liked to make phone calls to old friends on Saturday mornings, so when I worked for him I would say "Senator, if you're in, I'll come by Saturday and we'll make some phone calls." He lived right across the street from his Washington, D.C., office, in a comfortable old building called the Methodist Building. He just had to cross Constitution Avenue and walk down to Room 337 in the Old Senate Office Building (now the Russell Building). I'd get there and he'd say "Let's ring up so and so." Of course he could have dialed them himself but he had arthritis so it was easier for me to do it. This was back in the day when we only had the rotary phones. He had a whole shelf of phone books from all the little towns in North Carolina, and I'd look up the numbers and "dial them up" for him.

For example, he'd say, "Let's ring up Champ Davis over in New Hanover County." I'd have to ask him Champ's real name, then we'd be off. In those days everyone listed his name in the phone book. When I got the person on the line I never said, "Senator Ervin is on the phone," because he didn't like that. (I don't either.) I just handed the phone to him. We had this little Saturday routine. We'd make calls for a couple of hours. He loved to nurture his old friendships. I learned the value of this from him and sometimes late at night I will "dial up" an old friend and catch up.

Senator Ervin was right. Old friends are precious, and during hard times they may be all you have, especially when you are in politics. In political life, when you're winning, everyone's your friend. You have to learn who your real friends are and distinguish between the hangers-on—those folks who are there for something—and those people who are true friends. Nothing will put that truth to test more than political life—political failures, in particular. You find out who your true friends are when a crisis comes along. I've had at least three big crises in my life, which is why I have empathy for people who get into trouble. I've always felt this way. I find myself wanting to reach out. When you get in trouble, you need someone to validate that you're still a human being, still worthy of friendship, no matter how badly you might have screwed up. It is a painful thing to feel that you've let your family and friends down. You can feel completely worthless. That is the time when you need your true friends, and they show you who they are at exactly that time.

7

Watergate

The time that I was in Washington—particularly the time leading up to Watergate—was a tumultuous time. It was a turning point for America. A series of catastrophic events that began in the 1960s set the stage for a generation of strife, confusion, and change. On November 22, 1963, President John F. Kennedy was assassinated in Dallas. Five years later, in the spring of 1968, civil rights activist and minister Dr. Martin Luther King, Jr., fell to an assassin's bullet in Memphis, and that summer Sirhan Sirhan mortally wounded Senator Robert Kennedy in Los Angeles.

At the same time, a cultural revolution swept the nation that challenged the fundamental assumptions of many Americans and enflamed American youth with new ideas that many people found dangerous. Older Americans would have been unsettled by just the long hair and counterculture clothing—but it was the ideas that accompanied these fashions that truly frightened many of them. At the center of it all, the Vietnam War was raging, and many were questioning the role the United States played in this conflict. Protests deteriorated into riots as tempers flared and police officers trying to contain the demonstrations resorted to force. I could actually see the smoke and flames of Washington, D.C., riots from the balcony of my Alexandria, Virginia, apartment.

The Ohio National Guard gunned down four student protesters at Kent State University in the spring of 1970. People were frightened, angry, and often opposing factions had primarily one thing in common: a deep mistrust of the United States government. All of this added up to a kind of drumbeat of horror that led up to the Watergate conspiracy.

Richard Nixon had a long, complicated history. Richard Milhous Nixon grew up in Yorba, California, the son of Quaker parents. He decided early on that his calling was to be in public office. His kind of campaigning was established in 1946 when he ran for United States Congress during the McCarthy era, and while campaigning, took full advantage of the post–World War II "Red Scare" launched by Senator Joseph McCarthy by repeatedly calling his opponent Congressman Jerry Voorhees a communist.

This was Nixon's idea of the best way to start his campaign. Voorhees defeated him that year. He ran for Congress again in 1950, this time, against Helen Gahagan Douglas, then an incumbent senator. He used his usual tactics of character assassination and inciting fear in an attempt to manipulate the public. He maligned the lady, crudely implying that she was a communist by saying she was "pink right down to her underwear." (Nixon's own biographer referred to his campaign tactics against Douglas as "reprehensible.") In 1952 Dwight D. Eisenhower chose Nixon as his vice president, a position Nixon held throughout both of Eisenhower's terms. By the time he ran for president of the United States against John F. Kennedy in the fall of 1960, Richard Nixon's insidious pattern of trying to attain public office by scaring the hell out of people was well established.

When Nixon ran again for president of the United States in 1968, there was immense conflict on Capitol Hill over the Vietnam War, with body bags flowing into military airports in waves, flag-draped coffins accompanied by the military guard, and grieving families on the news every night. All of this was the result of a foreign policy gone crazy.

All throughout this time, Richard Nixon ran using his usual tactics: demonizing the former administration and the opposition, and portraying himself as the "great savior" and peacemaker. He won the presidency by a hair, and as historians have noted he vowed he would never let that happen again. So just before the Watergate scandal broke, things were brewing together in a very scary way. While claiming to be the peacemaker, Nixon had ordered vicious attacks on the Vietnamese and while claiming to be ready to end the war he instead escalated the war because as he said, he did not want to be the first president in history to lose a war. His first move was to order secret bombings of Cambodia. It was later revealed that prior to his election he went so far as to convince the South Vietnamese government (via back-door diplomatic channels) to delay peace negotiations until after he was elected so that he would look like the "grand peacemaker." This, of course, resulted in a tremendous loss of human life.

On September 3, 1971, Nixon "plumbers" (a code word for his group of covert agents who were paid to plug leaks to the press) broke into the Beverly Hills, California, office of Daniel Ellsberg's psychiatrist, Dr. Lewis Fielding. It was a sloppy job, so they decided to make it look as if burglars had torn the place apart. The reason for their felonious behavior (which today would get you decades in prison) was that Nixon was furious because Ellsberg, a former Defense Department employee, had leaked the Pentagon Papers. He wanted to find out what might be in Dr. Fielding's files that he could use to discredit and destroy Ellsberg. Why would the president have ordered this illegal action? Perhaps because he thought, as he told talk show host David Frost several years later, "when the president does it that

Long lines of people waiting to attend the Watergate hearings.

means it is not illegal." My take on the White House under Nixon is that it seemed that almost everything his staff did was calculated to help him get even with somebody for some offense, real or imagined. Richard Nixon was easily offended and always wanted to "get even." He dressed these attempts at revenge as "national security" operations.

Who, before the Watergate conspiracy broke, would have ever believed that this could happen, or that this egregious breach of the public trust would occur while secretly sanctioned by the president of the United States? We later learned that Richard Nixon not only hated those who opposed him but also saw the press as "out to get him." This man kept an "enemies list." It is no great wonder that during Watergate so many members of the press corps whispered to me that they couldn't stand Nixon, but would "try to be impartial." They may have tried to be impartial but human nature is what it is, or in the Latin, Res ipsa loquitur—"the thing speaks for itself."

Richard Nixon set up his own downfall. His personality itself led to his ruin. It's been my contention all along that he surrounded himself with a bunch of ad men who were better at creating advertisements for big firms on Wall Street than they were at attempting to govern a nation of diverse people. The Haldemans and Erlichmans of his administration had never so much as set foot inside a city council meeting, much less held any office. Anyone who has ever run for public office will tell you that people like this will never give you good advice. In addition to his own personality problems, Richard Nixon seemed to have had a mountain of bad advice.

My work with Senator Ervin on the Constitutional Rights Subcommittee and the Subcommittee on Separation of Powers was excellent preparation for Watergate. Long before the scandal arose, President Nixon was ordering government employees to take grossly invasive psychological tests, breaching their privacy by asking about their sex lives, and other kinds of personal things that disturbed Senator Ervin tremendously. In the Separation of Powers Subcommittee hearings, we talked a lot about the president using executive privilege as an excuse to refuse to turn over information to Congress and to the public. There was discussion of the impoundment of funds, in which Congress would appropriate funds and the president could just tell the budget director "don't spend it," thereby thwarting the will of Congress.

The Separation of Powers Subcommittee brought attention to the ways in which President Nixon was abusing the powers entrusted to him. For a while, it seemed to fall on deaf ears, but as it turns out many fine minds were catching on that this senator and constitutional scholar from North Carolina, Sam J. Ervin, Jr., had some smarts about things that really mattered to America. It was in this way that serving on the Separation of Powers Subcommittee was a scholarly exercise, and good preparation for what was about to unfold.

Before this time, most people had respect bordering on reverence for the office of the president. Watergate caused many to lose trust in that office. It was hard for the American people, seeing proof of profound abuse of power within the American presidency by the president of the United States himself. In the glare of a highly charged public forum, during a hot sweaty summer, the American people experienced revelations which still haunt us today. This shook the foundations of our democracy. Senator Ervin believed that Richard Nixon saw himself not so much as a public servant but as a king who possessed unfettered powers. As I drove the senator to an event in his old Chrysler he posed the rhetorical question, "How dare you, Mr. President? We don't have a monarchy here. How dare you do these things?" His grasp of the injustices the Nixon administration heaped upon Americans of every type was keen. He articulated these abuses of the United States Constitution so

With Senator Ervin, center, and Sam Dash early in the hearings.

well that Senator Ervin became something of a folk hero in spite of his past unpopular defense of segregation. (Senator Ervin's stance was that people should be able to *choose*. While I didn't agree with him on all the issues, I understood that his point of view arose from his deep and thorough knowledge of the United States Constitution and how the law should be applied so as to be in line with its principles.)

When the Senate Watergate Committee was formed, the world around us was in a frenzy about the Watergate news. Montana Senator Mike Mansfield, the pipe-smoking, gentle majority leader of the Senate, knew he had to choose someone extraordinary from the ranks of the Senate for the chairman of the Watergate Committee. He could see the thunderclouds on the horizon and knew the gravity of the situation. Some of those old-timers were without equal in their insights and ability to almost predict the future because they knew the political climate so well. They had seen a lot and knew how things worked. It was obvious that Senator Mansfield wanted someone who possessed great respect, who the Senate members would trust and who had no further political aspirations, like running for president. There was only one person that fit the bill and it was Senator Sam J. Ervin, Jr., from Morganton, North Carolina. Also appointed were Senator Daniel Inouye (Democrat, Hawaii); Senator Joseph Montoya (Democrat, New Mexico); Senator Herman Talmadge (Democrat, Georgia); Senator Howard Baker (Republican, Tennessee); Edward Gurney (Republican, Florida); and Lowell P. Weicker (Republican, Connecticut). Senator Baker was designated the ranking Republican on the committee.

Because of my own political aspirations and my relationship with Senator Ervin I wanted to be part of this committee. There were of course other staffers who also wanted in. I confess that my competitive nature came into play. Before Senator Ervin had even chosen a chief counsel I quietly launched a carefully executed campaign to become deputy chief counsel of the Senate Watergate Committee. I knew I was not qualified to be the chief counsel, but I also knew that I had a grasp of the workings of the Senate and that I would be a loyal and effective helper to Senator Ervin. I prepared a detailed letter that outlined all the reasons why I thought I would make a good aide for Senator Ervin.

During the hearings of the Separation of Powers Subcommittee we had chosen various scholars to study the principles that came to be dominant themes of the Watergate hearings. Arthur Miller, one of my professors from George Washington University Law School, was one of my recommendations for consultants to the Separation of Powers Subcommittee. He was a great constitutional scholar among several legal scholars on the subcommittee, some of whom are judges to this day. (Ralph K. Winter, Jr., Alexander M. Bickel, and Philip B. Kurland were all consultants to the Separation of Powers Subcommittee.) As the furor over Watergate increased and the time for choosing the chief counsel approached, Arthur said, "I have a suggestion for chief counsel. His name is Sam Dash. He's a very bright professor, from Georgetown University. He has been a federal prosecutor and written a book on various aspects of the separation of powers." This sounded good to me so I asked Arthur to set up a meeting with Sam Dash. Because I had recommended Arthur to the Separation of Powers Committee, I had a little leverage, and he liked me.

My office was then in the New Senate Office Building across from Senator John Tunney of California. Sam Dash was, as I expected, a little older than I was. He had a clipped, brusque speaking manner that was the opposite of Senator Ervin's mushy southern drawl and the slow cadence of his everyday speech. I was a little intimidated.

I told Sam, "My friend Arthur Miller here asked that Senator Ervin take a good look at you for chief counsel of the Senate Watergate Committee. I am willing to arrange a meeting between the two of you but I want something in return. Now I have a pretty good job right now and I feel sure I will be working on this new committee in some capacity. But I'd like to have the position of deputy chief counsel. In return for setting up a meeting with you and Senator Ervin, if he offers you the job, I would like to suggest that you ask him to loan me to you as deputy chief counsel. I've been here ten years. I worked for the senator during law school. Washington can be treacherous terrain for a newcomer, and I can be a great help to you." Sam agreed, gave me his word that he would, and it was arranged.

Happily, Senator Ervin was amenable to Sam's request, and said I could keep my present position on the Subcommittee of the Separation of Powers while I worked as deputy chief counsel on the Senate Watergate Committee! He said, "You can be both and save us a salary." That sounded just fine to me. Then he said with a twinkle in his eye, "Oh, and I told Dash you sometimes needed to be slowed down a bit." I knew this was as much a message for me as for Sam Dash. I felt like I was going to bust from both pride and fear. I knew this was a big assignment with a lot of possible pitfalls, but I didn't understand just how important it would prove to be to my life. I couldn't foresee what a tremendous impact my role on the Senate Watergate Committee would have on my life or the opportunities that would come to me as a result of serving on it. I truly had no earthly idea.

I was so happy I walked around feeling lit up like a Christmas tree. The hymn that came to mind was "The Sweet By-and By." The hardship and drudgery of law school was over, I had graduated and passed the bar in 1968, got my first job in Washington with the senator, and now this! I thought of all the people I should thank, my family and friends, the neighbors, my coaches and teachers, the Three Forks Baptist Church, so many people who had helped me along the way. What I wanted the most was to make Mama and Daddy proud. I thought how lucky it was that I grew up in Senator Ervin's part of North Carolina and that I had gotten the chance to work for him and to learn from him. I learned more just following Senator Ervin around than I had ever dreamed of.

Naturally there was some resentment among Senator Ervin's staff when I got the job. I couldn't blame them, but I felt I had worked hard for the job and won it fair and square. I had driven him thousands of miles, sometimes missing my law classes, I had spent so much time on the road with Senator Ervin and in so many different situations. I worked hard to get that job, and I was the only person who knew the senator well enough that I could pick up his comments midsentence and finish them. I knew I could help him better than any of them and I like to think he knew it too. There was no doubt that this job was a stunning opportunity that any young lawyer might dream of so early in his career. I remember humming "Amazing Grace" that night before I got to sleep.

I worked closely with Deputy Minority Counsel Fred Thompson, and we worked together well. He was a "good old boy" from Tennessee and he spoke my language. Both of us understood that our jobs had one overriding purpose: not to let anyone hurt our bosses, senators Sam Ervin and Howard Baker. We could not let them get roughed up in any way. We collaborated a lot and Fred understood that I was Ervin's man. We had a lot of southerners on staff because it made it easier for everyone to understand one another and work together. Fred and I had shared cultural heritage—we were both southerners, we understood the elaborate, subtle, but oh-so-sensitive code of behavior and social cues of southerners. Had Senator Ervin been from New Jersey, it might have been different. Sam Dash, while brilliant, just did not know how to take the "good old boys," and his discomfort and sometimes abrupt, confrontational manner was frequently at odds with us. I often stood up for Sam because I knew he had a good heart. He just didn't understand our ways.

In the end, Fred was much kinder to me when he wrote his own book than Sam Dash was in his book. Fred wrote in his book *At That Point in Time*:

> He [Dash] was sharing the office of Rufus Edmisten, a long-time political aide to Ervin.... Edmisten is the politician's politician ... easy going and gregarious, he was the man to see if you wanted to have someone hear your side of the argument.... Edmisten soon earned the reputation as the "fastest chair of the committee." In 1974 Edmisten was elected attorney general of North Carolina.... Edmisten and I developed an immediate understanding. Both of us knew politics and what was involved in working for a senator. It was to our mutual self-interest, and more importantly, to the self-interest of Ervin and Baker that we get along together ... and protect each other's flanks. It was certain that somewhere along the line our senators would have differences of opinion and that they would even cross swords on occasion. When this happened, Edmisten and I would do battle, fight hard but fair, and protect our respective senators with no hard feelings afterward.

Senator Baker was a young man when we met during Watergate and he became almost like a brother to me. We were comrades in arms, raised about the same way, and we used the same kind of idiomatic expressions. I could often anticipate exactly how he would say something. Long after Watergate, when I was running for governor, he came up to a campaign event. A Republican, he said to me "I know you well and I'll make you a deal. I'll come out for you or against you, whichever will help you. You'll make a good governor."

Howard Baker—along with Senator Ervin—in my view was the two biggest reasons the Senate Watergate Committee was so successful. It worked because they worked well together and they *made* it work. Two men of two different parties had that committee running fast and running smoothly. Hardly ever do you see discourse like this in Washington today because people cannot dislike a person's politics without disliking the person. Back then, you could have disagreements in politics in a very public way and still go have a drink and be social. The old atmosphere of camaraderie and good clean fights we enjoyed in past decades is gone.

When Sam Dash came on board as chief counsel to the Senate Watergate Committee his work place was literally the corner of my desk. We were fast getting into the thick of things. The telephone was ringing off the hook and people were rushing around, busy with a million things. The first thing I had to do was find a place for Sam to hang his hat. Sam begged me to give up my cushy office, so I told him I would. The fact was, Sam needed to be in the Capitol complex more than I did.

To find a place to hang *my* hat, I went to see my old friend Bill Cochrane, who was chief counsel of the Senate Rules Committee. Bill was from Chapel Hill, and a former professor in the School of Government at the University of North Carolina. He had so much sway journalists sometimes referred to him as "North Carolina's third senator." He got his start with Senator B. Everett Jordan from Saxapaw, North Carolina. Senator Ervin deferred to Jordan when it came to matters of commerce. I pleaded my case to Bill and told him that I was willing to give up my office to Sam Dash if we could find a suitable place for me. Bill took me to see a four-story house nearby that sat on a great big parking lot. I had seen this house before and noticed that people came in and out of it all the time. It was a mystery to me. Bill said it was owned by the Senate and asked me what I thought about it. I wanted it! Someone already occupied it, but I do not know who it was, to this day. I didn't care because I needed to give Sam Dash my office and find a new place to work. I had a look at the inside of this townhouse and saw that with a little work it would be fantastic. Bill helped me make it plush.

People often forget that along the way on life's journey you had better get to know the service people: the parking attendants, the police, the general service crew and other people who "make things work." On Capitol Hill the hardest thing to find is office space and parking. Louie Caraway, the sometimes crotchety head of the General Services Administration for the Senate, was a drinking buddy of mine. He outfitted the new house with everything I wanted. He even offered me a telephone in the bathroom, which I politely declined. After the work was finished, this luxurious townhouse became the new headquarters of the Senate Subcommittee on the Separation of Powers. Nobody had anything like it on Capitol Hill. It was a miracle of a space. I named it La Petite Maison Blanche. So in the end, Sam Dash got what he wanted and so did I. I felt I had once again fallen into a lovely condition.

The next question was, where were we going to put the committee staff? It was a daunting question. I went to the senator one day and he said, "Let's take a walk. We need to find some more space." I consulted with him as we walked the halls, which I really enjoyed. Finally, he said, "Well, we need to call Bill Cochrane," which was the right move. The senator did not have the time or the inclination to deal with minutia, so it fell to me. Bill and I then took the walk. As Bill and I walked around we came upon the Senate Auditorium. I looked at Bill and asked, "Why can't we take over this space?" I knew it was not used very much—just for certain special events and gatherings. At first Bill said, "No way!" It took a few days of persuasion but he relented, and he and Louis Caraway and their men began construction on converting the auditorium into office space. Because the auditorium had the usual gradually elevated seats, a platform had to be built over the seats and secured. Because the floor sloped downward as auditorium floors do, the platform for the new floor got higher off the original floor as it went outward, so that the outer edge was the least stable. I joked with Fred Thompson and said we ought to put all the Republicans out on the precipice.

Next came hiring the staff. This was primarily Sam's job but I had input because I suggested hiring and received the authority to hire some people from North Carolina. There was such a cultural divide. Dash's people were primarily from outside of North Carolina and many simply could not understand Senator Ervin.

Sam Dash had his choice of people and I had mine. I knew we had to have some people who understood the senator's distinctly North Carolina demeanor, approach, and delivery. Smart, experienced, capable people from close to home would be able to do that, would understand Senator Ervin's goals and assist me in implementing them. I stashed North Carolina people all over the place, because my job was to protect Senator Ervin so that he could best do his job, which was, to my mind, the job for which he was destined.

I was front and center, serving as Senator Ervin's right-hand man and managing logistics for diverse parts of the investigative body behind the hearings, and some folks came to think that's all I did. However, I also I conducted both private and public interviews of witnesses. Former Commerce Secretary Maurice Stans was the first witness I interviewed. Stans had resigned as Commerce Secretary in 1972 to work for the re-election of Richard Nixon. He was chairman of the finance committee of the Committee to Re-elect the President (which we referred to as "CREEP"). Money that Stans raised for the campaign was used to finance some of the illegal Watergate activities. He was indicted in 1973 for perjury and obstruction of justice. The court acquitted him the following year.

Before any public hearing, the staff of investigators routinely worked up a biographical sketch of the witness with some in-depth background, having had the benefit of the private interrogations in the "dungeon"—the windowless room in the basement of what is now known as the Dirkson Building. Every witness scheduled to testify in public was questioned in private, usually the day before the hearings. (This procedure lent itself to tremendous leaks to the press, who always seemed to know the story before the public testimony.) I received a binder full of information on Stans.

I was more than a little aware that there would be millions of people watching on TV—most importantly, my mama and daddy and all those folks in Watauga County. I wanted to show them all the big stuff I had learned in law school, and this was my chance.

Mr. Stans was a very dignified gentleman and reminded me of Gregory Peck. He was elegantly dressed and his bearing inspired respect. I began my questioning by asking about a million-dollar campaign contribution. Stans said he didn't know how it was spent. Part of my interrogation strategy was to show that Mr. Stans was a highly competent and detailed accountant, so his claim that he was not aware of how a million-dollar fund of this nature was spent while under his oversight would have been out of character. It was simply not believable that he did not know what happened to that much money.

The questioning went on to identify Gordon Liddy's role and detail some of the requests for moneys that came through his office. In particular, there were requests coming through and being granted with little questioning or knowledge of where the money was going or how it was to be spent. That was the climate of chaos among the president's men.

RUFUS: Now, Mr. Stans, in late June or early July did you receive a call from Mr. Herbert Kalmbach requesting money from you?

MR. STANS: On the 29th of June I received an urgent call from Mr. Kalmbach. He said he was in Washington at the Statler-Hilton Hotel, that it was extremely vital that he see me right away, and he wanted me to come over there, and I did. I dropped everything and went over there to see him. He said, "I am here on a special mission on a White House project and I need all the cash I can get."

I said, "I don't have any cash to give to you. Will you take a check?" He said, "No, I can't take a check, it must be in cash, and this has nothing to do with the campaign. But I am asking for it on high authority."

RUFUS: What high authority did he say?

MR. STANS: He did not say. "I am asking for it on high authority and you will have to trust me that I have cleared it properly." As I said, I had no cash belonging to the committee at that time because we had closed it all out but I did have two parcels of money that were available, and I gave those to Mr. Kalmbach. They added up to $75,000 of funds outside the committee.

RUFUS: Now, Mr. Stans, did you not ask him why he wanted this money?

MR. STANS: Yes, I did.

RUFUS: What did he say?

MR. STANS: He said, "This is for a White House project that I have been asked to take care of and I cannot tell you. You will have to trust me."

I went on to question why a man of Mr. Stans' reputation and background would have been so willing to act on blind trust and commit possibly illegal activity for someone who was not his direct superior. He never answered my question, but I knew the answer was that it was just blind trust that put many men in prison uniforms as a result of their involvement in Watergate. Years later, Mr. Stans asked a poignant question: "Where do I go to get my reputation back?" I never thought he was one of the bad guys.

My questioning of L. Patrick "Pat" Gray had memorable moments. A former World War II submarine commander in the United States Navy, Mr. Gray was acting director of the Federal Bureau of Investigation from May 3, 1972, to April 27, 1973. During this time, the FBI was in charge of the initial investigation into the burglaries that sparked the Watergate scandal. Gray was nominated as permanent director by President Nixon, but failed to win Senate confirmation. He resigned as acting FBI director after he admitted to destroying documents that had been stored in E. Howard Hunt's safe.

John Dean had contacted Mr. Gray and requested that he turn over files that had been available to him as acting director of the FBI.

RUFUS: You did understand, Mr. Gray, that Dean was speaking for the President of the United Sates. He said that to you, I believe.

MR. GRAY: No question about it. I asked him specifically on two occasions and maybe even three occasions. I can't be certain of the third occasion so I can't testify to it under oath but I specifically asked, "John, are you reporting directly to the President or through Mr. Haldeman and Mr. Erlichman?" And he told me, "Directly to the President."

RUFUS: ... That was the day Mr. Erlichman and Mr. Dean handed over to you the contents of the Hunt safe which had not been turned over to the FBI. Can you reconstruct that meeting a little better than you did in your answer.... I notice in your statement, there was no indication that you at any time made any resistance to taking any files.

MR. GRAY: I asked the question whether or not these files should become a part of the FBI files and I was told no, but if you are asking me did I resist and did I say no, I don't want to keep these files or you keep them yourself; no, I did not.

RUFUS: Now Mr. Dean said that the files had national security implications, they were political dynamite, they were absolutely not connected with the Watergate, and I know you have asked yourself this question probably dozens of times, why didn't you tell Mr. Dean and Mr. Erlichman to take their own files and destroy them?

MR. GRAY: I don't think the thought ever entered my mind to do that.... I was receiving orders from the counsel to the President and one of two top assistants to the President and I was not about to question those.

RUFUS: You held those files for approximately 6 months ... your final testimony is that you took them to Connecticut and you burned them with the Christmas trash. I just want to know what kind of state of mind were you in to hold those so-called explosive files for that amount of time and never look at them.

Mr. Gray: … In hindsight, granted, God knows, I should have looked at those files. I should have looked at them that evening in the office and if I had looked at them that evening in the office I would have said give these to the State Department.…

Rufus: When you had that little brief glimpse of these cables at that time with your Christmas burning trash, you saw that they involved the State Department. Did it occur to you at that moment, I can give these to the State Department now, I know they are not in my bailiwick and I haven't been the recipient of withholding something from my own Agency?

Why didn't you give them to the State Department at that time?

Mr. Gray: No, I didn't think in those terms at all.… I carried out my orders and I destroyed them, in fact I was ashamed of what I read in that dispatch to believe that my Government would be involved in that kind of an effort to assassinate the president of another nation.

The testimony went on to detail the conversations around Mr. Gray being told that he was going to be named acting director of the Federal Bureau of Investigation.

Rufus: During your confirmation hearings there was quite a bit of controversy about your "perhaps" involvement and they were digging into you heavily about the Watergate investigation. Sometime during that time, I think around March 7 or 8, you, in your statement, alluded to it, had a call with Mr. Erlichman and he seemingly approved of the way you were handling yourself. But, of course, unknown to you that same day, he called Mr. John Dean and therein ensued the famous quote that I think we ought to "let him hang there, let him twist slowly, slowly in the wind."

At what point in your confirmation hearings did you discern that attitude on the part of the White House?

Mr. Gray: I never did. The first knowledge I had on that was when I was shown in the assistant U.S. Attorney's office, that telephone conversation.

Rufus: What was happening? Do you know now, what was happening to you?

Mr. Gray: What was happening to me?

Rufus: As far as the White House was concerned?

Mr. Gray: Mr. Edmisten, that calls for a judgment you know, that I am not prepared to make because I know how, and knowing that other side, but knowing at least what I know now, and knowing that in the service of my country I withstood hours and hours of depth charging, shelling, bombing, but I never expected to run into a 'Watergate' in the service of a President of the United States and I ran into a *buzz saw.*

I remember, again, feeling empathy for him and the other very distinguished and accomplished men who in the service of their great country were deeply betrayed by the misdeeds of President Nixon and his closest advisors. Perhaps the saddest thing is that these advisors also felt they were serving their country. At the root of it all was the pervasive Washington power worship. It is of course alive and well today, and I wonder how many people may currently be in that same situation in the highest part of our government. History may change, but human nature does not. John Acton put it best, in a line you've all heard many times but if you're like me, never knew who said it until you looked it up: "Power tends to corrupt, and absolute power corrupts absolutely."

Gray remained publicly silent about the Watergate scandal for thirty-two years, speaking to the press only once, near the end of his life. Pat Gray had believed Mark Felt when he denied being Woodward and Bernstein's informant, refusing five separate demands from the White House to fire Felt. In 2005, when Mark Felt, who had been Gray's direct subordinate, unexpectedly proclaimed himself to have been "Deep Throat," the secret source to Woodward and Bernstein of *The Washington Post,* Gray said he was in "total shock, total disbelief," noting, "It was like I was hit with a tremendous sledgehammer."

Deputy Minority Counsel Fred Thompson and I often speculated about exactly who this mystery man might be. There were times when we thought Deep Throat might be entirely made up, just another leak, only in disguise. Other times we took it more seriously and pored over *Washington Post* articles trying to tie them to what we knew. I remember musing that I thought Deep Throat just *had* to be someone connected with the FBI. What other single agency had access to all that information from all those different sources? What one source would know the intricacies of things happening in the Judicial Branch, minute details of Executive Branch activity, and, most astonishing to me, things that I thought only Senate Watergate Committee members knew. Gray, with his son, wrote a book about his role in the Watergate scandal. In the book, which was published after Gray's death, he disputed the claim that Mark Felt was Deep Throat, and said that Woodward's own notes and other evidence proved that Deep Throat was actually a composite of several sources which included Felt.

The work of those behind the scenes is often overlooked by those writing about the Watergate. They were the foundation of the successful prosecution of the Watergate principals. Many members of the committee staff rarely got home before midnight just because there were so many preparations to make for the next day. The system we worked in was absolutely the creation of the federal government—complicated and cumbersome. It was something that is today all but unknown—a bureaucratic effort that actually succeeded. Its success demonstrated that the process created by the founding fathers can work in the right hands.

Senator Ervin was respectful and trusting of his staff and tended to give everyone a lot of leeway. Yet I witnessed people every day coming up to him to see what they could get. Everybody seemed to have an agenda, so mine had to be first and foremost to protect Senator Ervin and free him up from a lot of petty demands, aggravation, and unimportant details so he could best do his job—upholding the Constitution.

There has been a bunch written about how I did my job. If you read Sam Dash's book you'd think I did nothing but roll around in my chair and order lunch. Sam Dash knew nothing about the protocol of Capitol Hill and some of the things he proposed took up a lot of my time because he created such a furor on the committee. Dash was tenacious and competent—I won't hesitate to say that he was good at his job. He was direct to the point of seeming aggressive at times, and had a forceful way of talking and a big, easily bruised ego. None of these things made for smooth sailing and I was often the one trying to calm the waters.

Managing the media was another aspect of my job. Leaks proliferated. Most of us leaked to the press, whether we intended to or not. Senator Weicker was one of the biggest leakers of all. Various staffers provided information to Woodward and Bernstein, but I saw no evidence of anyone engaging in unlawful conduct that would have brought disrepute to themselves or the committee. I don't think anyone had a reason to want to make Watergate more of a circus than it already was. Everyone on the committee was sensitive to that. We were just pulled in so many directions. Managing these leaks was an ongoing challenge that we never fully mastered. There were just so many moving parts, and they were all moving really fast.

Given all of this, it amazed me that nobody gave away Alexander Butterfield's testimony—the smoking gun that nobody expected to emerge when it did—or possibly at all. Butterfield was called to the committee mainly to talk about administrative matters in the White House—who was where, who had what job. He was President Nixon's "get it done" man, much as I was for Senator Ervin. No one expected Butterfield to reveal the existence of personal recordings the president himself had made of conversations all over the White House. Like other witnesses, Mr. Butterfield appeared for an executive session the day

Reporters and staff behind the cameras during the testimony of John Dean (courtesy Brian Alpert).

before he was to appear in public. The procedure was that a senator swore in the witness then left the interrogation to staff members. To my great regret I did not attend the Alexander Butterfield interrogation because I thought he was a minor witness, and I had a staggering array of other things to do.

I sometimes attended sessions during which witnesses gave the private testimony that preceded the televised hearings. In the early stages of the investigation, former United States Attorney General John Mitchell came in for an interview. He was visibly nervous. Sam Dash and I were there with one of the senators to question Mr. Mitchell, who was visibly shaking and breathing heavily. He sat down in front of my desk and kept trying to light his pipe but his hand was trembling so badly he couldn't get it done. When I asked if I could help him, he seemed startled, but allowed me to hold the lighter for him and cup the hand in which he held his pipe, to steady it. "Young man," he said, with a look of genuine relief and appreciation in his eyes, "that was very kind." It was a tender moment. Regardless of their alleged role in the scandal, I tried to engage witnesses and make them feel at ease. I'd ask about their families try to make pleasant conversation when I could, because they were understandably jittery.

There were other times when I lost touch with my upbringing and who I was inside. Sometimes I got caught up in the glare of instant celebrity and people kowtowing to me because I was close to Senator Ervin. The influence that my relationship with Senator Ervin seemed to have on others was helpful when I had to do things people didn't like, but it was the kind of thing that could swell a young man's head. So many things were flying at us every minute, and it continued for so long. People react in strange ways to this kind of pressure in such a volatile arena. The actions of the Senate Watergate Committee and its staff would have made a great study of what this kind of pressure can do to people.

So, the burglars had been caught in the Watergate Hotel, had been tried and were ready for sentencing when Judge Anthony Sirica entertained a letter from one of them, James McCord. In his letter, McCord told the judge why he could not respond with candor to his questions. He wrote that he was "whipsawed in a variety of legalities" when he tried to respond to them. McCord made the case that because of these things, answering Judge Sirica's questions might violate his Fifth, Sixth and possibly other Amendment rights. On the other hand, he argued, if he did not answer the judge's questions he would give the appearance of not cooperating which might just land him a stiffer sentence.

Other problems cited by McCord: his family feared for his life if he told what he knew and he at the very least feared retaliation that might harm him, his family, and his friends, destroying careers and lives. In spite of all this, James McCord gave the judge the following statement:

1. There had been political pressure applied to the defendants to plead guilty and remain silent.
2. Perjury had occurred during the trial in matters highly material to the very structure, orientation, and impact of the government's case, and to the motivation and intent of the defendants.
3. Others involved in the Watergate operation were not identified during the trial, when they could have been, by those testifying.
4. The Watergate operation was not a CIA operation. The Cubans may have been misled by others into believing that it was a CIA operation. He knew for a fact that it was not.
5. Some statements were unfortunately made by a witness who left the Court with the impression that he was stating untruths, or withholding facts of his knowledge, when in fact only honest errors of memory were involved.
6. His motivations were different from those of the others involved, but were not limited to those offered in his defense during the trial.

McCord closed by asking for an opportunity to speak privately with Judge Sirica, telling him that he had not discussed the contents of his letter with his lawyers so as to protect them, and giving his word that his statements were true to the best of his knowledge. In my mind, his letter was the first truly explosive piece of evidence in Watergate because McCord was clearly saying that the higher-ups were doing things that were illegal. This was the first time we knew we were on to something that had long, sticky arms and was going to reach out and touch a lot of lives.

James McCord was a distinguished person. If you saw him coming, you might think, "There is a fine person who was raised right." I often thought he must have been conflicted about his role in Watergate. That said, we found that some of Nixon's men had criminal mindsets and truly were trying to run, as John Dean later said to me, "a little mafia shop" inside the Executive Branch.

I sometimes looked at a witness and thought, "How in the world did you get yourself in this mess?" Watergate burglar James McCord was a good example. He was a lawyer, a former CIA agent with a promising career. How did he get himself into this mess? Was he blinded by some strange notion that he was beyond the law? It truly baffled me. How were these distinguished gentlemen tricked into doing things that were not only stupid but carried criminal penalties? It was almost like some kind of group psychosis, the way these Watergate participants did daring and foolish things to win favor from President Nixon.

The awe of working in the White House can overtake a person, I suppose. John Dean recognized this, and once said, "I was a young guy, barely thirty, and there was an awe that came upon me. You see all this important stuff going on—the most powerful nation in the world conducting business of life and death for the planet and it does strange things to you." It is clear that he was not alone in feeling this way.

I remember telling John, when we met in my office during his recent book signing in Raleigh, that even just working in the Senate had a similar effect on me, because my hubris reached heretofore unattained levels. I became spellbound.

The Watergate hearings were high drama that played out in front of tens of millions of people. It was like a giant Hollywood production—all the pieces had to fit together for it to work. I was not fully prepared to be the chief operating officer and general "go-to-guy" for running a wildly dynamic circus like the Watergate hearings. I had a lot to learn and I had to learn a lot of it on my feet. We were all so busy. I felt overwhelmed a lot of the time, all the while putting one foot in front of the other and doing what I needed to do. A good number of the personalities involved might be described as prima donnas. I remember lying in bed practically every night with my heart pounding, thinking through the day. I think we all wished we had more time to take notes and preserve more details of the events that were taking place. I would just hope I could sleep every night, and some nights I had no luck.

There was an ongoing joke that I made a deal with the television and newspaper photographers so they would make sure I was in every picture. Now I admit, there was one guy, Jim, who made a lot of photos, and I had gotten him press credentials so I think he took a lot of photos of me as a return courtesy. I obtained credentials for all of the members of the press, and this certainly may have contributed some to why I was in so many photos, but the truth is, if you were anywhere around senators Baker and Ervin, you would be in pictures. I'm not going to go so far as to say I didn't like it, though.

I stayed close to Senator Ervin for a number of reasons—one being that my job was to be his right-hand man. I also stayed close to him because he had an arthritic neck, and had asked me to stay where he could pass information to me without turning around. (Senator Ervin had the usual aches and pains that aging brings to everyone, but some of his were made worse by the terrible injuries he sustained as a young man during World War I.)

Television was in its infancy in the 1950s when the McCarthy hearings were covered. By the time the Watergate hearings came along people were accustomed to watching television and millions watched the proceedings, some even watched them twice. The Committee received a deluge of letters and telegrams from Americans from all walks of life saying they watched the hearings during the day on one of the three major networks and again on public television at night. To this day people still walk up to me and tell me, "I remember being in college when Watergate happened. I couldn't wait for class to end so that I could run to the dorm television room and watch the hearings." The hearings also produced a large number of amateur sleuths who wanted to tell us how we should question people. People would say things like, "Isn't it obvious he was lying?"

The setting—the magnificently beautiful Senate Caucus Room—added drama and interest to the spectacle as it unfolded. Beautiful as it is, in those days this venue was technologically challenged. Obviously we didn't have the Internet, smart phones, and digital cameras and microphones—but we didn't even have enough land line telephones or electrical outlets!

Watching while Senator Ervin, center, confers with Sam Dash.

As the pace of the investigation ramped up, denials were coming from the Oval Office fast and thick. The administration first issued press releases denying any involvement in the illegal activity. Then President Nixon responded to routine requests for information from the committee by using executive privilege to refuse to comply. When he did turn over documents he thwarted the committee by providing material so heavily redacted it was virtually useless.

Then there was the problem of managing the crowds that wanted to attend the hearings. When word got out that a major witness was coming in, long lines snaked out of the third floor all the way down to ground level and onto the sidewalk on Constitution Avenue. Everybody and their sister wanted tickets to attend the hearings, and that alone was a big job for me. The crowds could be unruly once they got into the hearings, too. Capitol Police, sometimes taking direction from me or other staff members, quelled outbursts from spectators who made asses of themselves on national television by standing up and yelling out, "He's a liar!" and so forth. Senator Ervin often gaveled the place to order, shooting me a look that meant, "Go see Captain Blackstone about returning order to the hearing." Every day I learned to handle things I had never encountered before, so every day was full of improvisation—exhilarating and scary all at the same time. It was truly a trial by fire for me.

The staff was a hive of activity that did not end when the cameras were turned off. There were countless things to do just to keep the whole thing running. Diverse and often competing objectives meant that I put out little fusses all day long, trying to keep all that stuff away from Senator Ervin so that he could concentrate. There was regular tension between Fred Thompson and Sam Dash, along with many other conflicting personalities, so I constantly worried about staff members saying something in public that would throw the hearings into disarray.

People from widely different backgrounds were brought in as staff members, more often than not brash and young, sometimes older, opinionated and more experienced. Just as I did, these people knew that this momentous event might just be their tickets to fame and fortune. Competing interests caused conflicts—some worked for members of the committee other than Senator Ervin. I understood these competing interests, and how they might shape agendas, so I had an insight into how to handle them. It was part of my job to keep everyone working on an even keel, to keep the wheels of the hearing process rolling smoothly. I mediated lots of conflicts between staff members. For example, one of Dash's appointees, Assistant Counsel Terry Lenzner, was a bright and capable lawyer. Nevertheless, some conservative organization had convinced Senator Herman Talmadge of Georgia that Terry would be bad for the committee because he had headed the anti-poverty Legal Services Group. They said he was too liberal and that he should be fired. Talmadge insisted that Senator Ervin let Terry go. This was delicate, because in general you want to accede to the wishes of your Senate colleagues.

Sam Dash became frantic about this, so much so that I was worried about his health. He had placed great trust in Terry and named him lead attorney for a particular phase during the hearings. When he called me for help, his usually rapid speech achieved epic velocity. I said, "Sam, slow down," secretly glad he knew he could depend on me. Senator Ervin was prepared to follow protocol and fire Terry, though Dash begged him not to. Sam asked me to talk to Senator Ervin on Terry's behalf. I considered this, then went to Senator Ervin and said that Sam was having a terrible time with the prospect of losing Terry, and that he thought firing Terry would set a dangerous precedent and that it would be harmful to the work of the committee. After a long pause, I said, "I don't know if this is best. It could have a domino effect. What if someone demands we let some of our people go just because they don't like then? This would put an unnecessary burden on you."

I made these comments with great trepidation, because Senator Ervin had already made up his mind. It was a risky thing for me to do. This was probably the biggest risk I had ever taken with the senator, and I had to summon all my courage to disagree with him. He didn't say much other than, "I'll think about it over the weekend."

The following Monday morning Senator Ervin called Sam Dash and said, "I thought about it over the weekend and firing Terry isn't the right thing to do. I won't do it." Sam knew that I was instrumental in changing Senator Ervin's mind. Senator Ervin's decision set a precedent that nobody could simply demand to have anyone on the committee staff fired and expect compliance. More importantly, nobody was getting fired because of his politics or ideology. We saved ourselves a lot of headaches by focusing more on the work at hand and less on the personalities involved. Sam Dash later confided that if Senator Ervin had fired Terry, he himself would have tendered his resignation.

During Watergate, there were many times when everyone had conflicting interests they wanted to protect—that's just human nature. Republican Senator Howard Baker was a man who could always be reasoned with. I was often in the room alone with Senators Baker and Ervin when the conversations were frank. There were many times when Senator Baker was one of my heroes because when it came down to the wire he voted to do *the right thing*. He didn't just vote to look out for his party or the president. There was a lot of arguing going on and Sam Dash had a mistrust of Senator Baker. I tried to keep the peace during Watergate. Dash also mistrusted Thompson because he thought he was a pipeline to the White House. There was nothing inherently wrong with someone being a liaison with the president. Fred was not, to my knowledge, giving any advance information or warning to the White House. It was just a fact that someone would have a relationship with the White House. After all, nobody there was yet accused of a crime.

When President Nixon said, "They are out to get me," I had to agree. In all my time there, I don't recall a single reporter who sided with the president. I did not notice a lot of professional journalistic objectivity when it came to Richard Nixon. I remember some of them saying things like, "I can't stand that man." They *were* out to get him. But of course, he kind of brought that on himself by running a personal mafia out of the White House. The lengths to which some members of the press went in order to get a story just amazed me. I saw some things people did to get a story that might be roundly condemned today.

John Dean was a pivotal figure in the Watergate hearings. Sam Dash did a marvelous job getting into Dean's head and preparing him for testifying. Dash did most of that work in Dean's home under extreme secrecy because Dean was "public enemy number one," as far as the White House was concerned. They were terrified of him. They knew that John knew many of their secrets. Haldeman, Erlichman and company had woven him into the conspiracy so that he would be the scapegoat. There was no doubt about that. John reaffirmed that to me in later years. I give Sam Dash full credit for coaxing out the right details so that Dean revealed critical things about Nixon and his whole sorry operation that no one else could have brought to light. Only a mind like John Dean's could have put together the sordid machinations of the White House in such a way that the significance of the events became clear.

Around that time I was with Senator Ervin on a trip one day and he said, "I don't know how we have kept Dean's interview so secret. This is about the only secret nobody has leaked." Dash had to be so careful. It could not get out that he was talking to John Dean. For one thing, Dean was afraid for his personal safety. In addition, if news of his talking to the Senate Watergate Committee had leaked, John felt sure that the White House would destroy all of the incriminating evidence they had on hand. Dean's private interview was not unusual in and of itself. The Senate Watergate Committee routinely interrogated all witnesses prior to their appearance on national television. We needed to have an accurate idea of what they were going to say in public. Miraculously, as the clandestine interrogation dragged on, nobody leaked a word about Dash's contact with John Dean.

Prior to appearing in the televised hearings, Dean carefully prepared a statement, which he later delivered to the committee in his characteristic dry tone. The statement went into such minutia and was so intensely scrutinized that at one point, he said something like, "it was Mayflower Coffee Shop," and the White House tried to discredit him because he got the name of the coffee shop wrong. Bear in mind that the name of the coffee shop did not make a whit of difference to the outcome. There was simply no margin of error for John Dean. He had to be perfectly correct to withstand the assaults on his character coming from those who accused him of wrongdoing, many of whom might be found culpable as a result of his testimony.

Another reason was that he was the only one who knew the whole story. The other players in the Watergate affair had bits and pieces of the story gleaned from blindly following and trying to please a president who had lost his way. The stakes were high and the White House team took every opportunity to seize on the most trivial discrepancy, no matter how meaningless. John Dean's testimony went on for days, and it incriminated President Richard Nixon beyond any reasonable doubt ... *if it were true*. At that time, Alexander Butterfield had yet not revealed the existence of a recording system installed in Nixon's offices. John's testimony showed that Sam Dash had done a great job debriefing him. Sam later told me that he just could not believe some of the things that came out of John's mouth. While his delivery was deadpan, the content revealing White House misdeeds was riveting.

There was fierce competition among reporters to be the first to break any new development. Watergate made many reporters famous—Connie Chung, Maxine Cheshire, Sally Quinn, Leslie Stahl, Clark J. Mollenhoff and of course, Bob Woodward and Carl Bernstein are some examples. Every reporter worth his or her salt covered Watergate. Every famous media person in America at some point wanted a piece of the Watergate action. I want to stress that we had no Internet, no iPhones, no laptops—no means of instant communication at all. There was a single pay telephone in the entire caucus room. It was in an old-fashioned booth with creaky doors and there was usually somebody in it and a crowd waiting to use it. When a break came in the proceedings the press scattered like a covey of quail and scrambled to find a phone in some senator's office in order to deliver their scoop to their editors. I often wonder how today's technology might have changed the complexion of the hearings.

We all eagerly anticipated the midday break because we could escape the hot klieg television lights, get away from the tension, and have some lunch. Getting lunch was problematic, though because we did not carry food into the hearing room and it took too long to eat in the Senate dining room. We had to have lunch delivered to our respective offices. I have a secret to tell about this that involves a picture that newspapers had published of Senator Ervin and me looking at a copy of the Bible during one of the sessions.

Living up to my "always be prepared" motto, I realized early on that we would have to order something in advance for lunch before the break. I couldn't predict what the senator would want, and I knew that it would not do for Senator Ervin or anyone involved to be seen perusing a menu during the hearings, so I would put the Senate sandwich shop menu inside the nearest book. Senator Ervin would then take his finger and stop at a certain item as I looked over his shoulder and I could give an aide his order for the day. We were receiving thousands of pieces of mail a week during the hearings. The scrutiny was intense.

We didn't want to get flack about our lack of respect for the process due to our deciding on what to order for lunch while we were still in session.

While we studied the menu inside whatever book I used to hide it, we had to look super-serious, like we were reviewing something that might be pertinent to the case at hand. On this particular day, the closest to me was the Bible (please God, forgive me), which I used to hide the menu. One of the photographers snapped a photo, and that picture still tickles me when I see it.

The daily menu concealment and lunch selection with Senator Ervin.

During the long days of John Dean's testimony it seemed like every sentence brought a new revelation about wrongdoing in the White House. The press went wild. When it came time to question Dean, Sam Dash went first. Some committee members questioned this order of procedure. Dash, as was his practice, had again violated Senate protocol. The senators were used to having staff "clean up" after they finished asking all the good questions. Sam had convinced Senator Ervin that staff counsel should do the questioning to lay the proper foundation. I agreed with Dash that staff counsel should go first to get the facts out and then the committee members would build upon it. Senator Ervin could have easily chosen to ask the first questions, but the quality of the proceedings was the most important thing to him and he knew that Sam Dash was the man for the job. This was somewhat of a blow to some members of the committee, to have a mere staff member ask the more choice questions first. The order was usually decided by seniority, because by the end there were few questions left to ask which came as an embarrassment to those in that position.

You could always see so much of Senator Ervin's judicial training and experience come into play as he piloted those hearings. So many great lessons were in evidence. You can say anything you want in a committee hearing, but if you take an oath, you had better tell the truth. Many people involved in the Watergate affair went to jail just for lying to the Senate Watergate Committee.

With his response to one of Sam Dash's questions, John Dean provided one of the most poignant moments of the hearings when he testified that he had told President Nixon himself, "Mr. President, there is a cancer on the Presidency." I remember that response as the one that jolted me the most, and I could see by their faces that it had had a similar effect on many of the reporters, the committee members, and staff, and the spectators. This was not surprising. If what we were hearing was true, we had a president who had conspired to commit several felonies and as John Dean later put it, was running a "little mafia shop" in the White House.

A rare moment of levity at the hearings, with Senator Howard Baker, left, and Senator Ervin, right, who had a wonderful sense of humor.

Dean's testimony, if it were true, heralded the end for the Nixon presidency, and those who had tried to make John Dean part of Nixon's conspiracy probably rued the day they made that decision. John's intellect and photographic memory was their undoing and Alexander Butterfield's later testimony about the tapes corroborated John Dean's testimony and sealed the fate of the Nixon administration conspirators.

Raleigh, North Carolina, native Gene Boyce, who had come to Washington to work for Representative Ike Andrews, was ready to go back to North Carolina at this point, but I just couldn't let him go. There were so many people who had to be investigated, it was overwhelming. We still needed a fourth attorney on the committee and I wanted Gene. He kept talking about going home and finally I said, "For God's sake, don't go home!" Everybody in the world wanted to be on the committee but Gene just wanted to get home. After talking with Senator Ervin, he finally agreed to stay. To manage the investigations we divided up the witness chart into members of the Republican Campaign Committee, members of the Republican Finance Committee and finally, the White House Staff Committee—to which Gene was assigned, simply because it was the last group on the list and he was the last one to come on the team. So it was by accident that Alexander Butterfield was included on Gene's list. Butterfield was actually the last one on Gene's list. If Butterfield had not been on Gene's list of people to be investigated, we may never have found out about the White House recording system.

Items related to Rufus' time as chief deputy counsel for the Senate Watergate Committee.

Each investigative group was composed of a majority counsel, a minority counsel, an investigator and a court reporter. (At that time, everything was recorded using stenographers.) Don Sanders was the minority counsel and Gene was the majority counsel in their investigative group, and they worked together every bit as well as Senator Baker and Senator Ervin to uncover the revelation of the tapes. Don was a retired FBI agent, a likeable, straightforward guy. Scott Armstrong was the investigator.

Gene expected the investigation of Butterfield to be routine, but discovered that three findings made it significant. Paraphrased, from his words in an interview:

1. We knew that Nixon did not keep a diary, like many presidents do. We learned by accident that Nixon did a morning news report with his staff. It was a single sheet that included the top news stories of the United States and world. In the right-hand column the president wrote the initials of the assistant—(Haldeman, Erlichman, Mitchell and Dean, etc.)—who was to follow up and report back. These were all the notes he kept. We subpoenaed those and had copies of them.

2. In response to a subpoena, Special White House Counsel Joseph Fred Buzhardt, Jr., sent over the calendar that extended back 18 months into the administration, and it had the sequence of events and people, groups of appointments, how long they lasted and what happened the next day. All that stuff was there. The amazing and revealing thing was at the bottom of the page. There was a short summary of the subject of each meeting. All the summaries were written in the same handwriting and it was obvious that *all of the meeting summaries had been written at the same time—long after the dates indicated.* How could they have gone back 18 months and remembered all of that?

3. John Dean's interview revealed a connection between Hunt and Liddy. The case was tightening up. A review of John Dean's testimony to the committee revealed that Dean said that one time, when President Nixon questioned him, he felt as though Nixon was recording their conversation. This was a pivotal moment in the Watergate investigation.

This comment struck Gene. It stood out and ultimately raised a suspicion in his mind. Once again, Gene Boyce connected seemingly disparate elements and brought things together for the case. It became clear to Gene that his team had to raise that question of whether there were tape recordings of President Nixon's interactions in the Oval Office. The procedure was that the majority investigator asked Butterfield a question, then the minority would go second and Gene would fill in the details. Don Sanders ended up asking Butterfield the question about the existence of a taping system.

When Gene got home to North Carolina after the tapes were discovered, the Chief Justice of the North Carolina Supreme Court, Joe Branch, asked him, "Tell me, Gene, why do you think Nixon didn't destroy those tapes?" We all have theories about that. The disclosure of the existence of audiotapes in the Oval Office is the seminal event that determined that Richard Nixon would be caught red-handed. It was undeniable proof that he was running illegal and unconstitutional activities from the White House. I remember when John Dean came to Raleigh for his book signing, he autographed Gene's book with a note that said, "Thanks for finding the tapes!" What an ending to that story.

Having Gene Boyce on that committee was a godsend. I think the world of him and I will always value his friendship.

According to committee protocol Sam Dash was the man who would begin questioning Butterfield in the public hearing. However, Senator Howard Baker insisted that since minority staffer Don Sanders had asked the question in executive session, Chief Minority Counsel Fred Thompson should follow up. Sam Dash was not pleased at this request, to say the least. Nevertheless, in his usual fair way of dealing with people, Senator Ervin answered "That's only fair."

This change of procedure made a great deal of sense to me because it would seem less partisan if Fred Thompson propounded the question, rather than taking the usual procedure of Sam Dash asking the first question. So, that's what we did. Fred Thompson described it in his book *At That Point in Time.*

> After Armstrong concluded his questioning, Sanders said "John Dean has testified that at the end of one conversation with the president he was taken to a side of the Oval Office and addressed by the president in a very low voice concerning a presidential exchange with Colson about executive clemency. Do you know of any basis for the implication in Dean's testimony that conversations in the Oval Office are recorded?"
>
> Even before Butterfield replied, it was apparent that Sanders had struck home. With a look that was part consternation and part relief, Butterfield said that he had thought this question might be asked … then he proceeded, with no further prodding, to detail the entire White House recording system.

When the question was asked during the televised hearing, there was great hesitation on Butterfield's part because he knew that this would be the unraveling of the presidency. I don't think I have ever been in a room as jam-packed as the room was that day. People were lined up down the hall waiting to get into the hearing, and the line snaked down two flights of stairs. I remember sitting there, thinking, "I wish I had been in the interrogation room rather than being at a party." I wished I had been there for yet another act in the unfolding drama of the slow and inexorable destruction of a president by his own hand.

When Fred asked this question and Butterfield answered that there was indeed a recording system in the White House, the room was dead silent. Reporters were looking incredulously at one another. Some of my favorites were looking at me, like "What's the deal?" I have to remind the readers again that this was at a time when personal technology was not available and everyone was left to his own thoughts. In today's world, the beeping, bleeping, and chirping would come like a chorus from everyone's most important electronic appendages. Nobody stirred. We did not carry telephones around. There was nothing to do but listen because nobody could get to a phone. No one would dare leave because they had to hear it *all*. His first utterance had opened the door to God knows what. The wide-eyed expression on so many faces said, "What's next?"

Butterfield wore a pained expression. He didn't want to have to say it and later often said it was a dreadful thing to have to do. The committee insisted it come from him because he was the one who supervised the installation of the tapes. His next words opened the door to President Nixon's worst nightmare. As a result of his revelations Butterfield's name became inextricably woven into the worst misdeeds of Watergate.

We eventually discovered that there was a boatload of tapes and they were heavily laced with not only deep prejudices against certain people and some of the worst obscenities that not even my Aunt Jenny could come up with. Then there were the accounts of copious criminal acts, plain and simple. There are people today who still defend Richard Nixon mightily and say this was a frame job. My only response is, "Read his own words."

Radio and television news broadcasts all over the world announced at a fevered pitch that the recording system existed, and if the tapes were what we imagined them to be, they would show what occurred under Nixon's watch, and we would finally know the truth.

That set the stage for the committee to issue subpoenas—one for the tapes themselves, and another for all of the papers and other pertinent materials from Nixon's inner circle.

On Friday the 13th of July, the night of the discovery of the tapes, Gene left Washington and returned to Raleigh. Along with most other members of the committee I was attending a lively and pleasant after-work party at Senator Herman Talmadge's home. Gene had called to tell me about Butterfield's testimony and I knew I had to tell Senator Ervin, if indeed he did not already know. When I told him his eyebrows expressed his surprise and he immediately said, "Don't tell anybody else. We don't want it leaked."

The day before, on July 12th, 1973, in an executive session, the committee had met to determine what to do about the president's refusal to release books, papers, and other records (which would later include the tapes). Senator Talmadge asked Sam Dash if Congress had ever subpoenaed a sitting president, Sam replied "No, this would be the first time in the history of the country." A heated discussion ensued. "Do we have the right?" Senator Baker asked. Senator Edward Gurney of Florida said it would be outrageous and that we should not do it. Connecticut Senator Lowell P. Weicker was in favor of issuing the subpoena, saying, "The only thing President Nixon will understand is a subpoena from us. I am all for going ahead with it." As usual, Senator Talmadge deferred to Senator Ervin, saying, "If you think we should do it, then I am for it too." In the end Senator Ervin had the votes to go ahead and issue the subpoena. Little did we know that the very next day the committee questioned Butterfield and we had our evidence that the thirty-seventh president of the United States, Richard Milhous Nixon, had actually authorized the installation of the taping system and ordered its daily use. This meant that we would not simply subpoena the White House. We would have to subpoena the president himself. These were momentous days. The excitement was almost unbearable. After further discussion Senator Baker convinced Senator Ervin that he should first make a personal request to President Nixon for the materials. Later in the meeting Senator Baker said to Senator Ervin, "I think you should first place a telephone call to the president."

President Nixon's assistant for legislative affairs, Bill Timmons, was alerted that Senator Ervin wished to speak with the president. Mindful of protocol, Timmons called with the message that "it would be better if the senator called the president," and left the number. Senator Ervin said, "Well, Rufus, go dial up the president." He said it so casually, like he might ask me to call to see if his dry cleaning were ready. I dialed the White House directly asking for President Nixon and someone, I presume Rose Mary Woods, said, "Hold on, I'll be back."

I waited, expecting Rose Mary to come back on the phone. Much to my shock I heard President Nixon's characteristic gravelly voice on the phone, saying "Hello Senator Ervin, this is Richard Nixon." I was taken completely by surprise, flabbergasted and in a state of shock. I blurted, "Hold on Mr. President, Senator Ervin wants to GET YOU! ... uh, on the phone, sir." It was an unfortunate choice of words that was nevertheless really funny. President Nixon had been accusing Senator Ervin and the committee of being "out to get him," for months. Everyone in the room broke up. When the laughter subsided, Senator Ervin punched the right button and in his customary fashion said, "HELLO." I had been around the Senator for so long that I could tell his brain was in high gear because his eyebrows started twitching and moving up and down and his wonderful, expressive face became a little flushed. After what seemed like forever, but was probably just a couple of minutes, he said, "Well, Mr. President, there is no basis for you or anyone in the executive branch to exert executive privilege. I hope you will reconsider and cooperate with the committee."

Everyone in the room, including myself, was dying to know what the president said. The Senator ended the call by saying, "I appreciate talking to you and I'm sorry we can't work this out." The senator hung up, turned to us and said, "Well, the president is using executive privilege to try to keep the committee from finding the truth. As far as I am concerned, this is executive poppycock." At that moment, I knew it was certain that the committee would vote to issue a subpoena for the requested documents and other information, which later came to include the tapes.

It's astounding to think about how the effects of Watergate have rippled through our nation over the past half-decade. The sins of Watergate were most eloquently summarized by Senator Ervin himself in his book, *The Whole Truth: The Watergate Conspiracy*, published in 1980. To paraphrase his summary:

1. Taking enormous cash contributions from corporate executives for Nixon's re-election campaign, with implied benefits of governmental favors or avoiding governmental favors while President Nixon remained in the White House. A substantial portion of the contributions was made out of corporate funds in violation of a statute enacted by Congress.
2. Hiding these contributions and other campaign funds in secret deposits to conceal sources and identities.
3. Secretly dispersing these funds to finance the burglary and bugging of the offices of the Democratic National Committee in the Watergate complex in order to obtain political intelligence and to sabotage and "dirty tricks" to slander the opposing party in the election.
4. Using departments and agencies of the federal government as political playthings of the Nixon administration and using their resources to promote the re-election of President Nixon, rather than serving the welfare of the American people.
5. Conspiring to urge the Department of Justice, the FBI, the IRS and the FCC to pervert the use of their legal powers to harass "enemies" of the White House: individuals and members of the news media who dissented from President Nixon's policies and opposed his reelection.
6. Borrowing CIA disguises that E. Howard Hunt used in political espionage operations in order to spy on the psychiatrist of Daniel Ellsberg.
7. Assigning White House consultant E. Howard Hunt to falsify State Department documents to defame the memory of former President John F. Kennedy and discredit Senator Edward M. Kennedy in case he sought or received the Democratic nomination for president.
8. Used campaign funds to hire saboteurs to forge and release libels of honorable men running for the Democratic presidential nomination in the primaries.
9. Made cash payments out of campaign funds to be used as "hush money" for the seven original Watergate defendants.
10. Gave assurances to these same Watergate defendants that they would receive presidential clemency after serving short portions of their sentences.
11. Made arrangements with the attorneys who represented these seven Watergate defendants that their fees would be paid in cash from money that had been collected to finance President Nixon's reelection campaign.
12. Induced the Department of Justice and prosecutors of the seven Watergate defendants to assure the news media and general public that there was no evidence that any persons other than these seven were implicated in any way in Watergate-related crimes.

13. Inspired massive efforts on news media to persuade the American people that most members of the Select Committee named by the Senate to investigate Watergate were biased and irresponsible men motivated solely by desires to exploit the matters they investigated for personal or partisan advantage and that the allegations in the press were venomous machinations of a hostile and unreliable press bent on destroying the country's confidence in a great and good president.

As we discovered together, as a nation, President Nixon's efforts did not succeed. As the truth emerged, so did a picture of Richard Nixon as a pitiful human being—I truly felt sorry for him. While many members of the committee, including Senator Ervin, thought President Nixon should be tried as a criminal, I did not. I felt that enough was enough. I didn't want to see the man on trial, and I could never envision the president serving a prison sentence. I think it would have been a sorry "reality show" spectacle, and only serve to further divide the nation. The Watergate scandal had damaged the reputation of the United States government enough.

The Federal Elections Commission was created in the spring of 1975 in part as a response to the abuses of Watergate. It was designed to clean up dirty money in election campaigns, and it was an effective tool for true campaign finance reform. Not only is this commission now toothless, it seems to be a home for those who love the challenge of looking for esoteric loopholes to see how they can manipulate the truth so that no one knows who gave what to whom. What used to be a shield from corruption has become a tool to enable those who want to engage in the dark side of politics. Unfortunately nothing can be done about this short of asking for a constitutional amendment.

The United States Supreme Court *Citizens United* decision effectively gutted the Federal Election Commission, removing any powers the commission had to reform campaign finance. This decision polluted our political system so that it is again awash in money, just as it was during Watergate. This ill-advised decision, formally known as *Citizens United v. The Federal Election Commission*, was delivered in 2010. In a five-to-four vote in favor of the group *Citizens United*, the court decided that the United States government could not stop corporations from spending enormous amounts of money supporting or attacking candidates for public office. Political spending, it argued, is a form of free speech and as such according to the Constitution must not be suppressed. So suddenly money equals speech and corporations have the same rights as people. The four dissenting justices objected in part due to the very real possibility that this would allow wealthy corporations (simply large groups of wealthy people in many cases) to further their political agendas to sway elections on a large scale that *no average donor could ever manage*. I believe the dissenting justices were right. Although corporations are still prohibited from giving money directly to candidates, they can now spend unlimited amounts on attack ads. They only have to disclose who their donors are if they spend $10,000 or more per year on the ads. This has to be among the worst United States Supreme Court decisions of my lifetime. It is a ridiculous notion that money equals speech and that corporations have the same rights as individuals. This decision has made a mockery of our democracy. How about the little guy that gave me $50 when I was running for governor? That type of campaign contribution is so meaningless now, and it shouldn't be. It has resulted in an egregious tipping of the scales in favor of the wealthy, who are already favored enough. Having these corporate entities pour trainloads of money into politics amounts to stealing our democratic republic from the people for whom it was designed and to whom it truly belongs.

The very institutions we thought would protect us from another Watergate have vanished because of the large influence of dirty money. All the telltale signs are there—the influence of money, government secrecy, and the routine invasion of our citizens' privacy. The erosion of the zone of personal privacy we see now would astound and disappoint my mentor Senator Sam J. Ervin. Celebrity culture has spawned a generation of people who seem to compete to see how public they can make their private lives.

The lesson to take away from all of this is that people will do stupid and outrageous things when large amounts of money are involved. Democracy is in peril when a handful of individuals who hold most of the wealth in the nation use that wealth and the power it confers to advance their own political agendas, with little or no concern for the public good.

Another institution that arose from the Watergate scandal is the Special Prosecutor's provision, formally the Ethics in Government Act, created in 1977. Ironically, it was United States Attorney General Elliott Richardson who, at Nixon's request, appointed the first special prosecutor. (Nixon apparently thought an outside prosecutor would be more believable than his own United States Justice Department.) As the story goes, Archibald Cox, whose job was to investigate the Watergate scandal, proceeded to try to force President Nixon to turn over the White House tapes, and when he would not desist, the president told Richardson to fire Cox, and when Richardson refused, the president fired Richardson. The same fate befell Richardson's replacement when he refused to fire Archibald Cox. Nixon eventually found a way to fire Cox, but the incoming United States attorney general appointed Leon Jaworski new Special Prosecutor, and Jaworski took the demand for the tapes to the Supreme Court, where Nixon lost and was forced to turn over the tapes. At that time, the powers of the special prosecutor were limitless and undefined. This in and of itself could lend itself to abuse, as a prosecutor might have unlimited funds and unlimited time to investigate any aspects of an individual he pleased.

With Howard Baker, left, Senator Ervin, and Sam Dash, reading the president's response to our request for information.

The Ethics in Government Act better defined the role and resources of the special prosecutor, but still left the appointment open enough to invite abuse. This provision was intended to place a check upon the activities of political higher-ups but has become distorted and is now used as a means to persecute rather than prosecute. For instance, Kenneth Starr spent years hounding Bill and Hillary Clinton over Whitewater and created a cottage industry. It trampled over the lives of so many people—Republicans and Democrats. Another prosecutor harassed Colonel Ollie North in the same way, and even as far back as the Jimmy Carter era, someone accused Hamilton Jordan of being a habitual cocaine user and that was investigated via special prosecutor. I think it is outrageous to have a position that is authorized to investigate carte blanche any individual, for any length of time, using unlimited allocations of funds. In addition, everyone who feels there is even a possibility that they may be involved has to "lawyer up" and spend untold amounts of money that is largely money wasted and has put many a person into bankruptcy. The very process creates a climate of fear and has reinforced the public perception that everyone in politics is a crook. The excesses of the special prosecutor during Whitewater were so widely and well recognized that the Ethics in Government Act was allowed to expire under a so-called "sunset clause" in 1999.

After 1999, the Code of Federal Regulations oversees the appointment of a special prosecutor, giving much more power to the United States Attorney General in deciding when and if to appoint a special prosecutor, but effecting little other change. For my part, I have always believed that the United States Department of Justice is entirely capable of prosecuting those who deserve it.

8

The Attorney General Years

When I gave Senator Ervin my letter of resignation and left the Watergate committee I was overcome by emotion and feelings of insecurity, like the very ground was shifting under my feet. I was about to leave Washington and drive down that road not knowing what I faced. What I wanted was to get elected North Carolina Attorney General. I thought my role in Watergate might serve my goal well by giving me recognition and making me memorable. Earlier, North Carolina Attorney General Robert Morgan, who had been in the North Carolina Senate and earlier one of the youngest clerks of court in the history of the state of North Carolina, announced that he was going to run for United States Senate. He chose to step down as North Carolina Attorney General in August 1973, so that he could devote his full attention to his campaign. This was the day I had been waiting for—a chance to run for North Carolina Attorney General.

I headed down I-95 and branched off south of Richmond onto I-85—the long, familiar trip I had taken so often with Senator Ervin. When I arrived in Raleigh, I rented a one-bedroom apartment at Quail Corners. At first I didn't have any furniture to speak of, just a big map of North Carolina that showed every nook and cranny of the state. I put it up on my wall and started busily mapping out my plans to win the nomination for attorney general. The governor at that time was Jim Holshouser, a fellow Watauga County native who had been elected in 1972 along with Senator Jesse Helms. Governor Holshouser was the first Republican elected to the governorship since Reconstruction.

Skipper Bowles had just suffered in 1972 the same fate I would suffer in 1984. In the primary election, he was dealt grave political wounds which never healed, and that resulted in the election of Governor Holshouser. As a result Jesse Helms won his Senate race with a near landslide in 1972 over Nick Galifianakis who had a wonderful, ebullient, outgoing personality, and a fun sense of humor. For example he divided his name into two campaign buttons because it was so long. "GALIFIA" read the first and "NAKIS" read the second, and he wore them together. Whenever I think of Nick Galifianakis I remember the time Senator Ervin and I campaigned for him. The senator spoke at one of his rallies. Dear Ester Presnell liked to bring us boxes of homemade cookies, and at this time there was a lot of terrorist bombing going on nationwide, so when the security people saw the box, they thought it looked suspicious. So the whole rally was called to a halt when the bomb squad was called in, and in the end they blew that box of cookies to smithereens. It still makes me laugh!

Anyway, Nick ran a strong campaign that year but there was resentment about beating the old guard, so Helms won that race in 1972 and riding the tide, Jim Holshouser defeated Skipper Bowles, the Democratic nominee.

Galafianakis had defeated Senator B. Everett Jordan in the primary by running newspapers ads comparing the ages of the two candidates. Galafianakis was a much younger man. It did not help Senator Jordan's campaign that he was hospitalized with a minor ailment just before the election. Someone released a photo of him looking frail and unwell, seated in a wheelchair, and soon it was all over television. I often wondered how his campaign manager had allowed that to happen. Galafianakis, who was an indefatigable campaigner, simply wore out Senator Jordan, a textile manufacturer from Haw River and Senator Ervin's colleague and buddy. It was not a matter of age: Jordan had never been a particularly strong speaker or campaigner.

I've often thought Jim Holshouser was more surprised that anyone to find himself elected governor. He and I knew each other. He had attended high school with my older brothers and sister Betty. When Morgan resigned from the office of attorney general in 1974 to run full-time for the United States Senate, Holshouser had been governor for two years. North Carolina law called for the governor to select someone to serve until the next general election, which was in November 1974. He appointed Jim Carson out of Charlotte to fill the vacancy and serve as sitting attorney general when I moved to Raleigh.

The procedure for choosing nominees for each party in a situation like this was to require the statewide executive committee for each party to make the choices. Members of the executive committee were from all over the state, a diverse group. There were nine other candidates for the Democratic nomination, all of whom would be trying to sway the executive committee. When I looked at some of those people I felt a little shaky. I would be up against Herbert Hyde, who had served in the North Carolina House of Representatives, and other people with many years of experience. I was a young upstart and an "outsider" but I had some face and name recognition from being in the national spotlight during Watergate. I also had a grand plan that I thought would work.

When I began running in earnest I had to travel all over the state on a shoestring budget, sometimes staying with friends and sometimes even sleeping in my car. One time on a trip to Shelby to speak to the Kiwanis Club, I put down the seat of my old Rambler and slept most of the night there at the Kings Mountain rest stop. I cleaned up in the bathroom, changed clothes, dabbed on some cologne and went on to the speaking engagement. I didn't mind. I was fully *in* the race and I needed to win. I often joked at rallies that I was running for attorney general because I needed a job—which was really no joke. While I had just resigned from a good job, all of the other candidates were employed full time.

When I worked for Senator Ervin he often sent me to party functions to deliver his greetings, so I already had ample knowledge of the members of the executive committee and many contacts to tap. Wherever I went I made it a point to remember people's names and some little detail about them. I kept a Royster Fertilizer pocket notebook that Mr. Goodnight from the seed store back home gave us whenever we bought fertilizer and wrote down names and details about everyone I met. Things like the names of their children or mamas or pets, their hobbies, that sort of thing. Then when I saw them again I would ask them how so-and-so was doing or how thus and such was going. I jumped at every opportunity to get out and make myself known. The public exposure Watergate gave me meant that I was a bit of a sought-after speaker and that helped me.

I knew I had to wage a full-fledged, all-out campaign. Ken Wright, in later years a lobbyist for Blue Cross and Blue Shield, was my first campaign hire. We went to one of the office supply stores and got huge sheets of paper and tacked them on one whole wall of my apartment, which had become my campaign headquarters. We wrote down the names of everyone on the Democratic executive committee. When I made calls to executive committee members or people who could influence them, we noted what they said, whether they were hot, cold, or lukewarm on me. Soon there were over four hundred names on the paper that covered my wall.

If I knew the person well enough I might let the call suffice so I wouldn't have to travel so much. We handled many people by phone and I remember that nobody was ugly to me. I caught them just after dinner and never asked them to call back because it would cost them money to call long distance. Having met many of these people by way of Senator Ervin gave me a big advantage. I had always known that my association with him worked in my favor, and I admit, I used it shamelessly.

I remember calling a man in Chatham County whom I had met at a Democratic rally. He had mentioned that his daughter had just gotten a new pony. I wrote it down. Later when I called to ask for his support I asked about the pony. Before we hung up he said, "I'm for you 100 percent, put me down ." I didn't think anybody I was running against was as adept as I was at knowing and working the party apparatus.

In 1974 we sometimes traveled to forums that people held even though there was a gas shortage, what was called "the gas crisis." I drove an old diesel Mercedes, and there was no shortage of diesel fuel. So I never missed a forum for lack of fuel but I did hide the car as I didn't want the "Buy American" crowd to see I had a foreign car. I had gotten a really good deal on that Mercedes when my old Rambler finally died.

One time when I traveled to Lee County to drum up support and a man's wife said he was out plowing the field and directed me to where I could find him. I pulled over, took my tie off, climbed over the barbed-wire fence and went right through the muddy plowed field in my good shoes. I told myself, "Don't worry about the shoes, do like you do at home."

On the campaign trail in a vintage car with supporters.

He was out there on a red Farm-All tractor. When he saw me he got off his tractor and asked me who I was and what I was doing there. We had a nice talk about the difference between flue-cured and burley tobacco, and I got his support. Circumstances like this went on over and over again. Dogs chased me, kids eyeballed me, and mosquitos made many a meal of me. I got rained on and ruined more than one pair of shoes.

On the other hand, sometimes I met with top executives in slick, opulent office complexes. One was Charles Cannon of Cannon Mills in Kannapolis. He was gruff and kept calling me "son," but that was all right with me as long as I got his support. My opponents often had large pockets of fiercely loyal supporters, and I talked to them also. Most of the trips took a couple of days. When I got home Ken and I would fill in information on the big sheets of paper on my apartment wall—who was for me, who was against me, who was undecided. It soon became clear that my strategy was working, at least if I could believe the ones who said they were for me.

Some people hid from me, some people told me they would support me then didn't. Not everyone tells you the truth in politics. Still, I knew I had a good chance of winning. Unlike many others I never ran in a race if I didn't think I had a good chance of winning. By the time the executive committee was due to vote, Charlie Smith had become my campaign manager. Charlie was a brilliant strategist who would play a key role in my political campaigns. I had met him in Washington when he was working for First Union Bank in Charlotte. When I called him and asked him to work for me he took a giant leap of faith and quit his bank job to come work for me. I was eating a lot of Vienna sausages with crackers and vinegar to make sure I could meet campaign expenses. Sometimes I splurged on bologna sandwiches.

Greeting a young supporter during my run for attorney general of North Carolina.

As the day of reckoning approached the media predictions began. I made my own predictions. Because I had been such a "people person" my whole life, even though I was young, and had both engaged and observed so many different kinds of people, I knew that many who said they would support me would say the same thing to others. I took the number of people who promised me their vote on their mother's grave and cut it in half. I was off by two points when the final votes came in. I got two more votes than I thought I might.

I can't talk about my first election without talking about Jimmy Ervin, the political analyst whiz, aka Samuel James Ervin IV, now a justice on the North Carolina Supreme Court. Jimmy was a political and intellectual child prodigy. When he was just eighteen years old, Jimmy completed an excellent analysis of the 1974 Democratic primary for North Carolina Attorney General. This analysis, to me, presaged his career as a brilliant lawyer and jurist. I had to include it here. It is just an outstanding piece of work, particularly from a young man who was still in his teens.

Samuel J. Ervin IV's Analysis of the 1974 North Carolina Attorney General Democratic Primary Election

On May 7, 1974, the voters of the state of North Carolina went to the polls to determine the nominations of the parties for the United States Senate seat being vacated by the retiring Sam J. Ervin, Jr. The campaign had stirred little interest during its course, and this fact was reflected in the vote totals, which showed the lightest turnout in many years. The major candidates were the present attorney general, Robert Morgan, whose candidacy was supported by the democratic organization, former Congressman Nick Galifianakis, who was supported by some liberals and those who had a personal antipathy to Morgan, and Henry Hall Wilson, a retired Chicago businessman who had returned to his home state to make the race. At the time most of the citizens had gone to bed on the day of the election it was known that Morgan was the leader in the field of candidates, but whether he would win an absolute majority was unknown, and he had to do this to avoid being in a run-off with Galifianakis. At dawn, Morgan was still short of a majority, with the early edition of the *Charlotte Observer* having him short of the required 50%. A later edition showed that Morgan had 209,418, Galifianakis had 138,750, and Wilson had 44,590, with the remaining 24,459 votes scattered among a number of minor contenders. During the morning Morgan pulled over the majority mark and the afternoon papers showed that the results were conclusive, with Morgan the recipient of 292,676 votes (50.45%), Galifianakis the winner of 186,710 (32.21%), and Wilson coming in with 66,424 (11.46%) with the rest scattered among the remaining less serious candidates for the office.

The nomination of the incumbent attorney general for the Senate put the two major parties in a situation which they had not been put in before throughout the political history of the state. It was necessary to replace a sitting member of the Council of State whose term was not ordinarily expired and do it without the benefit of party primaries and on rather short notice. The Republican candidate, James Carson, a member of the North Carolina Court of Appeals, was chosen by Governor James Holshouser to fill the post upon the resignation of Morgan, which was to occur in the month of August, which was a little earlier than the attorney general had planned to step down and Judge Carson's nomination was expected to be ratified by the Republican Party Executive Committee without any difficulty.

The Democratic Party was in a different situation. Because of its severe setbacks in the general election of 1972, in which it lost both the governorship and a Senate seat which had been in its possession since the end of fusion rule in 1900, the party had no clear ruling force and was forced to do what it probably would have done anyway—choose its nominee to replace Morgan in a party executive committee fight with no holds barred just like a political convention with any number of political contenders trying to affect the outcome of the meeting. This was indeed what was done, and it produced one of the most interesting races in North Carolina political history.

The members of the executive committee began arriving in Raleigh on the afternoon on July 26, with most of them going to the Sir Walter Hotel, where the balloting was to be held. The prospective candidates were all in the hotel to do their last-minute politicking in an effort to pick up those badly needed votes. One last forum was held for the candidates, with the second floor meeting room where the talking was done filled to overflowing with listeners who wanted one last chance to hear all the candidates talk on the issues that they saw in the campaigns. The major topic of conversation by the candidates at this last meeting was the Holshouser administration and the "Broyhill machine" which was alleged to run the state's politics.

Judge Winner stated, opening the forum, that he was "going to talk about our opponents … the Republican Party and their handpicked, closed-doors candidate, James Carson." He went on to say that "The Holshouser administration had done nothing to meet North Carolina's problems. Can we expect Jim Carson to be any different?" The judge went on to say that Carson was the "hand-picked candidate of the governor and of the Broyhills who pull the governor's strings." Concluding, he stated the opinion that Carson was not qualified to be attorney general because he had threatened to fire SBI Director Charles Dunn.

Rufus Edmisten continued this series of blasts at the opposition by saying: "There's no doubt about it, the Broyhill family owns the governor…. The state is being run from Lenoir." He listed his own qualifications being his ten-year stay in the Senate fighting bureaucrats and trying to straighten out the problems of the nation. McNeill Smith said during his allotted time that "it's even more important now that we have a Republican governor that we have someone who can enforce the law." Stressing the nature of the office of attorney general, he noted that he had more legal experience than his opponents and that he was the only one to offer specific programs for the improvement of the services of the Justice Department to the people. Mitchell said that he would continue to fight for consumer protection and laws against lobbying, but that he was "scared to death of this crowd (meaning the Republican administration) because the executive branch is trying to work its will on the people regardless of the law." He went on to accuse the Enforcement and Theft Division of the State Highway Commission of illegally investigating Robert Morgan until the matter was leaked to the public and they were forced to put a stop to that kind of practice.

The only black, Mickey Michaux, continued his claim that he was a serious candidate because of "the aspirations and hopes of many people … who have never wavered in Democratic politics … people who have given their total allegiance." The older candidates, Hyde and Josey and Kivet stressed their experience and their backgrounds, with Kivett stressing also his Piedmont background, claiming that it would give strength to the ticket. Hyde emphasized his vote-getting ability and warned of the consequences of letting the Republicans control the SBI because they might use it for political reasons. Josey was fishing for the support of the undecided when he said to the gathering: "I have represented individuals and people in my advocacy."

After the meeting broke up the candidates swarmed out into the audience to meet those on the committee who they thought might be persuaded to vote for them on the morrow during the balloting. Then the men went back to their hospitality suites or floated around the lobby in search of more members of the committee who they could talk to or work on in some way. A tour of the hospitality suites revealed a great deal about the way that the campaign was going, for no one denied that the places which had the greatest and most enthusiastic crowd might not be the one that ran away with all the marbles.

The Edmisten suite, on the fourth floor in room 447 was alive with activity. The ever-present supply of alcohol and other beverages was in evidence, as was much food spread in a haphazard fashion along a lengthy table in the next room, which also contained a television set going at full blast showing the deliberations of the House Judiciary Committee on the subject of the impeachment of Richard Nixon. A crowd of supporters thronged through the two rooms and out a small entrance-hall into the hall, filling the whole wing of the building with merriment. They drank and talked and read literature praising the candidate and informing them about his good side. Down the hall of the same floor of the building was the headquarters of Judge Charles Kivett, where champagne was being served in addition to other, more ordinary kinds of beverages, both potent and otherwise. The television was silent in the main room and the candidate himself was in the next room talking to people quietly on a one-on-one basis where no one else could hear them. The people outside were not particularly enthusiastic and the room was practically deserted except for the few loyal supporters that were actually working for him. The atmosphere was depressing and dead.

The rooms of State Senator McNeill Smith were a little noisier and more jovial than Judge Kivett's, with a steady stream of well-wishers flowing to the bar and the supply of newspaper reprints which extolled the candidacy of Smith. The place was fairly full, but not inundated, with the candidate able to greet all who came in, but not talk at any length to anyone except those who showed some signs of being about to come over to his side. His aides hurried through the visitors and talked to them and sought to find out what they were thinking, sometimes succeeding and sometimes not. Kitch Josey's establishment on the third floor was full of people—supporters and family members and well-wishers of all kinds. There was a vibrancy and enthusiasm which we had not seen except in the Edmisten quarters and which radiated out into the hall. The candidate was greeting supporters and visitors in a steady stream which continued to flow all the time. The bar did a flourishing business during the evening. Of all the places in the building this was the place that had the look of a winner. Herbert Hyde's rooms [sentence drops off here and does not continue on the next page, which is in numerical sequence.]

The meeting opened a few minutes after ten o'clock with an invocation by ?, then got down to serious business. The roll was called and a total of 258 out pf 260 answered when their name was called by the Secretary. Chairman James Sugg then brought out the proposed rules of procedure for the meeting which were adopted after two amendments were defeated (they would have provided for the votes to be announced by Congressional Districts in order to let the eight candidates know where their support was and assisting them to campaign in the room. This was beaten with the argument that to do this would damage the unity of the party. The same argument was used to defeat the second amendment which would have dropped the requirement that the low man drop out, which some candidates didn't like because they were not doing so well. The two changes were easily defeated and the meeting began with a set of rules that provided that a majority was needed to nominate, that each candidate and one floor leader were all that could be on the floor during the balloting with the delegates, that the vote would be taken by secret, written ballot to be counted by a committee consisting of Mayor Lightner of Raleigh, Secretary of State Thad Eure, and Commissioner of Agriculture James Graham, that after the first ballot anyone who did not have ten percent of the votes would be eliminated, as would the low man on each ballot after the first one. The chairman allowed nominating speeches of two minutes each and no seconding speeches at all.

Mr. John Dees of Burgaw nominated Rufus Edmisten, saying that he would "sweep the state from Boone to Burgaw." Max Childers, a state legislator form Gaston County nominated Kitch Josey, a longtime member of the legislature and a friend from the time the two of them were in school together. McNeill Smith was nominated by Isaac "Pete" Avery from Iredell County, then Max Cogburn from Buncombe County nominated State Representative Herbert Hyde. Charles Kivett was put in nomination next, then State Senator Eddie Knox nominated Judge Dennis Winner. A defeated candidate for Congress, Robert Wynne, submitted the name of Burley Mitchell, a fellow citizen of Wake County. A Mr. Whaley from Durham County nominated the last contender, State Representative Mickey Michaux. The nominations were closed upon the motion of John Beasley and the balloting began at 11:45 as the marshals passed out the paper ballots which were in canvas pouches on a table in the front of the assembled committee.

The meeting went into an informal recess until the ballots were counted, a process which consumed approximately 35 minutes, during which all manner of rumors swept the floor. It was rumored that Judge Winner would withdraw after the first ballot if he did not have ten percent of the votes even though he was not required to do so until the second round. About twelve twenty the counting committee returned to the room and announced the results of the vote.

Edmisten	74
Josey	47
Smith	25
Hyde	33
Kivett	20
Winner	17
Mitchell	16
Michaux	24

Proving the rumors to be true, Winner withdrew without recommending that his supporters switch to any specific candidate. The second ballot was called immediately after Winner's pullout, but a point of order was made by Roger Cushee to the effect that the required fifteen minute caucus had not been held. The chairman sustained the point of order made from the floor, but the committee voted to suspend the rules and call for the second round of balloting immediately and this motion carried. The ballots were passed out and the counting committee went to count the ballots, with Burley Mitchell pulling out after the motion to dispense with the caucus round was passed. During this time most of the delegates retired to neighboring restaurants to eat a hasty lunch. The committee returned at some time around fifteen till one and announced the results of the second ballot:

Edmisten	83
Josey	47
Smith	34
Hyde	44
Kivett	28
Michaux	22

Michaux made a withdrawal speech and the caucus round began with a frantic scramble for the votes of Mickey Michaux, and with the Kivett supporters trying desperately to avoid being knocked out on the third ballot. Edmisten had picked up 9 votes from the losing candidates, Hyde had gained 11, Smith 9, and Judge Kivett had picked up eight, with Mickey Michaux losing two of his first-round votes. After the caucus had been concluded the ballots were passed out, written, and voided. During the absence of the counting committee the politicking continued at a furious pace until the ritual of counting the ballots was completed and the members returned to the hall with the result of the vote. The third ballot was announced at about 2:30 with the following results:

Edimisten	86
Josey	47
Smith	51
Hyde	45
Kivett	27

The black vote had been swung to McNeill Smith and Judge Kivett had been pushed out of contention, and like all other candidates before made a short speech after he had been eliminated from the contest. The caucus round was filled with wild attempts by the Edmisten floor team to keep on gaining votes and by the Josey supporters to keep their man from being eliminated and having the "too liberal" Smith from gaining the nomination. Edmisten and Smith expected to pick up the bulk of the votes belonging to Judge Kivett. Rumors swept the floor about some kind of deal between Representative Hyde and Senator Smith, altogether an unusual combination which at the time frightened the eastern Josey supporters. At about 4:00 the fourth ballot began and the same process was repeated again after a motion to pass another motion to dispense with the caucus round was defeated. The committee returned with the final results a few minutes later:

Edmisten	96
Josey	51
Smith	59
Hyde	51

The tie between the last-place finishers brought a ruling from the chair that neither was to be considered eliminated although the rumors at the time pretty much assumed that Josey was through for the day. The black voters held a caucus, and Representative Michaux came to Edmisten and said something to the effect that the voters favored the nomination of either Smith or Edmisten and that in his opinion the former could not win because of his too-liberal reputation among the party leaders, so the black vote was coming over to their second choice, which was Edmisten. The Josey supporters were in great confusion when rumors came that their candidate was going to withdraw from the contest. The rumors also stated that Josey and Hyde were in the washroom trying to work out some form of a deal with each other on the subject, although easterners were opposed to Hyde because of his opposition to the death penalty, and the Hyde supporters in the main wanted a western candidate to balance the ticket with Robert Morgan. Against this backdrop the fifth ballot was taken. The Edmisten supporters and floor workers were confident that they would be far in the lead and could possible take the nomination on this ballot. The vote came back and was announced as follows:

Edmisten	120
Josey	41
Smith	34
Hyde	59

As soon as the result was announced the two low candidates came forward and made concession speech. Smith, who was knocked out as the low man, came forward first and announced that the party was still healthy and that the competition of the day showed that fact better than anything else could. Kitch Josey voluntarily came forward and withdrew, saying that he didn't think he had a chance and that he did not want to prolong the session any longer than he had to. The caucus round wasn't wanted by many, because they thought that Hyde would withdraw at any minute, but he did not appear and the caucus was held as provided for under the rules adopted for the day. The last rumor to hold sway was that the long-rumored Hyde-Josey deal was being offered but that Hyde was confident that he could win without the deal and on that order turned it down. The caucus round was half-hearted, because most people assumed that the Smith support would go to Edmisten rather than Hyde because he was not one of the old-time party wheel horses, while Hyde was. The Josey supporters split between Edmisten (because he was not on record as being against capital punishment and because of his long association with Senator Ervin, who was revered in the eastern end of the state) and Herb Hyde (because of his association with the old leaders of the party in the state legislature and because he was older and more "mature" than Edmisten, plus the fact that someone was spreading the rumor that organized labor was supporting Edmisten and that the easterners were violently opposed to labor.) The ballots were passed out and the committee went into another informal recess while awaiting the result of the final vote. The counting committee returned about 6:00 with this report:

Edmisten	161
Hyde	92

Hyde came forward and moved that the nomination of Edmisten be made unanimous and that was passed. The nominee came to the front of the room and made a short speech pledging that the campaign would be waged successfully and that he would indeed be the attorney general. Claude DeBruhl moved that the chairman be empowered to submit the name of the nominee for that office to the State Board of Elections at the proper time in order to avoid a threatened Republican lawsuit preventing the election at all in order to ensure that the GOP would control the office of attorney general for two years and not two months for certain. This motion was also passed without dissent and the meeting was adjourned.

The nominee was quick to hit the campaign trail in his behalf and with the senatorial nominee and incumbent attorney general Robert Morgan. He appeared at a rally that night in Lenoir County and made approximately the same speech that he had made at the conclusion of the executive committee meeting that afternoon. He returned to Washington to see his wife that afternoon after the rally and took a week of to organize his campaign after that.

Most of the Edmisten support came from the Tenth Congressional District, which was his home area and the one in which he had done much party work during his life. He had all the votes in that district except for Sheriff T. Dale Johnson of Catawba County (who voted for Herbert Hyde on all ballots), Claude Sitton of Burke County (who voted for Dennis Winner on the first ballot and Edmisten on all succeeding ones), Lou Waddell of Catawba County (who evidently voted for Dennis Winner on all succeeding ballots), and Max Childers and Jerry Crisp of Gaston County (who voted or Kitch Josey until he was defeated and then switched to Edmisten). The district put a great deal of emphasis on supporting its favorite son over those of other areas and there was much talk of punitive action against those who did not vote for Edmisten after the first ballot.

The Seventh Congressional District was another center of Edmisten's strength. He had all the votes of New Hanover and Pender counties, and much support in the other areas which had no candidate after withdrawal of Hector McGeachy before the meeting convened.

Other Edmisten votes were scattered around the state in various places such as Pitt County, a few from Wilson County, and Mecklenburg, where he had 11 votes and the beginning of the meeting and picked up several votes during the course of the day, even though there was strong support for Herbert Hyde from some of the members of the delegation who were also members of the delegation who were also members of the state legislature and had served with Mr. Hyde in that body. The Forsyth County delegation also had an Edmisten supporter in its midst. The mountain counties of Ashe, Alleghany, Wilkes, Yadkin, Surry, and Stokes were also in Mr. Edmisten's corner. This support was the base from which he made his successful bid for the nomination.

The support that Herbert Hyde had came mostly from Buncombe County and the area west of it but one vote in Jackson County who voted for McNeill Smith until he was knocked out on the 5th ballot. The delegate from Clay County switched to Edmisten on the 5th ballot. Hyde also had some support in Mecklenburg and the central part of the state, but not enough to put him over the mark.

Kitch Josey had a hard core of supporters from the Second Congressional District except for Orange County, and had other help in other eastern areas of the state which gave him bedrock of 47 votes which held together until the rumors that he was about to withdraw split the ranks and they broke in confusion on the 5th ballot. The Josey supporters had the same problem that the other major legislative candidate had in that he was never able to expand his support out of his original sectional strength and the personal friends he had in the west who were unable to win any converts from the leading candidates in that area. Thus, he was dead on the second ballot after it became apparent that he was not going to be able to pick up anything from anybody else along his way.

The support that McNeill Smith had picked up was impressive numerically, but he weakened and the people who vied for him abandoned ship at the first sign of defeat. He had most of the votes from Guilford County, the labor vote which was present at the time, the votes from counties which had major colleges (such as Orange and Jackson, where student liberals had managed to get their candidates for the state committee elected), and the back vote which came over to him after the elimination of Mickey Michaux. His support was of the type, however, which repelled all the conservative powerbrokers who did not have enough votes to prevent his nomination. Thus his strength shifted to Edmisten at the end and did not stay long enough to do anything other than threaten the old leaders of the party and redouble their efforts to nominate a more "mainstream" candidate.

The small amount of support that Judge Kivett mustered was mainly from Forsyth and Guilford counties, with a small smattering of help from those in the east who were associated with the Terry Sanford wing of the Democratic Party and who were not in favor of Kitch Josey or any of the other candidates. His support was much smaller than the other contenders had given him credit for having, but much of it had been taken away by the entry of Senator Smith into the race, thus removing the home-town support that he had counted on to propel him up among the major contenders in the contest. Like the supporters of the other candidates who were running behind at the beginning of the balloting, his friends broke under the pressure and switched to other candidates—with most of his going to either Smith or Edmisten.

The Mitchell people were really the Wake County delegation, who were pushing their local boy. Like the other minor candidates no one knew why he stayed in the race, his support split up into tiny fragments, and he withdrew at the end of the first ballot. The vote for Dennis Winner came from Mecklenburg, Burke (one vote), Catawba (one vote), Randolph, and one vote from Robeson County. He never really had a chance and withdrew after the first ballot showed that he had no real chance for victory. Mickey Michaux made an impressive showing for a black candidate, with a bedrock strength of 22 votes which he was able to swing around as he chose all through the day even after he had been eliminated from the balloting. He lost only because he was unable to expand into the Piedmont's big counties because of the sectional vote in them for Smith and Kivett. One of the big factors in the Edmisten victory was the excellent organization he had set up for that day. He had one floor leader with a walkie-talkie who roamed around the floor persuading the delegates to come over to his side, staying in constant contact with the delegate from the east who had the other piece of that set of equipment (the former being Allen Dale of Drexel and the latter being Garland Garrett of Wilmington). Other friends of the candidate wandered around buttonholing individual delegates and working while one of the campaign managers stayed out in the area immediately outside the meeting room and tried to bring over larger groups of delegates to the cause. Others had only one or two people doing this while Edmisten had a small army working on the floor during the time the meeting was in session (Phil Hair, campaign manager; Michael Carpenter, Harvey Stuart, Jack Rhyne, Ron Baker, myself, Louis Faw, J.D. Baker, and many other delegates that were also part of the state executive committee).

My detractors said I had been in Washington for ten years, and that I had never run for any public office. True, but they did not realize that during those years I had regularly returned to North Carolina to speak to scores of Democratic groups, countless civic clubs, and had covered the state better than most of the other candidates during a campaign. I had been looking forward and laying the groundwork for a career in North Carolina public

Souvenirs from Rufus' first campaign for North Carolina attorney general.

service the entire time I was in Washington, D.C. The result of this and the hard work and brilliance of my crack campaign staff, after six rounds of balloting throughout the day, I won my first nomination as North Carolina attorney general by a healthy margin. My victory was sweeter because of the highly qualified and experienced candidates who ran against me: Judge Dennis Winner, Representative Mickey Michaux, Representative Herbert Hyde, Representative Kitch Josey, Judge Charles Kivet, and Senator McNeill Smith.

I don't think I can say enough nice things about Jimmy Ervin as a friend. As everyone knows, I idolized his grandfather, Senator Sam J. Ervin, Jr., and I've had the great pleasure of knowing Jimmy his whole life.

In a special election of 1974 I defeated James Carson, my Republican opponent from Charlotte, and was sworn in that November to serve the unexpired term (two years) of former Attorney General Robert Morgan, who had gone on to serve in the United States Senate. My wife, Jane, and I moved to a home in North Raleigh just after the election. Sadly, my marriage did not last. After a long separation we divorced in the early 1980s.

My offices when I was North Carolina Attorney General were in the Justice Building—the same building as those of the North Carolina Supreme Court. To me, this magnificent art deco building reflected the somber grandeur and magnificence of justice itself, and it inspired me every time I walked into it. Our offices were housed in the basement, first and second floors. My actual office and those of my deputies and administrative staff were on the second floor. The third and fourth floors not only housed the North Carolina Supreme Court, but also the stately Supreme Court Library which was at that time open to all attorneys. It was different then, more open and relaxed. Today it's like an armed fort. Terrorism, both domestic and foreign, has changed the nature of the world.

Shelley Castleberry was my assistant for ten years while I was attorney

Four generations of gifted jurists and statesmen: Samuel J. Ervin, an excellent lawyer (portrait); and from right, Senator Samuel J. Ervin Jr., a wonderful jurist and legislator; Samuel J. Ervin III, circuit judge of the United States Court of Appeals for the Fourth Circuit; and Samuel J. Ervin IV, North Carolina Court of Appeals Judge and now a North Carolina Supreme Court Justice.

general. She has a sharp political intelligence and along with her father, Shelton Castleberry, was always a huge supporter. We didn't have computers when we worked at the Justice Building. It was an ancient operation and she had a pedal-operated dictation machine! I dictated and she typed.

Shelley was with me through some wild times. My schedule was packed. I was being asked to speak and meet with aggrieved groups all the time. We even had the Wilmington Ten group in our office with Angela Davis at the head of our conference table. I was asked to be on the television show *60 Minutes* on four occasions and each time elected not to appear. I turned them down because, having watched the show for a number of years, I had noticed that whenever southern government officials were on they were portrayed at best as some kind of Foghorn Leghorn or backwoods clown.

A 1974 press conference shortly after I was elected North Carolina attorney general the first time.

With outgoing Governor Holshouser, left, and newly inaugurated Governor James B. Hunt, right, at the 1976 North Carolina Council of State and gubernatorial inauguration.

In February 1971 nine young men and one young woman were arrested in Wilmington, North Carolina, for arson and conspiracy in the firebombing of a local grocery store. You have to have some background here—Wilmington, like many other cities in the United States, was going through intense racial conflicts at that time. In response to desegregation of the public schools, the Ku Klux Klan and other white supremacist groups patrolled the streets and hanged the New Hanover County School Superintendent in effigy. Black students protested and students of both races were arrested for violent incidents in and around the schools.

Tension had been building for some time in the African American community. The Rev. Martin Luther King, Jr., was murdered in 1968, and in 1969 when the historically black, beloved Williston Industrial School closed for good, a lot of people got upset. The school board gave little notice to students, who were angry that they wouldn't be able to see their friends, play on their teams, or have their favorite teachers anymore, and Williston teachers and administrators of all races were simply laid off with no provision for new employment. While integration had been a matter of federal law since *Brown v. Board of Education* in the mid–1950s, the states and cities had leeway in how they implemented the new policies. Wilmington was not doing well with this task. A young African American man was shot and killed during a demonstration, and tensions reached explosive levels.

In retaliation for the police shooting of the young African American man, black activists firebombed a white-owned grocery store. When firefighters came to control the blaze, they said somebody shot at them from the roof of a nearby church. The National Guard came in and removed the people from the church—apprehending nine young African American men and a white female civil rights organizer. Now, no matter how anybody feels about anything, nobody can go around firebombing stores and shooting at public workers without consequences. The problem was not that the Wilmington Ten were arrested. The problem was the trial.

The first jury had ten African Americans and two whites. At that time prosecutor James "Jay" Stroud, Jr., said he was ill, and the judge declared a mistrial. When the second jury selected had ten whites and two African Americans, Stroud felt just fine, and tried the case. The Wilmington Ten were sentenced to a total of 300 years in prison. Public outcry was loud and long, and then in 1976 three of the key witnesses for the prosecution recanted their testimony, some saying they were bribed to say what the prosecution wanted them to say.

Eventually the case went to the federal Fourth Circuit Court of Appeals and that court found pre-trial misconduct. Stroud actually stated that his own conduct was not above reproach, so the case was overturned and sent back for a new trial.

North Carolina was roundly criticized nationally and ridiculed because the Wilmington Ten were not given a fair trial. We were catching hell from the media all over the country. To have the reputation of this state sullied in this way really bothered me. In a momentous decision I chose not to appeal the case to the Supreme Court. I looked at everything and just said, "I will not appeal. This case does not deserve a retrial. There was just too much misconduct."

I'll never forget when Chief Justice Susie Sharp caught me coming in to work and said, "What's wrong with you? You need to appeal this case." There was a general outcry among the citizenry for me to appeal the Circuit Court's decision to the United States Supreme Court. Still, the findings of the Fourth Circuit Court convinced me that the misconduct was so egregious that we really should not appeal. I told her, "Chief, there was just too much misconduct. The circuit court found this as fact. We don't want to go through this again. That's my decision, and I'll live with it." She was irritated with me, but I'm still glad today that I stood my ground despite heated and prolonged opposition. Had we appealed, we would have been seen as approving of and supporting the misconduct of the authorities who handled the original case, and that just would not do. If I had appealed it would have stayed in the national press, smearing the reputation of the North Carolina for years. There is substantive harm when people in positions of authority abuse their power and abandon the truth to achieve their own agenda. If the North Carolina justice system isn't answerable to the people of North Carolina, it is not doing the job it was designed to do.

Governor James B. Hunt, Jr., commuted the sentences of the Wilmington Ten in 1978, but withheld a pardon. Two years later the Fourth Circuit Court of Appeals threw out the convictions. In 2012 Governor Beverly Perdue issued a "Pardon of Innocence"—the fullest pardon, indicating that the defendants were not guilty of the charges—to the Wilmington Ten, although sadly, four of them had already died. A great many of my friends in law enforcement have told me that they were upset that the governor went so far as issuing the pardon with *innocence*, because all evidence proved that regardless of the mishandling of their case, the ten defendants clearly had burned down the grocery store and clearly had shot at the firemen who responded to the call.

There were also some high-profile, unsolved murders while I was attorney general that still remain unsolved. The State Bureau of Investigation was often involved in these murder cases, and part of my job was to oversee the SBI. Some of these cases were mighty mysterious and baffling. There is one case in particular that comes to mind. While I was still in Washington with Senator Ervin, on a cold, blustery, February night in Boone, North Carolina, a grisly murder occurred on the outskirts of town. I learned about it from the *Watauga Democrat,* which I received weekly while I was in Washington. Authorities found three bodies in a bathtub of a local home with their heads submerged and their hands tied behind their back. The victims were Bryce Durham, his wife, Virginia, and their sixteen year-old son, Bobby. Mr. Durham had moved to Boone from Mt. Airy, North Carolina, and was the proprietor of the Buick dealership in Boone. Mr. Durham, the father, had no known enemies. To this day, the case remains unsolved and still perplexes us.

When I was first elected North Carolina attorney general, I received a call from Mrs. Coy Durham, victim Bryce Durham's mother. She said, "Mr. Edmisten I know you are a good man. I wonder if you would help us try to find out who did this? I just want to know the answer before I die." I routinely flew to Wilkesboro on my way to Boone, and the Durhams sometimes met with me at the airport there. Mrs. Durham was a lovely silver-haired lady with azure eyes and hands that had seen a lot of hard work. Mr. Durham was a dignified, characteristically stoic mountain man, and seemed happy to have his wife do the talking. We discussed the case at length when we met. I really wanted to help solve it and bring them some closure.

I learned that the investigation had turned up nothing substantial and hence had kind of fizzled out. I created a new squad just for this case and authorized resources for the SBI to work on the case. I had strategy sessions with the sheriff, met with the chief of police and assigned SBI Agent Charlie Whitfield to help with the case.

There were many theories about what happened to the Durhams. At the time of the murders, there were military people training in the area. One theory postulated that they had been involved, based on the type of knots used on the ropes to restrain the victims.

Longtime SBI aide Larry Wagner, whose judgement tends to be spot-on, believed the murders had something to do with Bryce Durham's car dealership. Larry thought maybe

Mr. Durham knew something about odometer rollbacks and was killed to keep him quiet. Larry felt there may be a tie-in with Mr. Durham's former dealership in Mount Airy. The case is just so strange. Why this family, on a frigid Boone night? How did the murderer(s) restrain the victims before murdering them, especially a teenaged boy who was a strong high school athlete? The coroner ruled that all of the deaths were a result of either strangulation or drowning. The family had planned to go to a basketball game at the high school that night, but stayed home because of the weather. The whole thing just makes no sense. I still speak about this long-unsolved case with Watauga County Sheriff Len D. Hagaman every now and then. We never found any answers. I have to wonder, is the killer still out there? Is there anyone still alive who knows something that could help us learn what happened that night and who committed these murders? I truly regret that I was not able to fulfill Mrs. Coy Durham's dying wish and solve this mystery. To this day, the people of Boone remember the Durham murders.

Another unsolved case that fascinated me was the Bonnie Neighbors case. Bonnie was a beautiful lady who lived in Benson, North Carolina. She was married to Ken Neighbors, a successful accountant. One day she packed up their baby and went out to run errands, and simply never returned. A search ensued and on December 17, 1972, authorities found Bonnie's body at an abandoned migrant labor camp, her infant child there beside her, alive. The SBI was of course involved, and I reinstated the unsolved murder squad and intensified our efforts to find Bonnie Neighbors' killer.

This horrendous, well-publicized murder spawned lots of theories, each one wilder than the other. After Mrs. Neighbors' credit card turned up near Miami, many people thought her killer was a migrant laborer since her body had been found in a migrant camp. However, there were other theories involving romantic entanglement. Our investigation revealed that many people in Benson were suspicious of one another. When an investigative body turns over the information it has collected that material is raw—unverified and full of conjecture. Still, all information produced in the investigation must be preserved so that if the case is presented to the prosecutor he or she can review all of the evidence—so all the stories everyone in Benson told about one another and Bonnie are in the file. The things I heard in that investigation are too sordid to put in a soap opera. What people will say about each other is astonishing. Bonnie Neighbors' murder has still not been solved, and it haunts me to this day.

The unsolved mystery that garnered the most national attention was probably the Bradford Bishop case. I had a call in March 1976 from the sheriff of Tyrrell County in Columbia, North Carolina, who said, "We have a real mess down here. The Forest Service found a shallow grave with five bodies in it out in the country in Tyrrell County, not far from Columbia—a mother, her three children, and an older woman in a shallow grave with nothing else except a shovel." I quickly dispatched agents.

When they reported to me, these agents told me a few things that stayed with me over the years. First, they said they could tell the victims were from a financially well-off family by the condition of their teeth. He also told me that the shovel buried with the bodies had the word "Potomac" on the handle, which brought to my mind Potomac Hardware, a store just outside of Washington, D.C., that I had used when I lived there. Further investigation revealed that a man named Bradford Bishop, who was a ranking officer of the Foreign Service in the United States State Department, had purchased a shovel hardware personnel remembered.

William Bradford Bishop, Jr., had left his job with the State Department on the afternoon of March 1, 1976, complaining of a cold. Credit card receipts show that on March 2,

1976, he bought $15.50 worth of sporting goods in Jacksonville, North Carolina, a hundred miles or so from where the Forest Service worker found the bodies. Although the bodies were found on March 2, they were not identified until a neighbor called to report the family missing on March 8. Montgomery County, Maryland, police went to the Bishop home in Potomac, Maryland, and found a grisly scene and signs of a ferocious fight. There were bloody impressions of the children's bodies in their bunk beds and a bathroom door was broken down, leading authorities to believe that either the mother or the grandmother of the slaughtered children had locked herself in, trying to escape death. It was a truly horrifying crime.

The fact that Bishop was a security operative (what I call a "spook") who spent a lot of time overseas probably had a lot to do with how he got away, if indeed he did. On May 18 his car was found at a camp site in the Great Smoky Mountain National Park near Gatlinburg, Tennessee. There was blood in the trunk tire well. This meant that he had murdered his entire family in Maryland and drove with them all in the back of his bronze station wagon all the way down to Tyrrell County, North Carolina. Having made the drive from Washington through Richmond, Virginia, scores of times, passing through the toll booths just as Bishop would have done, I tried to imagine doing this with the bodies of five of my family members in my car. It was unthinkable.

Law enforcement searched the remote area of the park for days trying to determine if Bishop had become lost and starved to death, been killed by animals, or had himself met with foul play. They found nothing, even when they employed aerial searches. It truly was like Bradford Bishop simply disappeared without leaving so much as a footprint.

Authorities eventually charged him with the murders in absentia, and concluded that this man killed his mother, Lovellia, age 60, his wife, Annette, age 39, and his sons Brad, age 14, Brenton, age 11, and Jeffrey, age 5, put them in the back of the station wagon and drove to Columbia where he dug a hole, put them in it, burned their bodies then buried them. His last known whereabouts was the campsite in Tennessee. Where did he go? Bradford Bishop has never been found. People still have their theories that he went off in the woods somewhere, that he escaped to another country. For years, there were reports of sightings in foreign countries. The Washington press corps was eaten alive with this thing. Over forty years later, I still find this case both tragic and intriguing, and wonder what became of William Bradford Bishop, Jr. Where is Bradford Bishop?

As attorney general I enjoyed the consumer protection element of my office. It has been wonderful to have people come to me twenty years later and thank me for saving them from crooks. Being able to actually get results when people have been cheated is such a pleasure. The attorney general's office is not as mucked up by "red tape" as other agencies. It really is there for the protection of the people. I was successful in cracking down on false and deceptive advertising, and those performing bait and switch and similar dishonest maneuvers on uneducated consumers. The consumer protection division was really the brainchild of former Attorney General Robert Morgan and I set about to enhance it and hope I made it even better.

One part of the job that I did not enjoy was handling the condemnation of land and property for roads, highways, and other government needs. I hated that my name was on these records. I received a good many threats over this chore.

We had an active drug squad and I kept close tabs on it. It was a time when there were huge quantities of drugs sent from South America and North Carolina had become a favorite hub because there are so many nooks and crannies where people can hide on the "coast of pirates." While this was a serious problem, I noticed that lots of otherwise innocent kids were caught with a single joint of marijuana and locked up with rapists and murderers. Like it or not, it was a dope-smoking era. I had a friend whose kid was arrested with a joint in Chapel Hill, thrown in jail and roughed up. And no matter how we feel about the issue, it isn't right to have people barely out of their teens with no criminal record routinely locked up with violent felons.

I made what many saw as a controversial move and proposed to the General Assembly that we lessen the penalty for someone caught with just a joint. My staff warned, "Rufus, you don't need to be doing that." I said, "I'm going over to that committee and ask if anyone here can say with certainty that no one they know has smoked a joint." And that's what I did. I could see some of those lawmakers thinking about their kids and grandkids and maybe a little something they saw at a party they once went to. The law passed, reducing the penalty of simple possession of a joint to a misdemeanor infraction, so that offenders simply got a citation and paid a fine. It always felt good to recognize a problem, and work effectively to resolve it. I wish this had been the case with all my efforts as attorney general.

As attorney general I was very interested in the law enforcement aspect of the office. I worked hard to enhance the capabilities of the SBI, which was later transferred out of the attorney general's office and over to the North Carolina Department of Public Safety, which I think was a mistake. I believe it should reside under the state's chief law enforcement officer.

Every week I received reports from the SBI director, and it never ceased to amaze me what cruel things human beings can do to one another. I remember one time, this poor lady had been savagely tortured with a pitchfork and had over a hundred puncture wounds. When you see enough of that kind of thing, you can become hardened. I tried to not become cynical and jaded, but there really are some very bad people in this world. Or rather, people are capable of doing some very bad things.

When I traveled the state I usually contacted the local SBI person along with the local sheriff from each county. That way I could keep up with what was going on with law enforcement in the area. At that time the North Carolina attorney general was the chief law enforcement officer of the state. Since that time, it's been all scattered around. It seems like every governor wants part of law enforcement under his or her jurisdiction. One governor told me that he wanted a law enforcement division and sent an emissary over to me saying he was going to put legislation in to remove the State Bureau of Investigation from the attorney general's office. I let the messenger know that I opposed it and would fight it with everything I could muster. He never proposed the legislation he had in mind, and I had agents thank me for keeping the bureau where it belonged—in the attorney general's office.

During my early terms as attorney general, Susie Sharp was the chief justice of the North Carolina Supreme Court. She grew up in Rockingham County, North Carolina, and I saw her regularly as I came and went. I admired Justice Sharp a great deal. She had an office right above mine. She was a leader, nationally known, because she was the first female chief justice of the North Carolina Supreme Court, and one of the first in the nation. I remember my father talking about meeting Judge Sharp occasionally during his career when she heard wildlife cases in which he was involved. He said she was very fine judge and was impressed with her judicial manner and even way of treating everyone. This was my daddy's way of saying that females were just as qualified as anyone else. It never occurred to me that women couldn't do the same things as men. Senator Ervin's office was run by women and as attorney general I had many fine female staff members.

The attorney general office handled all criminal appeals from the various lower courts.

One day I was summoned to the office of Chief Justice Sharp. When her receptionist announced, "Chief Justice Sharp is awaiting you, Mr. Attorney General," I marched myself in there, wondering what in the world I had done wrong. There she sat in her regal way. "Have a seat, Rufus." She just pulled out a brief and said, "Take a look at this." I looked at it and it was four pages long—far too short to be anywhere near an effective brief for the defendant, who had been convicted of murder. I would have thought it was a joke if I hadn't known better. I said, "Chief, this is not a brief." She said, "Yes, it is a brief. From an idiot. This will not stand." She said, "What shall we do? You tell me."

I said, "Well, we could write one for the defendant, too." She said, "That's exactly what you are going to do." I said, "Don't we have a conflict here?" She said, "Justice is important here. This case needs some relief and I'm in a hurry. You get your folks to send a brief in here and I will take care of it if there is any problem." I said, "Okay." I walked back down to my office and spoke to the chief deputy and he said, "My God, that's impossible. How will we style this?" I said, "Style it as a friend of the court brief." So, we filed it and Judge Sharp and I never spoke of it again. I kept in touch with the case because this probably never happened in the history of North Carolina. That defendant got a great brief. Nevertheless, the court affirmed the imposition of the death sentence. I admire Judge Susie Sharp so much for her bold actions. She got the job done, and with style.

After Justice Susie Sharp died, Anna R. Hays wrote a book claiming that she had a pretty spicy romantic life. As it turns out she kept a diary in code and Ms. Hays cracked the code. One might expect this of an actor or celebrity, but in this case the person who wrote the diary was a brilliant, pioneering woman who passed law school, passed the bar, and became North Carolina's first chief justice of the Supreme Court.

A couple of years into serving as attorney general I read that Loretta Lynn was coming to play Dorton Arena at the North Carolina State Fair. I had grown up on Loretta Lynn and had attended her concerts. I had also helped her occasionally lead-footed bus drivers negotiate speeding tickets a time or two. It hit me one day that I knew exactly what I wanted to do. I wanted to sing with Loretta. About a month before she was to appear at Dorton Arena, I called her folks and said, "Do you think Loretta would possibly let me sing with her when she comes to town?" A couple of days later her management called me back and said, "She'd love to sing with you and Conway is coming with her." Conway Twitty! Now I had spoken before thousands of people but the thought of singing with Loretta Lynn and Conway Twitty both scared and thrilled me to death! I had never imagined anything like this. After a while Loretta sent word, "How about the old Hank Williams song 'Hey Good Lookin'"?" I would sing Conway's part. I thought that was a great idea. I got a copy of the lyrics and practiced over and over.

I thought I had it down pat. It was so hot, and suffocatingly humid that day. When I arrived at Dorton Arena with long-time aide Larry Wagner, Loretta was already up there singing. I was beyond nervous. You couldn't have gotten a pin up my butt with a sledgehammer, as my daddy used to day. For the first time in my professional career, I was terrified to face the lights and the microphone. Before this day I had never met a microphone or camera I didn't like, whether or not it liked me. But Loretta was such a big star, and I was and am such a big fan. I was stricken by panic that I might embarrass both of us, and that Loretta might regret her graciousness. I silently prayed, "Legs please get me up the stairs, voice let me get through this, and please Lord, don't let me faint."

My worst fear came true. Loretta brought me on and said, "This is my good friend, Rufus Edmisten. He is your attorney general and he's been mighty good to us. We want to do a little song together." Dorton Arena was absolutely packed and it was hot, hot, hot.

There were buckets of sweat coming off of me and I could hear shouts of "Rufus, Rufus, go Rufus!"

She started with her part, then it was my turn. Loretta looked at me and I froze. I absolutely froze. My mind went blank. Here was my big chance with my favorite country music star Loretta Lynn and I was blowing it. I was mortified. A moment passed and then she said, "Hold it honey, let me help you out here. We're going to start this over again. You'll be all right." Conway said kindly, "You want me to help you a little bit?" The band cranked back up and I belted out that song. Conway stopped singing and said, "You got it, you got it!" This was the first time I had ever frozen on a stage. I will never forget that feeling of total helplessness and embarrassment. When I got through with the song Loretta said, "That was real purty." After that people started calling me the Singing Attorney General.

I vividly remember attending the Davidson County Chamber of Commerce gathering at the former Velvet Cloak Hotel one evening in 1976. Thirty-five years old, I had been attorney general for a couple of years. It was one of those convention-type dinners where the chicken bounced and the boozed flowed. After the festivities were over I asked my traveling companion Larry Wagner to take me to Charlie Smith's apartment in Raleigh to go over the activities of the next day. When we arrived at Charlie's apartment he said, "Come on in!" and my eyes went immediately to the most beautiful creature I had ever seen. She was sitting on the floor with her feet tucked under her, her long flowing mane falling over her shoulders, the most entrancing blue eyes, and silky, flawless skin like a Breck Girl. She was a goddess!

When Charlie said, "This is General Edmisten," she gave me a puzzled look devoid of

Above: Singing with Loretta Lynn and Conway Twitty at the 1977 North Carolina State Fair. *Right*: Singing with Loretta Lynn at Dorton Arena in the 1980s.

any trace of recognition or deference and said, "What branch of the service are you in?" She'd never heard of me before, which I found intriguing. Mind you, she was Charlie's date that night.

As the evening went on I discovered she was a Raleigh woman who had been here longer than I had, that her dad was the head of the Air Quality Section of the Environmental Protection Agency in Research Triangle Park. Eventually I asked Charlie whose little bitty toy car was outside and Linda said, "It's mine. His name is Reggie." What an interesting woman! What could I do but ask her to take me for a ride, right on the spot!

After I had folded myself into quarters and pulled the car all around me I managed to get my right foot in. If seat belts had been mandatory I may not have made it. I liked the purr of the engine as Linda took it through the gears and the way she whipped that smart little car around. When Linda said she would take me for a spin around the block, she meant one block. She had an air of intelligence and reserve. As we walked briskly back to Charlie's I tried to engage her, to learn more about her. I could tell that this woman had more on her mind than listening to a politician trying to impress her. She sure wasn't trying to impress me.

I don't remember how I convinced Linda to give me her telephone number, I may have said I wanted to discuss historic preservation. I do know that once I got it, it was hard to wait a respectable number of days before I called. (In those days, the man always called the woman, and you didn't want to seem too eager, but you didn't want to wait too long so that they forgot about you.) I just couldn't get my mind off of this lovely, mysterious, quirky woman in her forest green cashmere. When I called, Linda said, "Why don't you meet me out at the stable where I board my horse Diana? It's called MacNair's Country Acres."

My attorney general basketball team at a match with Governor Hunt's team. We beat them. In fact, we beat just about everybody I can recall except the North Carolina Central Prison basketball team, and I suspect they beat us just because they had a lot more time to practice.

Once I arrived at this lovely country oasis so close to the city, there was Linda in her English jodhpurs and gorgeous riding boots, the sun glinting off of her glorious mane. She said "Diana, this is Mr. Edmisten." I was happy to note that Diana seemed slightly more impressed with me than Linda had. In later years Linda told me this was a test—if Diana didn't bite or kick me, then she must have thought I was okay. I'm glad that horse was in a good mood that day! Linda was spectacular as she expertly rode dressage around the ring, controlling Diana with soft words, barely touching the reins, directing the horse with pressure from her knees. She segued into jumping, and had me set the poles for her. It was a perfect October day with warm sunlight tempered by a cool breeze. This was the extent of our first date, but I knew there was more to come. Linda intrigued me. I loved her edginess, sharp, dry wit and independent mind, and that long, gorgeous hair. She reminded me of a lioness.

After several weeks of courting I decided I wanted to try to impress Linda with my horsemanship by attempting a jump. I had of course ridden horses growing up on the farm, but I had no idea what riding English was like. The saddle was different, there was no horn to hold on to, and I had to learn the heels down, toes pointed out, riding style and posting—the most unnatural thing in the world to me, riding along and bouncing up and down in the saddle.

One day I decided I was going to show off. I set everything up, and once mounted, approached a low jump, and Diana and I went over it. So far so good! I asked a hand to raise the bar a couple inches higher. We circled around and approached the jump. I had no helmet on, just a pair of jeans and a heavy coat of hubris. I knew Linda was watching and I was ready to impress her. Just before we reached the jump, Diana abruptly stopped.

Unfortunately, I kept going, sailing over the jump with grace and style. I later joked that Diana was a polite horse, so she simply had to let me go first over that jump. I hit the ground head first and saw sparks and flashing lights. Terrified, I thought "Am I paralyzed?" I wiggled my fingers and toes and I realized that I and my ego were merely bruised. At that moment, watching Diana graze placidly a few feet away, my ego seemed to be in far greater peril than my hide.

Linda scolded me a little as she helped me up. (She had told me not to try the jump.) She assisted me as I hobbled over to sit on a log and asked if I was all right. I told her I thought so, but after a while things began to hurt all over, from my head to my toes—so we went over to Rex Hospital.

My cousin Geraldine Hollar from Boone was the chief nurse on the shift that night. She took one look at me

My wife, Linda, around the time I met her.

and said "Rufus, what the hell have you been into? Showing off?" I had mud on my head and looked as if I'd been thrashed with a blackberry briar. I said "Yes." Geraldine grew up down the road from us, and was well-versed in mountain talk. She said, "You're a sorry sight. You could have paralyzed yourself. We are going to keep you overnight for observation." She explained that the only bed that was available in intensive care, and they took me to a chilly, sterile white room filled with frightening tubes and machines.

As it turns out I had a room-mate, an old man who kept saying over and over on about a count of four, "Oh Lord don't take me now." I got no sleep, and after a while could not help but think "Lord, you don't have to take him now but could you just make him hush!" The next morning I asked the nurse on duty to call Larry Wagner. She got him on the phone for me, and I said, "Wagner, no matter what you have to do, please get me out of this room." Somehow he managed this and they moved me out of there. Geraldine had left

With Linda and her horse Diana, the one that was so polite she insisted that I go first over the steeplechase jump-without her.

instructions that if I did not seem right, to keep me. She had no way of knowing that I would have paid her good money to let me go home no matter what shape I was in. Wagner drove me to my cute little cottage, a temporary home near Ravenscroft Academy that my friend Willie York loaned me until I found a permanent Raleigh home. Linda came to visit, showed the proper pity, and told me that I would never get back on one of her horses again. I have not. The things we do to impress fair young maidens!

Regardless of my monumental failure as an equestrian jumper, my next effort to impress Linda was more successful. I found out that Elvis would appear at the Greensboro Coliseum in April 1977 and arranged for two tickets. I had always loved Elvis, particularly when he sang hymns. Once the arrangements were made I asked Linda if she would like to go to an Elvis concert, and she said she would, though she was not as excited as I had imagined she might be.

I arranged for us to have a picnic at Coker Arboretum on the UNC campus on the way to Greensboro. I went to Southern Seasons and procured the fanciest picnic basket they had—it included china, silver, and all the goodies we needed for a lovely, sophisticated picnic. Fancy cheeses and imported meats, fresh fruits, a bottle of fine wine, the works.

Linda (Harris) Edmisten the equestrian riding her horse Farthing, named after my paternal grand-father Rufus Farthing Edmisten. Linda has loved horses since early childhood.

There were no Hershey bars, sardines, potted meat, saltines or Vienna sausages at this picnic! There was even a lovely picnic blanket to spread on the grass. This was a fine spread and pricey.

With my driver Larry Wagner at the wheel, I showed Linda some of my old Chapel Hill campus haunts, and eventually said, "Why don't we have a picnic?" Linda replied, "But we didn't pick up anything!" I then unveiled the basket and as we partook, Larry sharing with us but sitting on a bench nearby, I think Linda was finally just a little impressed.

Afterward Linda asked if I had tickets to the concert, and I pretended we had to get some when we got there. When we arrived we went to the door all the entertainers used. Larry Wagner took a police officer aside and the officer escorted us to the back of the stage. Linda was surprised to see that we were seated on the stage where Elvis would perform! We had seats on the side of the stage, the only people sitting there. Elvis came on to the accompaniment of shrieking women and great applause. Although his career and his life would be ending soon, he could still belt them out. Just before Elvis left the stage, Linda bolted from her seat to shake the King's hand and I got up to give him the honorary Attorney

General's badge I had made for him. I finally had the feeling that I might have impressed this fascinating woman! But it took twenty years before she admitted it.

Even now, it's hard to write about the man whose brilliance and good heart had a lot to do with my success in North Carolina politics. Charlie Smith was my mainstay for the ten years I served as attorney general. I got to know him when he was a public relations man for First Union Bank in Charlotte, and he and his crew came to Washington, D.C., several times a year to take the North Carolina delegation to dinner. It didn't take long for me to realize what tremendous political acumen he had. Like me, Charlie had been interested in politics early, working for the Young Democrats in his youth, and had later worked with the famous Burt Bennett, a political strategist who spearheaded Jim Hunt's successful campaigns for lieutenant governor and governor. Charlie had also become a well-known sports reporter for the *Asheville Citizen Times* in his twenties. He was brilliant, superbly articulate, and generous with his time and his vision. When I knew for certain I would try to capture the nomination for attorney general, I knew Charlie would be my right-hand man. We had a long, close friendship and we trusted one another.

Charlie was masterful at figuring out the best way to handle politically sensitive situations, beginning with my nomination race before the executive committee. Ferrel Guillory from the Raleigh *News & Observer* wrote, "Edmisten won by out-professionalizing the party pros." Charlie was responsible for that winning strategy. During that particular race, I was the outsider in today's parlance. While being very much a part of the Washington establishment, I was not in the day-to-day politics of North Carolina. Charlie defined my strategy this way: "These are all the insider politicians in the Raleigh establishment and you are the bright new face who has been a service to your state in a different way. We are going to play them against each other. We'll say 'It will just be the same ol' same ol' if you nominate one of the other people.'" As many observers noted, the branding was brilliantly executed, and I attribute that to Charlie's masterful political chess game. Charlie was the king strategist, in his fair and gentlemanly way.

With my dear friend and brilliant political strategist Charlie Smith.

Rufus ran for North Carolina attorney general for the second time in 1980.

After I won the nomination and the final vote was taken on the sixth ballot (the last being between Herbert Hyde of Asheville and me) I was so relieved! We had won! I was always very thankful that Herbert was a gentleman of the first order who stood up after the final tally and moved that the executive committee nominate me unanimously. Herbert made a wonderful comment—that we could be proud to have another mountain man up there running. He was the real thing—a mountain gentleman and he never said a negative word about my character. I learned a great lesson watching him, and I am forever grateful to him. It was one of the most exciting days of my life.

I also learned from Charlie how to better build coalitions at that time. There were times when groups of people huddled around in rooms trying to figure out how to "stop Edmisten" because I kept picking up votes here and there. We needed to counter that with groups of our own. Through him, I learned how to put the right people together, how to appeal to different people and how to bring people together around a unified goal. Charlie's strategy worked flawlessly and served me well later in life. He would always ask, "How can we work this out together?" That was a good primer for my later political life, although I failed at it for the race for governor because I couldn't control the dynamics.

Charlie stayed with me and became my administrative deputy. He ran the office, and while there were attorneys there who had amassed a tremendous amount of legal knowledge, they all deferred to Charlie on anything of a political nature. He ran that office without prejudice, rancor or discord. He knew how to run stuff and he knew how to keep stuff running smoothly. He was smart enough not to meddle in legal affairs, too. He didn't like to waste time, either. I remember when someone wanted us to give them a job he would grow very agitated if they had a bunch of people calling on their behalf. He would tell them to "cut the crap—we don't need all the calls." He always shot straight, and he was with me for many years. He was my political touchstone.

Years later, after I had won the first Democratic Party primary for the governor's race, Larry Wagner and I had flown to Charlotte where I appeared before the North Carolina Rest Home Association. I gave a fifteen-minute campaign speech. We were getting ready to fly back to Raleigh and the SBI agent in attendance, a strange, pained look on his face, whispered something to Larry. The rented plane carrying some of my campaign people to a final strategy session had crashed in Asheville, North Carolina. The caller thought everyone had survived, but was not sure. Remember, this was long before cell phones and internet. We commandeered the local SBI agent's car because we didn't have a car in Charlotte. There was no quick way to get to Henderson County Hospital where Charlie was being treated. That ride was so long. I kept hoping everything was okay. The people on that plane were very dear to me and they had gotten on that leased plane to attend a fund-raiser on my behalf.

We were going at breakneck speed with blue lights and siren on. We were so worried. Naturally, you assume the worst. We finally arrived at the hospital in Hendersonville and I asked the attending doctor, "Doctor, how is my friend and campaign manager Charlie Smith doing?" This miserable excuse for a human being, without even looking at me or shaking my hand, said, "He's dead," and walked away. I cannot describe my shock and dismay. My heart was about to pound its way right out of my chest. As I tried to console the survivors, I grieved myself, knowing that I had not just lost a wonderful friend, but that part of my political heart had been taken away that night. It would be long after my campaign and my loss of the election before I began to heal from the tragic death of Charlie Smith.

On a much happier note, I came to be known as the Singing Attorney General for a reason. I learned to love music from an early age and I always loved to sing. I guess I was a singing Secretary of State, too. I remember as a boy, on cold, sometimes subzero days, we could catch WBT radio out of Charlotte and listen to Grady Cole, the morning announcer. Sometimes we listened to country music singers, while my daddy was down below the kitchen sink with a blowtorch trying to thaw the frozen pipes.

When I sang country music as a boy, I liked to imitate people on the radio. I loved hearing all the beautiful sad and dramatic stories these songs told, and I was still unexpectedly breaking out into song during my days at Carolina. Fortunately, my roommate was also a country music fan. We listened to Merle Haggard and Faron Young. I learned the lyrics by heart and I especially loved the song I remember so well by Porter Wagner called "Satisfied Mind." I know all the words to that one.

I also loved the poignancy of "Knoxville Girl," which is an Appalachian murder ballad made popular by the Louvin Brothers. The lyrics are haunting.

This love of singing stayed with me and no matter what stage of life I was in, if there was a band, I would jump up on the stage, grab a microphone and go at it. I did it in Washington, D.C., too—major breach of etiquette. Nobody wanted to hear their very serious political person who was charged with weighty matters of grave import belting out a country song in the local honky tonk! One night at the Cellar Door nightclub I had a few drinks and asked if I could sing with the band. I started singing "The Wild Side of Life" (aka "Honky Tonk Angel"), and someone said, "Throw the bum out of here!" It was the early 1970s and this was a rock and roll bar, I guess. Nobody in there looked like they had ever been to the mountains or would admit it if they had.

I sang my way through life as a young man. I never stopped singing. When I lost the governor's race, Mama said "Son, if you had sung a lot more 'Amazing Grace' and a lot less 'Honky Tonk Angel [Hank Thompson's 'The Wild Side of Life'],' you might have won." Mama was right. I had tried to jump up on stage with every bluegrass band I saw. After I lost the election I figured I might just as well keep singing, what did I have to lose? At some point right along at that time I had a friend from Eastern North Carolina who said, "I would love to go to the Grand Ole Opry in Nashville." I thought to myself, "Maybe I can find a way for us to go. He could get his wish and I'd like to go too, and maybe go backstage." I started asking around and someone said, "Rufus, I know a gentleman in North Carolina who goes every Saturday night. He married Roy Acuff's daughter. Why don't you call him?"

I called the gentleman and I told him of my desire. He said, "I've heard of you. A lot of my folks back home in North Carolina know about you and I'll set things up for you. I'm here every Friday and Saturday night."

So, it was arranged and I got to take my friend and a couple of their friends to Nashville to see the Grand Ole Opry! That day we landed in Nashville, took a cab to the Opryland Hotel and were greeted like celebrities. We stayed in luxurious rooms and the manager even gave us a discount. After we had checked in the manager said, "The security staff will take you and your party to the Opry when you are ready. Just call." I thought, "WOW!" My friend George Parrott remarked that this was going to be a lot more fun than the economic development trip we had taken the week before.

George went just about every-where with me in those days. We were out there one time and during the show George disappeared backstage. I went to look for him and I saw George and this old man who was sitting in a recliner just having a big time. I motioned for George to meet me in the hallway and I said, "George, do you know who you were talking to?" He said, "No, he was really nice and asked me to come in and talk to him." I said, "That's Roy Acuff!" We were both agog. I loved those trips and George.

When we were ready they took us to the back door of the Opry. There was a big, stoic looking security man

"The Singing Attorney General" belting out a song during a campaign event hosted by the extraordinary Marvin Speight. After I lost the governorship, my mama said I might have won if I had spent more time singing "Amazing Grace" and less time singing "The Wild Side of Life" (aka "Honky Tonk Angel"). She may have been right.

at the door who waved people on if he knew them and stopped them and checked their credentials if he didn't. Men and women with guitars and banjos and other equipment filed past. The security man said, "You can go anywhere you want, just remember, no drinking back here." We all looked at each other. I had some mini bottles in my pocket, and I'm sure I wasn't the only one. That was just how we rolled in those days, when we went out to have some fun. We thanked the guard and began to wander past rooms with the likes of Bill Monroe and Loretta Lynn. We saw Roy Acuff fiddling around with a yoyo, and just all kinds of stars and notables, some of whom I did not recognize. I thought, "This must be Sugarland!" We all wandered around, wide-eyed. Everyone was busy preparing for the show.

After we took our seats, Porter Wagoner came out on stage and I was thrilled! What I loved the best is how down- to-earth all the performers seemed. There was a single band that played behind all the singers and there were three stunning backup singers. I loved the simplicity of it, and we stayed for both shows. It was so awesome I went back every chance I could and one time got to visit the home of Charlie Louvin, who sang with his brother Ira as the Louvin Brothers. I had been at the show and he invited me back to his humble home. The next night he gave me a shout-out, saying "I want to welcome here tonight my friend and a fine friend of country music, North Carolina Secretary of State Rufus Edmisten!"

There was a spattering of applause and a little commotion, then some people stood up and yelled "Rockin' R! Yay for Rufus!" It was a bunch of people I knew from North Carolina—T. Jerry Williams, the head of the North Carolina Restaurant Association, and Reed Parrot, then president of the Nash County Community College. It was a rip-roaring time. In the years since I'll sometimes see Jerry and call him "Jumpin' J" and he'll answer back "Rockin' R!" and we'll remember that fun night in Nashville.

I went back a few times and did some radio interviews on WSM and took my friends with me. We were there one night when Bob Hope did his Christmas special, and I got to meet some of the legends. I even made Bob Hope an honorary Secretary of State.

While I was still attorney general Linda found that the house we now live in had become available. She had done the research on it and strongly urged me to buy it. This was in 1979, and it was, and is a beautiful house. It took me years to convince Linda to marry me—she finally agreed to be my wife in 1983—and I like to think I passed an important test which earned major points when I bought this house. Our forever home is a Craftsman-style bungalow built by a dentist named Elmo Lawrence in the 1920s. I love this place. I wish I could be buried in the back yard next to the dogs under one of my mama's plants—preferably after I die. It sits on two and a half acres on the southeast side of Lake Wheeler Road in Raleigh. In 2005 our house was added to the National Register of Historic Places. It is a rare early example of a hollow-core concrete block bungalow, beautifully proportioned, broad and low slung, as the best bungalows are. From 1926 until his death in 1959, Dr. Lawrence operated his dental practice from an office at 123 West Hargett Street. I think it notable that both Dr. Lawrence and I traveled back and forth from this home to an office on Hargett Street.

In the 1960s the owner added a sun porch but other than that, we have just tried to maintain the integrity of the original structure, like any good preservationist. I have certainly filled it up with all my old stuff. Linda throws things out as fast as she can.

My favorite part and the area of the property I find most impressive is the garden. We filled the house itself with interesting items, but the garden is my safe haven. Fittingly, the good dentist's first wife was named Flora, and she was a member of the Raleigh Garden

Our Elmo Lawrence house and good dog Jasper.

With family on the steps of the Three Forks Baptist Church on the day we got married, December 22, 1983.

Club and responsible for most of the ornamental trees and shrubs around the property. I have tried to add to the existing plantings to enhance the natural beauty of this wonderful house. It has been a soothing touchstone, an oasis of peace and beauty in my rollercoaster life.

Linda finally agreed to marry me at the Three Forks Baptist Church. After I brought her home as my wife, my house became our home. Just three years after I acquired this house I ran for governor, and the way that turned out would leave me needing all the soothing I could get.

9

The 1984 North Carolina Governor's Race

Before Jim Hunt became Governor of North Carolina, people holding this office were limited to a single term. The people of North Carolina were leery of placing too much power in the hands of the governor—a lesson learned from the tyranny of the Royal Governors. During his first term Governor Hunt sought legislative approval of a constitutional amendment allowing governors to serve two successive terms. He succeeded by a very narrow vote.

Before this time, there was a kind of natural order among politicians aspiring to the governorship. Everybody paid his dues and bided his time until the party decided it was his turn for the nomination. The new constitutional amendment messed up this natural order of things. As a consequence the normal system of would-be governors "waiting their turn" was disrupted. Hunt's two terms created a "bottleneck" of Democratic candidates vying for the nomination for the next election. The result was that there were a lot of people contending for the 1984 Democratic nomination for governor. Not only had Hunt taken two terms, he had arranged that anyone who got elected might serve for two terms. Eight years is a long time to wait for another chance.

Jimmy Green was the 28th lieutenant governor, serving from 1977 to 1985. He was a crusty elder military guy from Virginia who had moved to Elizabethtown in Bladen County, North Carolina, and set himself up a tobacco kingdom. He was elected to the House of Representatives, served as Speaker of the House from 1975 to 1976, and then he ran for lieutenant governor and won. Because of Hunt's constitutional amendment, Jimmy became the first lieutenant governor to serve consecutive terms. For the latter office he campaigned principally against Carl Stewart (one-time Speaker for the North Carolina House Of Representatives). Now, there was an unwritten rule among veteran politicians that you never endorsed any candidate for any office in a year when you were running. My first mistake was that I not only endorsed Jimmy Green in his quest to become lieutenant governor, I pulled a lot of strings to help him get elected. I was able to get most of the sheriffs on his side.

At that time, sheriffs had more political power over their counties. I knew all of them due to my job as attorney general. Once Jimmy Green won the election, as a matter of protocol my office provided SBI personnel to him, and they carried him around wherever he needed to go and provided him security. Now, Jimmy was a very cutthroat politician—he punished his enemies and rewarded his friends. He rarely smiled, had a gruff, deep voice, and left every meeting early that I remember. His wife, Alice, seemed like the kindest woman in the world.

A rally during my campaign for governor of North Carolina in 1984.

Due to the backup from Hunt essentially "cutting in line," there were ten Democratic candidates in the primary. Myself, H. Edward "Eddie" Knox, James C. "Jimmy" Green, Lauch Faircloth, John R. Ingram, Robert L. Hannon, J. Andrew "Andy" Barker, Thomas C. "Tom" Gilmore, J.D. Whaley—and Frazier Glenn Miller, who was a member of the Ku Klux Klan and has since been convicted of murder.

I entered campaign mode in high gear, all the while fulfilling my duties as attorney general. Many will tell you that they don't campaign while in office. Don't believe them. Chickens scratch and chicken eat corn.

Monday, February 3, 1984, the day I filed to run for governor, was just such a big day. Mama and Daddy were there and they were so proud of me. I worshipped my mother, and I so wanted to make her and Daddy proud and win that race. I filed along all the rest of the candidates. Hell, we had more than enough men for a baseball team. We were all making speeches and going to forums all over the state. We were all going to a lot of functions in packs, even riding in busses together.

As our campaigns went along tensions developed between Jimmy Green and me. Jimmy would say, "Why don't you wait? It's not your turn." I would answer, "I can't wait, it might be two terms before I get another chance." Jimmy would say to me, "You're not old enough," and I would think to myself, "Maybe you're tool old," but I would reply, "Well, I think people have gotten over that."

As the election drew near all kinds of allegations began coming up against Jimmy Green. The Federal Bureau of Investigation had been running a national investigation into public corruption and organized crime code-named ABSCAM and Jimmy was indicted. He and the undercover agent, who was posing as a businessman who wanted to pay Jimmy $10,000 a month in bribes, had lunch at the Western Sizzler on Peace Street (now the Mellow Mushroom) and the agent recorded Jimmy accepting the bribe. Part of the exchange went like this, and was amazing to me, because Jimmy indicated that he had already been approached by undercover federal agents in the past.

Addressing supporters on the Capitol grounds after winning the Democratic nomination for governor in 1984.

"Are you with the business, or are you with the FBI?" Green asks.

FBI agent: "We're an investment firm. We're with an investment firm in Detroit."

Green asks the agent four more times whether he is with the FBI.

"It could be another ABSCAM," Green says.

"You're paranoid," replies the undercover agent.

District Attorney Randolph Riley came to me one Saturday morning and said, "I want you to lend one of your special prosecutors to prosecute Lt. Governor Jimmy Green." I said, "Not on your life—they will think I am doing that to remove him from the race. I won't do it." I declined because it put me in such an awkward situation.

Then just when primary campaigning was at a fevered pitch, there was a huge investigation about barn burning and allegations arose that Jimmy had burned down his own tobacco warehouses. The SBI, then under my jurisdiction, was called on to investigate. There was no way I could have or would have stopped this from happening, but Jimmy took it like I had become his archenemy. I was sitting in my office and got a call from the lieutenant governor's office saying that Jimmy wanted to see me right away. I was apprehensive because we were not on the best of terms. I knew something was up, but I thought it might have to do with the legislature. I dutifully walked over there and Jimmy's secretary had a nervous look about her when she said, "Go on in, they're waiting on you." I expected to see Jimmy alone, so I was taken aback. I opened the door and there were at least eight powerful senators standing there, but no Lieutenant Governor Jimmy Green. Their hostile glares seemed rehearsed. Nobody even said, "Please sit down."

As if he had been chosen to begin my inquisition, one senator, a man I had counted as a friend, demanded, "What the hell do you think you're doing? The stuff you're doing to Jimmy Green has to stop, and stop NOW. You're going to ruin him and we won't have it." Standing in silence, all I could think was, "This is an attempt to obstruct justice." I did not say one word, though the accusations and demands went on for about fifteen minutes.

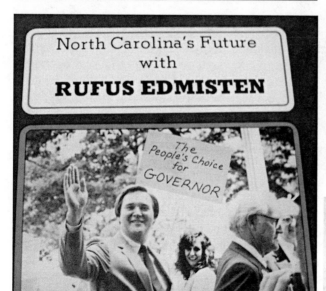

Rufus ran unsuccessfully for governor in 1984.

My second inquisitor was by far the meanest. His verbal abuse and accusatory questions seemed to go on and on. I stood in silence, until everyone had stopped talking. My heart was pounding when I finally said, "Are y'all finished?" When nobody spoke, I waited another long moment and then walked out.

This was so far out of the realm of decent conduct, such a blatant attempt at obstruction of justice, that I found myself at a literal and philosophical fork in the road as I left the Legislative Building. I could walk to the right to my office or I could walk to the left to the United States Attorney's office on New Bern Avenue and report the offense. I wished I had someone wise to consult, like my mentor Sam Ervin. It was a formidable career decision and a crucial fork in the road in my heart and in my mind. There is no question that the FBI would have taken my report seriously. There would have been harsh consequences. My mind was working so fast, going over everything I knew so that I could make the right decision. I rationalized, "These guys don't even know what they're doing, they're just saying what Jimmy told them to say. And he had to know this is obstruction of justice."

I went to Charlie Smith's office and told him, "You will not believe what just happened to me." As I was telling him the story my friend called and confirmed my suspicions that he had not known why he was called there until the first senator opened his mouth and lit into me. His call meant a lot to me that day.

In 1991 insurers Lloyds of London, filed a civil action against Jimmy Green. Jimmy was never convicted of conspiracy to commit arson, but was indicted for income tax fraud. (Jimmy's son who managed the warehouse admitted to setting the fire "as part of a scheme to collect insurance money"). In 1997 Jimmy was placed on house arrest for thirty-three months in his Clarkson, North Carolina, home. Back in Raleigh, his former aides despised me, sure I had caused Jimmy to lose the race for governor. It still bothers me that anyone would think I had done anything underhanded to damage Jimmy's chance at the governorship. He billed himself as the most honest man running, and I'm just not sure people thought that was true.

Sometime after I left public life, I was sitting in my office one day and thought, "I want to call Jimmy Green." I knew he hated me and blamed me for his losing the race for governor. I wanted to call him and tell him I didn't want him to hold a grudge, and that I didn't, even though he refused to support me after I secured the nomination. When he answered the phone. I said, "Jimmy, this is Rufus Edmisten. I think about you a lot and hope you don't still hate me. We had some mighty good times together and I think you did good things for North Carolina." He uttered a growly grunt and said, "It's all right," and hung up the phone. I felt better. He died in 2000.

Contrary to what many people thought. I did not enjoy running for governor. I was not a happy warrior. It was the most intense, furious-paced thing I've ever done. But the wonderful people I worked with during the campaign were a joy to me. Johnsie Setzer from Catawba County was one of them. She lived in the little town of Claremont. Her husband, Willy, was a well driller. Johnsie loved me like a son and I returned that love. She helped me so much, and she never failed to show up at events. I don't remember a meeting or a rally that she missed. She burned the roads up driving miles and miles for political meetings. I met her when I worked with Senator Ervin and she brought a busload of 4-H kids from Catawba County to see the sights of Washington, D.C. Johnsie had dark, dancing eyes. She loved being in the thick of politics. She was also a church leader. Johnsie contributed a lot of money to my campaign. Her poor husband complained that he was going to go broke, but they never let me down.

Forums were rarely my favorite part of campaigning, and this was especially so during the governor's race because there were so many people running so every forum would be L-O-N-G. For some of this pack of candidates, these events might be the only public appearances to which they would be invited. Every single candidate always showed up. Every single candidate had to give a speech. Along with too many candidates, there were just too many forums! Every organization had a forum and in the primary we had to attend all of them unless we wanted the organization to badmouth us. All of them! So I'd be there with Tom Gilmore, Jimmy Green, the KKK guy, and others, at endless events. One of my favorite fellow candidates was Andy Barker, who was mayor of Love Valley north of Statesville in Iredell County, which has been made up like a Wild West town. There are two saloons, hitching posts, lots of horses and horse manure. His granddaughter Tori is now on the town council there. She and her mother are friends of mine.

I liked to sit next to my friend Lauch Faircloth because he was funny. He created nicknames for all the candidates. Lauch called Tom Gilmore "Brezhnev" because of his eyebrows. He referred to the Klansman as "fruitcake." I couldn't help wondering what nickname he gave me when he sat with someone else. We all gave our speeches, then there would be questions and each candidate had to answer the question. Some of the questions were doozies!

Then there were the speaking engagements—it seemed like hundreds, to give to the civic organizations alone, the Kiwanis Club, the Rotary Club, the Elks, the Civitan International, the Women's Club and on and on. Everyone seemed to want a candidate to come and speak to his or her group. There were too many to even keep up with. There were so many it was easy to lose track and get a little confused. (I'm a hard worker and a hard campaigner, but this was an exceedingly long, tough campaign.)

I was addressing the Kiwanis Club once, and I made a regrettable faux pas. Arthur Goodman, a fellow lawyer, introduced me, and I said, "It is so great to be here with you Rotarians today." Arthur delivered a swift kick to my shin and hissed, "This is the Kiwanis Club." Judging from the glares I saw on their faces, I was going to have a job of recovering from this, but I had to try. I said, "Please forgive me. I've eaten so much barbecue my mind is cloudy."

Candidates running in the primary in those days had to receive a majority of the votes (50 percent plus one) in the primary to win. With so many candidates in the race, this was nearly impossible. Four of the candidates running against me in the primary had high name recognition (Knox, Green, Ingram, and Faircloth) so I knew getting a majority wasn't going to happen for anyone. The first primary was in May. I led the race, and it did not surprise me because I had worked so long and so hard. Still, I knew I wouldn't take the large cities because I didn't have the business access, and because I ran a populist campaign. I had to. At heart I am a populist politician. I got the most votes and the runner-up was Eddie Knox, then mayor of Charlotte. We had a month between the first and second primary. The second primary, in June, was a race between Eddie Knox and me. One time during a televised debate Eddie said to me, "You know nothing about the government. You've been a sorry attorney general." He rattled me. I should have been expecting that, but I didn't. Then he added, "You don't know anything about the budget." It was tough stuff, and hard to take. I had thought that Eddie was a gentleman. I didn't take any nonsense from him from that point forward.

The second primary was hard-fought and bitter. For months I campaigned all over the state seven days a week, and one Sunday I campaigned at four churches. I was relentless. I knew Eddie would carry counties along the Interstate 85 corridor, so I focused on less populated areas with rural people, because these were the people who would identify with me, and if I hit enough places I knew the votes would add up.

After a month of back-breaking campaigning I beat Eddie in the second primary. I remember that when the results came in that night, I was out at The Royal Villa Hotel that used to be on Glenwood Avenue near where Pleasant Valley Promenade is now. I held a lot of rallies there. The first thing you do when you beat somebody in a primary is call and ask for their help. I called Eddie Knox and said, "Eddie, I appreciate the campaign you ran. Obviously, I want to help you all I can to pay back your debt." He was very cold about it and made no pledge to me. Jim Hunt was the nominee against Jesse Helms that year, and was Eddie's college buddy.

Knox thought all along that Hunt should be helping him—but Hunt was fighting for his political life and couldn't help anyone at that point. I thought Eddie was a little naïve to expect help from Hunt under those conditions. Eddie mistakenly thought that anyone who was for Jim Hunt should be for him. This reminds me of one of my staunch supporters, Marvin Speight, who was the head of the North Carolina Alcoholic Beverage Control Commission (ABC). It drove Eddie crazy that Marvin had been a Hunt supporter but supported me and not Eddie in the 1984 primaries. This just laid waste to Eddie's scheme of things. I knew Marvin for years, and I liked him. He had dark curly hair and there was this one fat coil at the front of his head that bounced all around when he got excited.

I find this next story a little funnier now than I did when it happened. One night I gave a speech in Asheville. Larry Wagner had flown me to the venue in a little twin-engine Beechcraft Baron that could take off and land in the smallest places. After the event we were driving to the airport to return home. As we approached the airport we saw a group of twenty or so former Knox supporters marching in a circle holding signs that said "ABR" in huge letters and then in small letters underneath "Anybody but Rufus." A scuffle broke out between them and my supporters who were there to see me off. Eventually the large, imposing figure of the airport manager emerged from the building and ran them all off. He said, "This is the first time something like this has happened and I am not going to have it." He said the people with the signs started the trouble. Later we managed to get some of those ABR signs, and after I lost the election we created a bonfire and burned them one night. It was cathartic.

From the time I won the nomination for Democratic candidate for governor, I criss-crossed the state and met with everyone I could. I was on their schedule, not mine. For one solid year, I didn't have a sick day or day off. You were not allowed to get sick. You trudged on and you became numb. You ate whatever people put in front of you and at most campaign events in North Carolina that is going to be barbecue. As my friend Bob Garner wrote in his wonderful book *Bob Garner's Book of Barbecue: North Carolina's Favorite Food*, "Barbecue has long been the staple food at North Carolina political events." Boy, is it. Now, I like barbecue. I like all kinds of barbecue. But if you have to eat enough of any food, even your favorite, it will wear you down.

This brings me to the one thing that a lot of people still seem to remember about my campaign, which I find funny. I was out at the North Carolina State University Faculty Club for the North Carolina Recreation Association meeting. Three or four hundred recreation directors from all over the state were there. I gave my talk about how I believe recreation is good for us and of course mentioned that at one time my cousin was the recreation director in Watauga County. I sure could have used some recreation at two hundred and thirty-five pounds, but I didn't say that. I also didn't tell them that I called my cousin Joe, who was the Watauga County recreation director, "Fat Jack" because he was a big boy even when he was young.

I was really getting them, I could feel it. I had them. I was doing great, right in the groove, and felt like the Golden Boy of the Recreation department. Plus the polls said I was way ahead. After my fifteen-minute speech (I rarely spoke over fifteen minutes) I called for questions, as usual. A gentleman at the back of the room yelled, "Are you getting enough barbecue?" Before I realized what I was saying, I blurted, "That damnable stuff! You know, I'm sick and tired of it. I wouldn't mind if I never saw another drop of barbecue as long as I live." I'm still not sure what made me answer the question in that way, but I felt confident that it had come off as a joke. OH NO, it did not. The next morning the *News and Observer* article announced "Edmisten Attacks Barbecue." I thought, "What have I done?" Wilbur Shirley, of Wilbur's Barbecue, said, "What is wrong with you? Have you lost your mind?" The North Carolina pork producers said they were disappointed in me. "But I was joking," I moaned.

Boy, oh boy, if only I had paid attention to Proverbs 21:23: "Whoever guards his mouth and tongue, keeps his soul from trouble." If I could arrange for this proverb to appear before my eyes when I am about to say something I am apt to regret, I would get into a lot less trouble. I found out the hard way that people in North Carolina are dead serious about barbecue. They do not want some homespun politician disrespecting their barbecue and they don't want anybody messing with their particular style of barbecue. You've got eastern barbecue and western barbecue, and you don't take sides if you're in politics. In *Holy Smoke: The Big Book of North Carolina Barbecue*, by John Shelton Reed and Dale Voleberg Reed with William McKinney, Dennis Rogers of the Raleigh *News and Observer* is quoted as follows when discussing the merits of "down east" barbecue over that weird stuff out of the west. "The piedmont stuff is made with John Kerry's wife's ketchup vs. God's own apple cider vinegar, salt and pepper Down East." He added that "somebody who would put ketchup on barbecue and give it to a child is capable of pretty much anything."

As for me, it was clear I was in big trouble. I had not taken sides, I had actually disparaged *all* barbecue. People left phone messages asking me what I was coming out against next, mama and apple pie? The flag? Finally, I said, "This has gone on long enough. I am going to call a press conference on barbecue." Everybody showed up for it. I said, "I know I said something that was intemperate. The devil made me say what I said about barbecue. I have already taken precautions to cure myself of this malady. I've had an exorcism and I've had these demonic notions about barbecue removed from me totally. I'm back on barbecue maybe three or four times a day!" It went on and on, and even to this day, I still get called out on it.

Barbecue expert Bob Garner later wrote "Rufus should have known better than to say such a thing, no matter how much barbecue he had been forced to consume during the campaign." How right he was! For that unfortunate comment, I must forever be mentioned in every North Carolina barbecue book ever published. The barbecue wars in North Carolina are crazy. The authors of *Holy Smoke* also note that Jim Auchmutey once called the Carolinas "the Balkans of barbecue."

I advise my friends who are about to run for public office, "Don't condemn it and don't take sides." Barbecue is barbecue. Beef is a Texas thing. To me, barbecue is pork and I like piedmont *and* eastern—still do. West of the piedmont we have a mix of all kinds of barbecue from across the country and I like that too.

I am often called upon to judge barbecue contests and you can hear people saying "Look who's judging the barbecue!" So it's a standing joke. They still write articles about it.

Shortly before my victory in the second primary I was campaigning in Charlotte, hoping that the people who supported my opponents in the primary would come around and support me. The polls said that Jim Martin didn't have a chance because he was an unknown.

The polls also said that a good many Jesse Helms supporters were on my side. However, in North Carolina, Republicans historically got at least forty-five percent of the vote so I was wooing the people of North Carolina's biggest city, hoping to get those who had supported Eddie Knox and Jimmy Green on my side.

I was getting some dinner in a sports bar at the airport with some campaign friends when I looked up at the television to see a crowd of Reagan Administration functionaries disembarking from Air Force One. There were so many people coming off that plane, it was like one of those clown cars at the circus. Then I spotted Senator Jesse Helms come off of that plane, with *Eddie Knox* right behind him. This is how I learned that Eddie was not supporting me in the general election. I came to find out later on that Eddie was angrier with Jim Hunt for not helping him during the primary campaigns than he was at me for beating him. I wasn't surprised that Ronald Reagan's people supported Jesse Helms, since he was a Republican, but Eddie Knox? I had no idea Eddie could be so brazen.

The polls were tightening up, the campaign was in full swing, and suddenly the polls showed that Jim Martin had not only caught up with me, he was surpassing me. I had started out so high in the polls that I had nowhere to go but down. It was awful. I felt so bad for everyone who supported me. Reagan came to North Carolina twice in the closing days of the campaign. North Carolina history shows that when we have a strong candidate in the presidential election, the elections that follow go to that candidate's party—the coattail effect, as it is called. Reagan had such sticky coattails he swept both me and Jim Hunt away from our dreams. We were not alone, either. The sweep was broad and far reaching.

I was not elected governor of North Carolina. For me, the loss was like losing a loved

This photo is the perfect symbol of the heart of my gubernatorial race. I spent many days slogging through fields and down dirt roads trying to reach the "little guy" (photo by Mr. Frank Lewis of Angier, NC).

one. I had coveted that prize so much for so long. Though I know I made mistakes, I truly believe the biggest reason I lost was because Ronald Reagan, an immensely charismatic candidate, was running for president that year. I do not regret running because of the many friendships that I made and what I learned about human nature. I found out who my friends really were after that race.

The most important thing in life was to make my parents proud. Because of my natural propensity to engage people and my interest in politics, the governorship seemed like a shining beacon of the ultimate professional accomplishment. In high school, I was even nicknamed "Governor" because I was so active in politics. Even after I was grown I heard Mama say one time, "My boy Rufus would be a good governor." I agreed with her!

As a result I was crestfallen after the election, and I also felt abandoned by many. The ache in the bottom of my stomach was so great nothing appealed to me except finding some dark place to crawl away and hide. It was a truly overwhelming grief over what was the largest loss in my life at that time. In general, North Carolina has rarely been good to those who run for governor and lose. I swear I saw people cross the street so they wouldn't have to talk to me.

I know I'm whining, but I want to make this point: politicians are people. I've heard people say, "Well, they chose to be public figures, they knew what it was about." But when someone runs for office, he or she has usually spent years planning and preparing, weighing decisions, and formulating policy. During the election they can endure endless indignities, not to mention the grueling physical and emotional stress of the campaign trail. The pace

My campaign staff during my unsuccessful run for governor. This was the most dedicated, poorly paid campaign staff ever (many were volunteers).

and intensity of even an average campaign drains the body, the mind, and the spirit. The travel and the sleepless nights, the constant attacks from our opponents, some of which get way out of hand, especially these days. Then there's the bad food! (None of it barbecue, of course. I love all barbecue.)

It was all over in the blink of an eye, and the Golden Boy was suddenly a loser with a capital L. I felt worthless, like a cheap old piece of busted political baggage. Then there were all of the people I had let down, and all the money everyone had spent on my campaign. A lasting feeling of anguish swept over me. I thought, "All those years with Sam Ervin and as Attorney General and now you might as well be pond scum for all the appeal you have for public office." Very few politicians recover from losing the governorship in North Carolina.

Because they were and are such wonderful people my loyal supporters often said that they felt like they had let *me* down. At first this made me feel worse because it surely was not their fault, but then these people, who were still by my side even in failure, helped give me the loving shove that helped me climb out of the valley of despair. I understood that I was a lucky man who still had a solid group of friends who did not desert me, and as it turns out, would not desert me over a lifetime. This is a precious gift—a golden asset, and the finest one to have in any kind of undertaking in life.

The day after I lost the race my longtime friend Marvin Speight said, "Here, take my new car and you and Linda go somewhere and just get away from it all." Linda and I packed up and drove down to South Carolina and Georgia. Together we owed over a quarter million dollars on notes we had signed for the campaign. Among the agonizing moments: standing in the lobby of the Planter's Inn watching the victorious new governor address his jubilant supporters. Still stinging, I said, "Let's take a walk." We had planned a lovely dinner at a great restaurant near the Battery, but I asked Linda if she would mind if we just grabbed some sandwiches and went back to the hotel. I was sick with worry over the money we owed. Unlike many losing candidates, I was determined to pay my debts.

Meanwhile, I had not driven myself much in years and found myself in the pedestrian position of having to find a parking space and about a thousand other things that had been handed to me on a silver platter while I was in office. And then there was the little problem of a job—I had to support myself. I thought the primary campaign had been so bitter that no law firm would want me, so I didn't even ask around. I also noticed that nobody had said a word of consolation that included any job offers.

Once again I was saved by my fantastic friends. I partnered with a magnificent individual named Reagan Weaver. Reagan and his wife, Ardath, are both dear friends to Linda and me. Reagan and I set up shop in the Commerce Building on Hargett Street and waited for business. The partnership worked well for many reasons, one of which was that Reagan was "laid back" while I was "high strung," as we used to say. Today my old friend and partner is well known as one of the finest mediators and arbitrators in the North Carolina legal community.

As appreciative as I was for all my good fortune, good friends, and opportunities after losing the campaign, my heart was still broken. Maybe I should feel foolish for how much this meant to me. Maybe I was foolish, but I honestly had a hard time moving past it. For a while, I could hardly stand walking past the Capitol. Linda, ever the perfect, loving person to have by your side during a crisis, coolly and calmly went about setting up the offices along with Ardath. My good friends never let up in their quest to lift me up. My good friend Robert L. "Roddy" Jones, a successful entrepreneur and builder, got about ten people together and said, "Rufus needs some clients." They met at a restaurant in Crabtree Valley and shortly thereafter some badly needed clients came my way. I remember fighting back tears the day I learned of this.

10

My First Private Law Practice

As I settled in to my "fresh start," I was anxious to pay back my debt. Humiliating as it was, I held fund-raisers to do it. I would do whatever I had to do to pay back the money. We had a big Christmas party and people came in and we raised a hunk of money then. People really came through for me. It was a long haul and I had to swallow whatever pride I had left, but we paid back the debt. One person I hold dear is my friend and former aide in the attorney general's office, John Elmore from Wilmington, North Carolina. John approached me at the Christmas fund-raiser and said, "I have a check for you here. My business is coming along, and right now you need this more than I do." I knew he had been working hard to develop some property, but I was astounded at the number written on that check. There were a lot of things he might have done with that money, just like the rest of my steadfast supporters and friends. I will never as long as I live forget these people who stepped forward and gave so much when I had so little.

John Elmore wound up doing all right. He developed Shell Island and other magnificent properties. Some years later when the recession came, like so many others, he was wiped out and having a hard time. I called John and said, "Let me quote something back to you. My business is doing just fine and right now you need this more than I do." This wonderful man wouldn't accept any money from me, though I would have given him any amount he needed. Of course he recovered his losses and is back up and running, more successful than ever now. I can never forget his kindness and generosity.

After a little time of working hard and reinventing my life, Linda, being the entrepreneur of the family, as well as the one who makes the smartest bold moves, said, "Let's buy a building. Since we've paid back our debts, there are loans and mortgages we can get. We should do it! It will be a good investment." So we did. Now Linda has a shrewd eye for real estate, and since her heart is in historic preservation (and mine is too, now) of course the building was historic—it was a beautiful 1890s Eastlake cottage that had once housed Preservation North Carolina's headquarters. Reagan Weaver and I moved out of the Commerce Building and into the Bresch House, as it was known. Preservation North Carolina had moved this endangered house to the corner of Morgan and Blount streets. It was elegant and lovely and really added to our law practice. There were chandeliers there that are said to have come out of an Egyptian summer palace. We loved working in that house. Another great thing: there were fourteen parking spaces! This was unheard of in downtown Raleigh. We rented some of them out to help with the mortgage.

I loved working with Reagan Weaver, who is one of the finest human beings I have known, though I did not enjoy the sordid nature of domestic relations cases like divorce and custody battles. The other problem was, I gave away too much of my professional time to people in need. I think the role of public servant was so deeply instilled in me that even after I withdrew to private practice I still behaved like a public servant. This was not exactly fair to my partner since we were in business together to make a living. It didn't help that many people still asked for help and seemed to *see* me as a public servant. Reagan is such a nice person and he was a terrific partner. So kind and large-minded he could have been a clergyman.

It was a constant struggle for me to bill enough hours. I wasn't in public office any more but I still had contacts that could help and I still cared about the little guy. Linda sometimes said, "You have to *charge* these people." We had lots of divorce and small personal injury and cases and I had "settlement Fridays" where I settled a bunch of little cases amounting to maybe $5,000 apiece. I spent a lot of time negotiating with insurance companies and working up settlement offers. We won a few trials but I must confess, I would rather flip hamburgers for a living than take on any domestic cases again.

Here is an example of what divorce lawyers have to deal with on a daily basis. One case had two state employees. One day, the guy walked in my office and said, "I ain't giving her the plastic Santa Claus. We bought it from Firestone Tire Company and she's not gettin' it." This went on and on. I was so tired of the whining and couldn't believe this Santa Claus was the holdup. I got to thinking, my family has been friends with the Firestone people in Boone for years. I called a buddy back home and asked, "Do you have any of those plastic Santa Clauses? I need one." He said, "Oh sure, they are $14." I said, "Great. Will you please put it on rural transit and ship it to me soon as you can?" When it arrived, I brought it to the office and I called the husband and said, "I have this thing settled." He said, "Where's my Santa Claus?" I said, "I've got you a new Santa Claus just like it. She can have that old nasty one and I have a new one for you." He said, "Hell, yeah!" He was thrilled. I was more thrilled than he was to be done with the whole thing.

From that day on I have never taken another domestic relations case and I never will. Most attorneys who practice domestic law have similar stories. Divorce does not bring out the best side of people. Money and child custody are the main areas of conflict. Settlement talks in domestic relations law are often really about getting even. How many times did I hear a client say, "It's the principle of the thing." The first thing I found out

After Rufus lost the gubernatorial election, many of his supporters rallied around and became his lifelong friends.

about practicing this kind of law is that I am just not cut out for this kind of personal strife on a daily basis.

Still, Linda was right—practicing law was just what I needed. I was on my own, independent, and feeling whole again after a little while. I've often said you can do some things better as a regular citizen than a public officeholder. I could now make things happen more quickly because public office puts constraints on you that individuals don't typically have. I still had the opportunity to meet lots of wonderful people, and I felt that some people were more honest with me, and trusted me to be more honest with them because I was not looking for a vote.

At the same time I was not ready for the political trash heap yet. I still attended political meetings, and I walked in to every event with my head held high. Once I overheard one person say, "There's Rufus Edmisten. What is he doing here?" It hurt, but I knew I was a favored public speaker and I missed public life. I was feeling awkward and doing some moping at one gathering and my old buddy Steve Wordsworth came up and said, "Can I ask you something? How many people are in North Carolina?" "About seven million, I guess," I replied. "That's about right. Now let me ask you this: how many of them got the Democratic nomination for governor of North Carolina? I can answer that for you, too. One. Just one, and it was you. Now quit moping and be proud of that." It was as though he had suddenly shined a bright, clear light that gave me a new perspective. He was right. I stepped up my participation at political events, and when I heard that Secretary of State Thad Eure might not run again, I had an inkling of what I might do if he didn't.

11

The Secretary of State Years

When longtime Secretary of State Thad Eure formally announced he would not seek re-election—he had been one of my mentors and at that time had been North Carolina Secretary of State for longer than I had been alive—I announced immediately that I would seek the nomination.

In the weeks leading up to his decision, as speculation swirled, I had remained tightlipped, very mindful of Proverbs 21:23: "Whoever guards his mouth and tongue, keeps his soul from trouble." When anyone asked me about it, all I would say was, "I'm for Thad Eure." I was secretly hoping that Mr. Eure would not seek re-election. First, because it would allow me a shot at redemption after my crushing defeat in the 1984 gubernatorial election, and second because I was worried that if he did decide to seek re-election, he might not be able to fulfill the duties of his office because of his advanced age. I respected him so much.

Thad earlier told me that if I ran and won, I would become one of the few people in the state who had lost a bid for the governorship to come back to win a statewide office. I had spent four years practicing law after losing the governor's race, and I may have fallen into a false sense of entitlement. I had worked my heart out to become governor of North Carolina only to have time and circumstance—fate, if you will—snatch it from me.

I needed to prove to myself and others that I could fight my way back and win. This, and the fact that I thought I would be good at the job, is why I ran for North Carolina Secretary of State. Please forgive me when I say that for this reason, the Secretary of State office in 1988 seemed like winning second prize when what I had dreamed of was first prize: the office of governor. (Don't get me wrong, I loved being attorney general, but I also really wanted to be elected governor.) So it was like, "Hey, look at me, I've come back, there must be something special about me." The "high" of winning four years after such a crushing defeat led me to do reckless things. I was careless.

I ran against John Carrington. I knew John from my days as attorney general because he ran an outfit that manufactured police equipment and riot gear. John had actually been a contributor to my campaign for governor in 1984. We had a strange relationship. We occasionally had drinks and dinner and talked about his company. (He was later convicted of selling various kinds of law enforcement equipment to regimes the United States government considered "unfavorable.") When he asked me to write a letter to the judge asking for leniency, I was happy to do so. He had been very decent to me. He was tall, quick-witted, a confirmed supply-side Republican, and independently wealthy.

John's idea of campaigning seemed to be to stay home and watch his money pile up and buy ads. In one of his campaign ads against me, he began talking about his numbers in the polls and how he was inching up on me. When I asked if he would share his numbers he said, "Gladly." I believed him. I just had not raised a lot of money for the Secretary of

State campaign because I felt I had exhausted everyone I knew asking for money with the failed campaign for governor. I was hoping my name recognition would carry me through. John once said to me, "Rufus, if I win, I'm going to ask you to run it for me." I laughed and said, "John, I don't have time to do that."

Some of his ads were pretty ridiculous. He ran one saying that I would take away everyone's guns and oppose the death penalty. I shot back in a television interview that my father was a wildlife officer and that I had been around properly used weapons all my life. John and I laughed about it the next day. As for the death penalty, I remember saying that I imagined those people I put on death row kind of wished I wasn't for the death penalty. I also joked that I wondered if John would demand that death penalty for some notary whose license had expired. I could be pretty ridiculous myself.

John came very close to catching up with me in both races because I did no advertising. I have to say, there were times I thought John's ads related more to outer space than the Secretary of State race. Voters may have thought the same thing because I won the election. John later became a North Carolina state senator and I would go over and have nice chats with him. We really liked each other, even while we were duking it out over the campaign. Even when adversaries we always had a congenial relationship.

Glen Wells was my campaign manager. He had been one of my former aides in the attorney general office and he knew about campaigning. Another aide was Christine Reddin, a young woman of Spanish descent who had a truly winning way about her and was the go-getter in the campaign. Christine scheduled me for various events and if I couldn't go I would send her. The audience loved her. She was always charming and represented me well. At this writing, she is still active in Democratic politics and has two fine young sons. It was wonderful of her to be so gracious and kind to me on my first attempt to come back to political life.

Being elected North Carolina secretary of state gave me great joy and peace because I was back where I liked to be. I was elated to be back in office. I felt like I had returned from political death. The same year I won secretary of state, Jim Gardner won lieutenant governor. Jim was a former congressman and entrepreneur from Rocky Mount, North Carolina. It was also a jubilant day for Governor Martin, who was in his second term as governor of North Carolina. Here was the man who had handed me my hindquarters in the 1984 governor's race, still governor while I served on the Council of State. I have always liked Governor Martin and being in the Capitol meant I would see him all the time. I would be working closely with him.

I had many times visited the great Secretary of State Thad Eure, the longest serving official in the country at that time, in his magnificent office in the State Capitol Building. Thad's office had so many wonderful things, including a statue of the woman from the old State Seal of North Carolina. He had served as North Carolina's Secretary of State for fifty-two years. Thad was a state treasure, my buddy, an old-time orator, and in many ways, to me, a mentor. (Senator Ervin told me, when I was first elected, "You let Thad Eure teach you how to do things.") The Capitol, built between 1833 and 1840, is a monumentally lovely building that has survived the ages with tremendous grace. I could not wait to have my office in that stately, reverently simple building. Our State Capitol was finished right about the time North Carolina finished building its first railroad! Imagine that. It was no small wonder that I was eager to be ensconced in Thad Eure's beautiful old office and make it my own.

Shortly after the election, I was traveling to Durham for an event and the car phone rang. (Car phones, the first cellular phones, looked like giant humps between the two front

Being sworn in as secretary of state in 1989.

seats.) It was Governor Martin. He said, "Congratulations on winning the Secretary of State Office, Rufus! I have some news for you that you won't like, but I need to tell you. I'm going to take the offices of the Secretary of State in the Capitol and give them to Lieutenant Governor Jim Gardner. I need to have him over here to protect him from those Democrats over there in the Legislature." I thought to myself "No!" I was getting kicked out of the Capitol building before I had even gotten in there!

My heart sank. I was crushed. I said, "Governor, I hate that. I don't know what I'm going to do." He said, "Don't worry. We'll hunt you some space." I thought, "Okay." Well, word got out that Martin was kicking me out of the Capitol, so I decided to have some fun with it. I held a press conference in my law office and I said, "The governor has kicked me out of the Capitol. I feel like Moses of old wandering in the desert for forty years. However, I have had several kind North Carolinians offer to move a double wide onto the grounds of the State Capitol for the Secretary of State's office."

The governor called pretty fast and told me, "Cut it out! Even my friends think I'm treating you badly. Come on over here to the Capitol and let's find you some space. I can give you some space on the second floor." I went on over there and we went upstairs and looked in all the nooks and crannies. The governor said, "You can have any one of these."

I picked the one fronting on Hillsborough Street. "I can live with this one," I told him. I made it my ceremonial office, the place for giving the oaths of office and other functions. The governor had to kick out his scheduling secretary, Kim Shope, and another assistant in order to make room for me, so I appreciated it. We got loaner paintings from the North Carolina Museum of Art, and I had use of Governor Daniel Lindsay Russell's desk. (He was the 49th governor of North Carolina.) I had a window overlooking Hillsborough Street and another overlooking Fayetteville Street—the prime and most historic intersection of the City of Raleigh. While small, my office was just fine.

We had wonderful gatherings at this office. The balcony was one from which it was said that William Jennings Bryan had once spoken to the people of Raleigh. I sometimes had intimate gatherings there. Out on that balcony on a spring night, in the glow of candlelight, with the scents of the beautiful flora on the grounds sweetening the cool air, you could almost feel the presence of long-gone dignitaries and workers. I fell even more in love with the Capitol even though I had not achieved my goal of having Thad Eure's office for my very own. When the children came through on field trips I had little brochures made for them that they could stamp with Thad Eure's wonderful old State of North Carolina seal.

When I was attorney general I got to help mostly individual citizens, but as secretary of state I dealt primarily with businesses large and small. One of my jobs was to help businesses get started. I believed that if we had one-stop licensing and permitting it would streamline the process. It was one of my first legislative aims. We established the Business License Information Office and it worked very well. Small business people could contact that office and get everything done right there. I had borrowed that idea from the secretary of state of Washington. It worked so well that Harvard University invited me to present the details of the program at a national seminar.

Another thing I proposed that passed was limited liability corporation legislation, which is used by tens of thousands of people today. I was very proud of that one. We also established a regulatory office for sports agents, and beefed up the securities division. This is the entity that regulates the sale of stocks and bonds and business ventures. I ordered a crackdown on securities fraud and we indicted people for all kinds of schemes. One thing that amazed and distressed me was how consumers often got angry when we shut down a business for their own protection because we had uncovered fraud. They seemed to think we wanted to stop them from making money when we really wanted to keep them from getting ripped off and losing more money.

Trey Garrett, then in his twenties, was my enthusiastic traveling companion. He travelled with me to almost every county in our great state. When I was a member of the North Carolina Film Commission we once traveled to Fontana Lake, a remote part of Western North Carolina in Graham County, during the filming of the Jodie Foster movie *Nell*. Now, I might have been an Eagle Scout except for my aversion to swimming. (Thank you, brothers, for throwing me into that deep, cold river.) Understandably, I did not feel completely confident during the long, long boat ride to the film site. Trey teased me then and still gives me guff about that overwater journey. Despite my trepidation we survived and made it back to report that the newly formed North Carolina Film Commission was a success.

I have often been asked if there are ghosts in the Capitol. I would like to answer that question here, once and for all. Listen up! *There are ghosts in the 1840 North Carolina State Capitol Building!* For those of you who have not had the pleasure of visiting our state Capitol, it is made entirely of smooth, thick blocks of gneiss, beautiful, striated granite that is indigenous to Wake County, North Carolina. I often found myself alone inside the cool walls of this fine old beauty when I was working late into the evening. At those times I knew there was not another human being in the building. Mr. Owen Jackson, the guard for over a decade, left at 11 every night and made sure everyone else had cleared out. Yet I often heard loud bangs I couldn't explain, and phantom doors slamming.

This was unsettling. I asked Mr. Jackson if he had ever heard anything in his years of guarding the building. He said he had heard blood-curdling screams when there was nobody but him in the building, and loud bangs like I heard, and had once even heard the old elevator going up and down by itself, with nobody in there when the door opened. He said he had even heard the tinkling sound of glass breaking upstairs on the second floor one night when nobody was there. Or maybe it was the musical tone of champagne glasses toasting.

One night I was writing a letter at my desk and all of a sudden I heard chamber music wafting under my door. I thought, "Okay, who is the joker?" It sounded as if it was coming from the House Chamber. It was a Vivaldi composition and I got up to see who had snuck in a recording trying to get my goat. As soon as I got to the House Chamber the music ceased. I looked everywhere, I opened up desk drawers and looked on every shelf, I knew all the hiding places but after a thorough search, I found nothing. I walked back to my office and closed the door. After a few seconds, it started again. All I could think was, "Okay, that's a ghost. I might as well enjoy the music." It went on three or four minutes and then it quit. It was bone-chilling. If I were a dog, my hackles would have risen. It was an overwhelming feeling, and left me with the distinct impression that there is something to this ghost business.

Former President Bill Clinton won his first elected office as Attorney General of Arkansas in 1976. At that time, the terms of all statewide offices in Arkansas were only two years. I first met William Jefferson Clinton at a meeting of the National Association of Attorneys General in San Francisco. There is much pomp and ceremony at these kinds of meetings, not unlike the National Governors Association meetings. They are filled with flags, badges and ribbons. There I was, the youngest attorney general in America, being elected at thirty-three years old. Or so I thought. At that time I was thirty-five, and I was sure I was the youngest of the attorneys general at the event. I remember coming down to the meeting early and noticed that the configuration was that of a horseshoe. The table wrapped around with an oval in the front and two sides going down. Each of the attorneys general had a nameplate that also identified his state.

I sat down proudly behind my North Carolina nameplate with the North Carolina flag in the background. I always tried to be prepared at those meetings by going over the agenda and noting where in the program I might learn something, which was the true purpose of the event. As I sat there pondering what would be coming out for lunch, a very young man came up and sat down beside me in the seat to my right which was reserved for the Arkansas attorney general. This guy looked like he might be a little over twenty years old. I said, "Hello, I'm Rufus. Where is your attorney general?"

The fresh-faced kid turned and looked at me gravely, and said, "I am the attorney general." I was taken back because this kid looked like he had just given the valedictorian speech at Little Rock High School. Without even thinking, I said, "Well, how old are you?" He replied crisply, "I'm 27 years old." I blurted out without even thinking, "I *hate* your ass!" At the time, I did not know I was telling the future president of the United States that I hated him. I had thought I was the youngest guy there and here he comes in at twenty-seven years old and obliterates my record. Clinton laughed, and we became friends from that day on.

Later on, when Bill Clinton was running for president, he was about to speak at an Asheville, North Carolina, fund-raiser in a private home, and the host of the gathering, former mayor of Asheville Leni Sitnick, asked me if I would like to introduce him. I got up and gave him a proper introduction. He ascended the long staircase and when he got to the top said, "This is the guy at one time that told me, 'I hate your ass.'"

A couple of years ago, President Clinton was in North Carolina at a fund-raiser for Secretary Hillary Rodham Clinton's presidential campaign. I attended the pre-event meeting for the "FOBs" (Friends of Bill.) We had a wonderful chat, made pictures and reminisced about old times. When President Clinton began his speech he gave me a shout-out: "There's my friend Rufus and he will tell you that being attorney general is the best job we both ever had." We have said that on many occasions. Bill said that it was an office where you could flourish and grow and do good things for people. I heartily agree.

Toward the end of my secretary of state career I served as president of the National Association of Secretaries of State. I instituted a new policy of having annual meetings of the association in Washington, D.C. Prior to the trip to Washington, I had asked the White House for a meeting with President Bill Clinton to receive the secretaries of state, speak to them, and show them around the White House. President Clinton's staff approved our request and we were all giddy with excitement. It is a big deal to be invited to the White House to meet with the president.

On the day of the event, we took a charter bus to the White House and happily went through all of the tight security procedures. The president had agreed to meet with us for fifteen minutes but I knew Bill Clinton well enough to know that we would have more time than that with him. Before the president came in, Vice President Al Gore spoke to us in the Roosevelt Room. I was up there fielding questions for him and all of a sudden someone comes up behind me and gives me a big bear hug. I thought, "This can't be anyone except Bill Clinton." Delighted, I turned around and said, "Mr. President!" He said, "Rufus, you have lost a lot of weight." I was so pleased! President Clinton, who is admittedly a hugger, still doesn't hug *just anybody*, after all.

Since we had President Clinton in the afternoon, I had asked Senator Jesse Helms to talk to us in the morning. Although Senator Helms was complimentary of me as a fellow North Carolina native son, he wound up blasting President Clinton, railing on about some of his more liberal policies. This was of course in high contrast to the ideas President Clinton set forth, and I loved it, because the exchange of different, sometimes conflicting, ideas is what it is all about. It's what I think of as the spice of life—and the heart of political discourse.

After the talk we all returned to the hotel. When I went to my room to collect some materials, I found that Linda was out—I knew that she had planned to visit the office of the National Trust for Historic Preservation. (At that time, she worked for the State Preservation office, and historic preservation has been a lifelong passion for her.) The hotel phone rang and a lady announced, "The White House is calling." I just *knew* this was a joke. I could just see some of the secretaries of state pulling this one, getting one of the women to make the call.

When she said, "The president and his wife would like for you and your wife to come spend the night at the White House." I said, "Yeah, right!" and I hung up the phone! The front desk called back and left the message "Please ask Mr. Edmisten to call the White House." I called the number and the lady, whose name I later learned was Mrs. Huber, said, "I am the executive housekeeper for the White House." I said, "For real?" She said, "Yes, please don't hang up." She said, "The president and Mrs. Clinton want to invite you to be their guest tonight. Navy personnel will pick you up at half past 4 at your hotel. Look for a black car." I was ecstatic—absolutely beside myself that the president and first lady wanted us to spend the night in the White House. A few seconds later a messenger from the hotel knocked and confirmed that it really was the White House on the phone.

However, much to my chagrin, Linda was still gone and I had no idea when she was coming back. I was buzzing with anticipation and anxious as hell. It was getting on about 3, she was not back yet, and I had no earthly idea how to find her. I wasn't sure what to do. Should I try to find her before the car showed up? Should I ask the driver to stop at the Preservation office? Since Linda has always refused to own or even use a cell phone, I had no way of knowing exactly where she was and Washington, D.C., is a right large city.

To my great relief fifteen minutes later she casually walked in. Once I had convinced Linda that we were really invited, we started packing our essentials once we figured out what to wear. As the time approached for the car to arrive, a bunch of our colleagues were peeping out their windows. Then a beautiful, shiny, black car appeared and two navy guys in their crisp dress whites greeted us. "Gosh they're gorgeous!" Linda whispered. On the way to the White House I was already thinking "How can I commemorate this?" I wanted to preserve this memory, but didn't have a camera with me, so I asked the drivers to stop and I went into drugstore and bought a disposable camera with as many exposures as I could find. When we arrived at the White House I recognized the entrance, which faced the Washington Monument, as one I had seen on television when the president and first lady received diplomats and foreign dignitaries.

Our escorts sprung lightly out of the car to open our car doors for us. There to meet us was Mrs. Carolyn Huber herself, a lovely, personable lady. She greeted us warmly, and mentioned that she had been with the president when he was governor of Arkansas. As she gave us identification badges she said, "As the guests of the president, please make your-selves at home. You can do anything you want except for two things: you cannot go into the Situation Room and please do not try to take the stairs up to your quarters on the second floor. If you do that, something bad will happen. Nobody takes the stairs. Take the elevator only."

Trap doors, false walls, and secret passages flashed through my mind. I imagined Secret Service agents mowing us down. On the way to the elevator to the second floor we passed the Plate Room and the Portrait Room and other rooms with all kinds of beautiful, elegant objects. I felt like I was in the middle of a documentary film. When we got off at the second floor Mrs. Huber said, "You will be staying in the Lincoln Bedroom." The Lincoln Bedroom! I turned to Linda, bug-eyed with excitement. She was cool as could be, taking it all in stride, as usual.

After we got settled in, we just had to go exploring. Mrs. Huber said that as long as we had our identification badges we would be fine walking around. Crews were working on part of the White house wall that faced Pennsylvania Avenue because somebody had shot it up the week before. The guest book was open, inviting our signatures and after we signed, we just had to look at some of the names of those who had been there before us. Caroline Kennedy was the most recent. I thought, "I am a long way from the farm now!" In the midst of all this glory, my ever-pragmatic wife was most concerned about how she was going to get her cup of coffee in the morning. Linda has to have a cup before she gets out of bed. It was easily arranged. We soaked it all in and took pictures of one another with everything. I could not get enough of sitting at President Lincoln's desk!

When the time came that night to go up to the secretaries of state event on Capitol Hill, we saw lots of familiar faces. Jim Hunt beamed a greeting out to us by way of satellite television. Jesse Helms and Strom Thurmond dropped by. My Aunt Katy observed that Senator Thurmond was flirting with her. She whispered, "That man had the biggest feet on any person I've ever seen." We laughed. I kept looking at my watch not because I was impatient but because I wanted to get back to the White House.

After the Capitol Hill event I had another engagement, and Linda went back to the White House. (She later told me that when she told the taxi driver where she wanted to go, he looked incredulous and said, "Are you sure about that, lady?") When I came back the White House was lit up for the night, and I saw guards patrolling with German shepherds and snipers walking the roof. I just walked right in the front door, happy that everyone knew I was supposed to be there. When I told Linda about it she asked me if I had lost my mind. She had gone in the side door where we first entered.

Once back upstairs in the Lincoln Bedroom I wanted to explore some more. Linda was already in bed reading, but I have always been a night owl so I decided to wander around. I was careful not to forget to use the elevators to avoid any type of unfortunate incident between myself and the Secret Service. I wandered down toward the President's room, stuck my head in a little doorway where I saw about ten pairs of sneakers. I suddenly realized this was Bill Clinton's bathroom! Before I could back up and apologize I heard that familiar, distinctive voice say, "That's all right. How are you? I'm sorry I didn't have time to come visit." He was in the bathroom and I was just outside the door! Now, we're both known to be talkers, so we talked a while. Eventually the President said, "I'll see you in the morning." Just outside the president's quarters there was a briefing book. The briefing for the next day was written by North Carolinian Erskine Bowles, then chief of staff. The president was scheduled to meet with the German chancellor. History was everywhere. It was so exciting. I still couldn't sleep and didn't want to lose a moment so when I went back to our room I wrote a letter to my mama and daddy while sitting at the Lincoln desk. My daddy died three weeks later.

It must have been well after midnight by the time I settled down enough to even think about sleeping. I remembered that Mrs. Huber had said that breakfast would be served in the solarium at 8 a.m. I arranged a wake-up call for 6 a.m. and, still unable to cast off the excitement of the day, fell into a fitful sleep.

We awakened to a crisp, snowy day. The White House butler brought Linda's coffee to our room, then we went to the solarium for breakfast. The snow sparkled on the lawn and the surrounding historic buildings as we ate our pancakes and sausage, and I just thought to myself, I wish I could preserve this moment forever. I was filled with the wistfulness of being in a wonderful place I knew I would likely never experience again. Just before 9 we gathered our things and headed down to the car that would take us back to the hotel. We saw the president on the elevator on the way out and thanked him again for his hospitality. I hated to leave!

Back at the hotel we were besieged by questions from our curious friends. One of my cheekier colleagues wanted to know if Linda and I got lucky in the Lincoln Bedroom. We just felt lucky to be there. That night was one of the highlights of my life.

Over the years, President Clinton has been a delightful friend, even welcoming my last-minute request to watch the last Final Four basketball match with him and his guests at the White House in 2000, when Carolina played. I was in town with friends and took a chance we might be able to watch the game with the president. We had a wonderful time. I was in Washington in the spring of 2000, the year before President Clinton left office. I was staying at the Marriott and walking through the lobby when I spotted a good ol' boy from North Carolina. He said, "Any way we can get one of them tours to the White House?"

I said, "Nah, I don't think so." But he gave me an idea. I remembered that it was the final hours of March Madness and Carolina was playing in the Final Four. You had Maryland, Arizona, Michigan and Carolina that year. I knew that President Clinton was a basketball nut and loved to watch the games, so I put a call in to the White House and got ahold of my friend Diane Liesenger. I said, "Diane, is the president around this weekend?" She said, "Yes, he is going to be watching the ball game." I said, "Oh my gosh, I'd love to come. I've never watched a ball game with him. Why don't I write a note to the president and see if you can get it up to him." Diane said, "Good idea! I can't go up there but the ushers can." I wrote the note and it said, "Dear Mr. President, we'd love to watch the ball game with you tonight. Here's my number."

Diane got me in to talk to the ushers, who were these two guys who looked like they had been there since Coolidge, each in his own cubby. I have their cards in my office to this day. I asked them to deliver my note, and Diane added, "Now, this is a friend of the president and he would like you to take this note up there if you will, please." One of them looked at me doubtfully and asked, "Who's he?" Diane gave him my ID, motioned to the computer and said, "Check him out." I guess I passed because after a while he said "All right, I'll take it up there."

I returned to the hotel and went to the bar wondering if I'd pulled it off. I had no idea if the president would be able to respond on such short notice. I ordered a round of drinks, and we waited. About twenty minutes later, I got a call from President Clinton's social secretary. She said, "Please give me the names, Social Security numbers and addresses of the other members of the party." There were four of us, including myself. I didn't know the exact criteria for the security check, so wasn't sure everyone would pass inspection, but we all passed and promptly prepared ourselves to watch the NCAA Final Four Championship of 2000 with the president of the United States, William Jefferson Clinton! I felt like the man of the hour because all my friend had asked for was a tour of the White House, and we were going to get to watch the game with the president!

When we got to the White House the secretary told us we would be having dinner with the president. She escorted us to an area on the first floor that had a theater on the right and said, "This is where you will be watching the games. Dinner will be served at 6:30. There will be some interns here and folks associated with the teams represented in the Final Four, including some members of Congress and cabinet secretaries." My friends seemed transfixed by the stately grandeur of the White House, so I thanked her and we moved forward.

I have observed that there is something about the White House that makes country people like us realize how country we really are, especially mountain folk like me. We walked in and my companions peered up into the elevated theater area with eyes big as saucers. Invited guests started coming in and sitting down at tables set up outside the theater in the hall. Dinnertime comes and an aide says, "You will be sitting here with Attorney General Janet Reno and Secretary of Health and Human Services Donna Shalala." After a while I realized that everyone there had a hometown team in the Final Four. My friends were sitting back at another table with Representative John Dingell, from Michigan, who at that time had the longest congressional tenure in United States history. All the teams had a cheering squad at the dinner.

They were serving wine so I asked the server, "You couldn't find any vodka, could you?" He promptly brought out a bottle of Grey Goose. I was pleased. The president had not yet arrived. We enjoyed delightful conversations at the tables. I told Janet Reno about the people I knew in Florida and mentioned that when I was with Senator Ervin, I knew

Senator "Gorgeous George Smathers," who was the best man at John F. Kennedy's wedding. I was now "Rufus" to both of them. Secretary Donna Shalala told me, "I'm going to speak to NC State University in the next couple of weeks. Tell me something unique to say." I said, "You have to say … 'and don't we love Jim Valvano?'" Sure enough, I asked several people who were there at NC State when Secretary Shalala spoke and when she said it, the audience erupted.

It came time for the ballgame and a hush fell over the room when someone whispered, "The president is coming!" President Clinton came down the hallway by himself, which was striking because we usually saw him in a phalanx of Secret Service agents. His hair wasn't white at that time and he was wearing a maroon open-collared shirt, the picture of a young, brilliant president. He greeted all of us warmly—I was delighted to see a spark in his eye when he shook my hand—and went to sit in the front row of big, luxurious theater chairs. While the game was on, one by one, honored guests were summoned to go sit with the president in the front row of the theater, where there were four empty seats.

When it was Janet Reno's turn to sit with the president, I noticed a change in his demeanor. He seemed cool and he hardly said a word to her. I remember that at time he had reportedly been unhappy with some of Attorney General Reno's comments to the press on various matters. When the games were over we assembled to wait our turns to thank the president. Abruptly, as though it was something he had had on his mind and needed to say, President Clinton said to Attorney General Reno, "I want you to know one thing. I am still the President. I want something done about that boy *now*." She said, "I understand, Mr. President," and seemed to shrink before my eyes. Then he turned to wave goodbye to all of us. In just a couple of days, Elián Gonzalez—a boy involved in an international custody dispute—was sent back to Cuba. Attorney General Janet Reno had ordered the return of Elián to his father and set a deadline of April 13, 2000.

12

Hubris

I came upon a word—hubris—when we studied Greek tragedy. Hubris is defined as excessive pride toward or defiance of the gods, leading to nemesis—the inescapable agent of one's downfall. Hubris is sometimes referred to as the pride that comes before a fall. A wise old man in the mountains where I was born didn't use the word hubris, but he explained hubris intoxication well when he described the three stages of drunkenness:

Stage 1. You think you are the most handsome dog in the pack, and you hold your head that way.

Stage 2. You think that you are the richest man in the world and you yell to the entire bar, "Drinks for everyone, on me!"

Stage 3. You feel you are so powerful that you have gained the ability to become invisible, so you think you can do anything you want, without consequences.

I could find any number of excuses for my bad behavior as secretary of state but the truth is, it was nobody's fault but my own. This has not been easy to accept, but sometimes the truth isn't easy to take. Ironically, when I look back, I see that I fell under a similar self-aggrandizing spell that captured some of the key Watergate figures. This is particularly embarrassing, but there it is. I had been one of them—the people who brought catastrophe upon themselves in part by becoming full of themselves, feeling a false sense of entitlement and making unwise choices.

Once hubris gets a foothold it grows incrementally and accelerates until it is expanding exponentially, and in leaps and bounds takes over. No doubt the sycophants of the world recognize the hubris-infected when they see one and scamper to that person like crows to a fresh corn field. They converge and the convergence only adds to the inflated sense of self-worth of the Terrible Toad of Hubris because they are all paying attention to him. I forsook the humility that my upbringing instilled and became enthralled by the deluge of flattering attention.

I was in the last year of my second term as secretary of state after serving as attorney general for ten years, and before that spending ten years in high profile positions in the United States Senate. Getting too impressed with myself resulted in bad things happening to me. When you hold public office or any position others perceive as one of power, a lot of people say a lot of nice things about you. While some of them might be true, many of them are simply intended to win favor. This works about as often as you might expect. You really can catch more flies with honey than you can with vinegar. It can also really puff a person up. Everybody wants to be liked, after all.

It was 1995 and I had been doing some things that were foolish, to say the least. As I perceived myself to be more and more powerful I danced closer and closer to an edge I should never have gone near. I didn't intend to do wrong, I was just playing loose and easy with some rules by which I should have abided. The trouble began when allegations of inappropriate behavior in my office emerged in the press. While I take full responsibility for my mistakes, I do need to say that some of the allegations were not true.

My name was on the front page of the *News and Observer* for several weeks. Now I may be a little bit of an attention hound, but these were not good articles. Nobody wants this kind of attention. Three-term North Carolina State Auditor Ralph Campbell thought he should do an audit and he proceeded with one. The accusations in his report were devastating to the office and to me. The accusations included misuse of employees, misuse of state car, and abuses by subordinates. There were allegations that I had strayed from proper hiring practices and given positions to the children of political friends. Worst of all, of course, NOBODY had ever done this before! I mean, it's not like people in every state office imaginable had been helping their qualified friends and relatives with jobs from the beginning of time.

These were embarrassing things. I remember going home and vomiting. I thought to myself, "What have you done? Why have you thrown away all those things you worked so hard at?" My wife, always a lovely portrait of grace under fire, simply said, "We are going to get through this and you are not going to whine." As the newspaper pieces and television commentary became more and more brutal, deep depression set in. I slept maybe two hours a night and sometimes hoped I would not wake up. I was reaping the fruit of my super-sized need for adulation. The repeated allegations, over and over, each time seemingly louder and more detailed than the previous, were horrible. There was no way to combat it.

I announced that I would not run for re-election in 1996. I just didn't want to put my family and friends through it. I knew I had brought it on myself. There are things I should not have done and I only blame myself. I did nothing illegal but my carelessness was inappropriate and caused inappropriate events in my office. In the midst of the deluge of criticism and ridicule, I actually thanked God my daddy had died before this mess started.

When I got myself into a pickle, I sang hymns. When I had serious trouble, I always headed to the hills. I went to Mama. I went alone because Linda knew I needed to do that by myself. The drive had never been longer. There was no escaping the shame I felt, not even for a moment. The thought that I had embarrassed my mama crushed my soul. I dreaded facing her but I needed her, too. When I got there she looked at me with kindness on her wonderful face and said, "You are having a hard time, son." She patted me on the head and said, "It will be OK. What do you want for supper?" She was tender, but not indulgent. She was saying, "It will be all right. People have been through worse, son." Just the day before I had done an interview with Steve Ford of the *News & Observer*.

The call for me to resign sounded from every newspaper in the state. I went to see my mother one more time and by the time I got there, she was in the hospital with a minor problem. I got home to Boone that night and started to go down the stairs and I tripped on the steps. I fell straight down to the basement and injured my left eye so badly I thought I was going to lose it. It looked so gruesome, and knew I couldn't go see Mama in that state. It was utter misery. I called Linda and said, "I need to get home and get to the doctor in Raleigh." One eye was totally closed and I could only drive for twenty minutes before I had to pull over. Not only was I at my lowest emotional point but I was trying to drive with my one good eye full of tears. It took me seven hours to get from Boone to Raleigh. When I got home, Linda took me to the doctor, who said my eye was swollen almost out of its socket but that she thought my eye would be fine. I felt like the most disgraced person on the earth that day. I recalled the book of Job and tried to keep Mama's comforting words in mind.

There was worse to come. My shame deepened because so many articles said, "he must not have learned from Watergate." It would be bad in any case but it was worse for me because I had always cared so much what other people thought of me. The editorials were endless, and yet there were hundreds of letters and telephone messages saying, "Don't resign!"

One day shortly after I returned to the office I received a call from my friend Allen Thomas, a fellow lawyer from Wilson who was one of Jim Hunt's close personal and political friends. He wanted to have breakfast with me at the Farmer's Market. "We'll get in a corner," he promised, understanding that I didn't want to attract any attention. Besides being panic-stricken, I was still all bruised up and still had a big gizmo on my eye. I knew as soon as Allen called that there was something up other than a simple breakfast invitation. During our meal he said, "They are throwing some serious charges at you, Rufus. I know you didn't do anything criminally wrong, but you might want to think about resigning." I thought, "Oh God, am I going to be the first person to resign from this office in North Carolina?" I said, "Thank you." Allen never said he was speaking for Governor Hunt, but I knew he was there on his behalf when he uttered, "What's next?" I had met with Hunt weeks before and he had used that very phrase—"What's next?" That was a signal. I didn't (and still don't) resent Jim Hunt or Allen for any of this. I just knew that it was time to go after that conversation. Still, it cut me to the bone to say, "I am leaving."

I went back to the office and told the staff just that. Dick Carlton, my chief of staff,

One of the truly exciting times during my tenure as secretary of state was when we traveled with a delegation of other secretaries of state to Israel where I met Yitzhak Rabin, planted a tree in the Golan Heights which I hope is flourishing today, and dipped my feet in the River Jordan. It was moving to see in person so many places from the tales of the Bible that Grandma Nan read to me as a little boy. With me are Billy Guste, former attorney general of Louisiana, second from left, and Mr. and Mrs. William J. Brown.

had weathered the storm and endured so much pressure. I was not the only one who felt a great relief when I resigned. I walked out of that office on March 13, 1996, with my head high and drove *myself* home for the first time in a long time to my house on Lake Wheeler Road. I said to Linda, "I guess we have to start all over." She looked at me with kindness in her beautiful eyes and reminded me, "What did your mama say to you?" I said, "Worst things have happened to other people."

She said, "OK! You will not moan and feel sorry for yourself. It's Friday, but the day is not over yet. Call over to the Raleigh Building and get an

With Yitzhak Rabin in Israel at a meeting of the Israeli Autism Society, for whom his wife served as chair. He was assassinated in Tel Aviv just two weeks after this photo was taken.

office. I want you out of this house on Monday. I have a $5000 check to start you in your law practice." I was stunned and overwhelmed by this gift, and I did as I was told. I called Larry Bewley and asked about space. By Monday at lunch, I had a 300 square foot room and a desk. Margine, the secretary for the offices, was out front answering calls for everyone in the office. On Tuesday, my phone came. I was in business, but I was also in something like a state of shock for a good while. All I could do was keep my head down and say, "I am going to get through this. One foot in front of the other, one day at a time."

The moral of the story is that nobody is immune to the intoxicating sickness that power can bring. Richard Nixon demonstrated that even the president of the United States may fall prey to it. I had become impressed with myself and with the importance that others assigned me. The power of my position attracted people, they lavished attention and praise upon me and I loved it. Yet I was someone who had done chores and milked cows on the farm every morning of my childhood and I spent my formative years with decent, honest, humble people. Thinking back to those simple days eventually served to get my feet back on the ground where they belonged—after the swift and devastating blow of public humiliation jarred me out of my prideful stupor.

Flawed as I am, I do think I accomplished some things as secretary of state that I can be proud of. We modernized our corporate division, established a one-stop licensing and permitting office, gave the securities division additional powers to stop unethical investment officers, and recovered tens of millions of dollars of ill-gotten gains by securities firms. We established the concept of the limited liabilities corporation (LLC), and created a boxing commission designed to prevent the injuries and harm that happen so often in unregulated bouts. We set guidelines to regulate sports agents that were designed to keep people from exploiting young athletes. My friends in the legislature helped with this.

I've heard that we become best known by our worst act. I sincerely hope this is not true, and that the mistakes I made as secretary of state do not come to define my entire career.

13

Friends of Rufus (FOR)
to the Rescue

After I resigned, I knew I had to make a living, and I wanted to gain back a measure of respect. I didn't have any money except for the love offering Linda made. I could never pay her back enough for that act of love. There is just not a high enough interest rate in the world.

About two weeks after I had begun my private practice, I went to Washington, D.C., to ask for help from two of my Republican friends. I didn't feel entitled to anything, but I hoped they would help me. First I went to see my old friend and gubernatorial primary opponent Senator Lauch Faircloth. I said, "Lauch, I would like for you to consider helping me become a lobbyist for Phillip Morris." He said, "You are a good man as far as I am concerned and I stick with my friends." Among the many other things I am grateful for, my heart is so thankful that for the people I knew who did not jump on the bandwagon and join the "feeding frenzy." So many people said I was still a good man, and that everybody makes mistakes. It still brings tears to my eyes to think about it.

Then I made my way over to see Senator Jesse Helms, with whom I had worked to save the New River and who I had known for years as a fellow Mason and in many other capacities. Although I did not always agree with some of his stances on social issues, I knew he was a man of his word. The day I visited, Senator Helms was conducting a hearing as the chairman of the Foreign Relations Committee. I first connected with one of his aides, Jimmy Broughton. Jimmy, always kind, said, "Let me just tell the senator you're here." Senator Helms went so far as to recess his hearing for a moment to speak with me." When I asked him the same favor I had asked Senator Faircloth, he just said, "Why don't we call Howard Liebengood from Phillip Morris?" He picked up that phone and said, "Howard, this is Jesse Helms. I have our friend Rufus Edmisten here and I hope you can find something for him." Howard said, "Have Rufus come on down here and let's sign him up." That this busy man would do that for me was amazing. I could hardly believe it.

Within two weeks I had acquired two Fortune 500 clients by way of "a little help from my friends." And yes, they were Republican friends. (For some reason, some of the state's most influential Democratic leaders suddenly seemed to be too busy to return my calls. When I ran into them, I wondered if I had recovered my superpower of becoming invisible.)

The retainer from Phillip Morris amounted to almost as much as I had made as secretary of state. I have reminded Jimmy Broughton and Senator Helms' granddaughter so many times about this kindness that I will never forget. I am reminded of Samuel 16:7 which says "For the Lord sees not as man sees: man looks on the outward appearance, but the Lord looks on the heart. " I can say from personal experience that Jesse Helms had a good heart.

George Taylor was the vice president of West Publishing Company. At about the same time I was talking to Helms and Faircloth, I called George and said, "I'm in a fix. I'm in a bad way." When I explained my circumstance, which I am sure he had heard a little bit about, he said, "You want to work for us?" I said, "I certainly do." He signed me up right then and there. I represented West for many years—for as long as Taylor was there. Because of the kindness of my friends and well-wishing acquaintances, within a few weeks I had two clients and was making more money than I had as secretary of state. I've learned so many times, you can't be afraid or too proud to *ask* for what you *want* when you are in need. Sometimes they want to help but don't know what to do. Sometimes they might just be waiting for you to ask.

Though I needed money, it wasn't the money that made me happiest. It was the fact that my friends cared enough to help me when I really needed it. I didn't feel like such a lowly wretch any more. No matter what else you do, or how mad or frustrated you may feel, be good to people. While it is not true that everyone you are good to will be good to you, many will. All of us, at some point, find ourselves in the valley of despair, but we can climb out if we have people who will stretch forth a helping hand.

I especially want to thank former Senator Terry Sanford, Congressman Bob Etheridge, then Commissioner of Labor Harry Payne, and District Attorney Howard Boney for offering moral support when others deserted me. I suspect some of my colleagues were afraid because they might have done the same careless things and that their association with me might put them in the same boat in which I found myself.

There were also buckets of letters that were heartwarming, supportive and kind. One person said, "There are only two people in North Carolina known by a single name, and that's you and Andy." People reached out to me to tell me they were praying for me, and to give me love and support. It was humbling and healing. I will always be so grateful for these kindnesses.

I pushed on. Once you get way down in that valley of despair, it's easy to stay down there. You have to understand how you got there, learn from it, and move on to face the public. I walked right back in there. Believe me, my stomach was in my throat, but I said, "I'll be damned if I let this define me for the rest of my life." I showed up in my office every day and got on with the business of living.

At around this time, President Bill Clinton sent me a personal letter that I treasure. He said, among other things, that having been through his share of bad times, he had found that he could only feel truly happy when he let go of all the bad feelings those times created. I'll never forget this generous gesture, made just at the time when I needed it the most.

14

Exoneration and Rebuilding My Life

I was coming back slowly from the calamity I had caused by what was justly called mismanagement on my part. Still looming over my head was the fear that the District Attorney might charge me with something. The investigation the SBI had begun before my resignation went on for months and was exhaustive. All of my accounts were scrutinized. More than one hundred people were interviewed and the final report was approximately three thousand pages long. I had earlier met with the SBI for two days straight to address the allegations of abuse. They were formal and professional and certainly gave me no preferential treatment because I had once been their boss. The questions were tough. In short, they did their jobs.

By that time, I was mentally and physically drained. My dear friend and law partner, Woody Webb, stood by me as my attorney and my friend. I can never thank him enough for his encouragement and his steadfast belief that nothing would come of this legally. He had faith in me because he knows my character. Still, it was scary. I imagined being hauled off to jail and serving time. I lived in mortal fear and my only true escape from the pending investigation was my garden, my beloved wife, Linda, my friends, and my sweet dogs Moses and Lily.

I have always used my garden as my one steady crutch and friend. The earth is there for us to grow things to help us forget sadness. I was at home in my garage hideout with my good friends Trey Garrett and Galen Newsom. We turned on the radio and were listening to live coverage on WPTF. We had heard that District Attorney Colon Willoughby was going to make the announcement about the investigation. I could tell the room was full of members of the press. There was bustling around and microphones coming on. Although I was nervous enough to knock back a strong adult beverage or two manufactured in the mountains of North Carolina, I felt sure that Colon Willoughby would evaluate all the facts and determine there was no criminal wrongdoing. He came on and said, paraphrased, "There is a mess over there and they need to fix it, but we don't see any criminal wrongdoing." I will always be grateful to Colon Willoughby for bringing an end to a hellish episode of my life that at the time seemed like it could have gone on forever.

I threw my hands up and shouted, "I'm free at last!" and joined the boys, who were mountain-style buck dancing. I must have sung every redemption hymn we knew. The long ordeal was over and now I could get back to the work of repairing my tattered soul.

Woody requested a formal letter of exoneration from Willoughby's office. It arrived on December 23, 1996, and I still carry it in my briefcase to this day.

Gradually I came fully to life again. It truly was akin to rebirth. I dove right into it, too, often working sixteen to eighteen-hour days as a lobbyist in the General Assembly, and otherwise representing my clients. I got to travel more than I had when I was in office and for the first time in my life, I was making big money. I was a long way from the days on the farm where it would take me two weeks to save up fifty cents. My father never made a lot of money, and he had six mouths to feed, but he always saved and he taught me to save. He was thrifty. The astounding thing is that when we settled my father's estate he had nearly half a million dollars in a CD. I tell Linda this must be why my garage is stuffed with every extra piece of twine, rubber band, and spare wood. That's what growing up with Great Depression–era parents will do. Linda tells me I'm just a pack rat. Whichever it is, I saved and saved and we eventually bought the building where my office is now. It feels wonderful to be debt-free.

When I left the secretary of state's office, I had first thought about going back into business with my former law partner Reagan Weaver and moving back into the beautiful historic building where we started out. Reagan, for reasons I did not then understand, said, "You really don't need to be doing that. You need to go over to the Raleigh Building and find an office and start anew there." This is what Linda said I should do, too, but I was shocked and hurt because I thought my friend, who has always been such a saint to me, was rejecting me. I reluctantly took his advice and later found out that he was doing me a favor. It wasn't that he didn't trust me or thought I would taint him, as I had feared. It was that he thought I would be better off with a fresh start. Oh, how right he was. Within a few months, the building at 132 South Salisbury Street came up for sale. It was just a stone's throw away from the humble office I rented. It wasn't advertised, but my wife's career in historic preservation gave her an inside line to opportunities to acquire historic properties. She heard about it and we went to see it.

It is a 1920s era building on the corner of Salisbury and Hargett streets that once housed a bank, and later a beauty school. There is still a bank vault in the basement. When we bought it, it was structurally sound and had been remodeled in the 1960s, but it needed a lot of work, and had this funky little spiral staircase going up to the third floor. When we got up there, though, it was all splendor. The space was perfect and we could see everything that was happening on Salisbury, Hargett and even Fayetteville streets from the third-floor windows high up on this corner-situated building. We found photos of the ladies who worked in the bank way back, all in their white gloves, navy suits, and white summer pumps. I love thinking about the history of the building and imagining the people who worked in it and did business in it almost a hundred years ago.

We renovated with lawyerly wooden paneling and a new staircase. I filled my office and conference room with memorabilia from my life and career. It brings me so much pleasure, along with some grief, to go back and think about all the years, events, people and emotions that makeup a lifetime. Here I can think of a time that meant a lot to me and cherish it even more because I can see a picture, read a kind note or touch an object from that time. Reminders that in my life, people said to me, "We admire you. We believe in you." Hooray for packrats, I say! Do not let the anti-clutter people deter you! My wife Linda may tell me that I should go on the reality show "Hoarders" but I am a happy man with my stuff.

So at the age of fifty-five, I put aside all petty things and began a new life. There have been challenges since, but I have never had the slightest urge to go back into public life. I got my head back and almost all of my heart. I'm a different person. I liked old Rufus just fine but I like this Rufus better. I try my best not to revert to any of the behaviors that put me squarely in the middle of what was at that time the worst time of my life. Little did I know, there would be an even more devastating time just ahead.

I had practiced law by myself for several years when I met a striking young man named Gardner Payne, who had worked as a lobbyist/lawyer in the General Assembly for a couple of years. My friend Garland B. Garrett, Jr., who was then secretary of transportation under "Governor for Life" Jim Hunt, introduced me to Gardner. Gardner was immediately likeable. He was a good lobbyist, and had the potential to be a good trial attorney if necessary. I asked Gardner to come be an associate with me and the firm became Edmisten, Webb, and Payne. He attuned to the office flawlessly. Cheryl Mattingly, my executive assistant, and I adored him. He fit in with us beautifully. He was not a stuffed shirt and was not averse to having a sip with me occasionally after work. I appreciate Gardner and enjoyed the time he was here with us.

Becoming a lobbyist was a departure from my days as an advocate for the little guy. Now when people ask me what I do, I sometimes say, tongue-in-cheek, of course, "I represent rich, corporate America so I can keep my wife in horses." Then I explain, "I'm still a lawyer I just apply the legal principles I learned over all those years to issues that arise between companies and the government."

Lobbyists have acquired a bad name. Mama asked me once, "Son, just what is it you do?" "I'm a lobbyist," I replied. She said, "Isn't that bad?" "I answered "Well, no, Mama, not necessarily. Unless you think someone trying to help the Red Cross or the Watauga County Humane Society is a bad thing." She said, "But it seems like every time they say something about a lobbyist on radio or television, they make them out to be bad people." Mama was not alone in thinking like that.

The truth is there are good lobbyists and not-so-good lobbyists, like anything else. There are lobbyists who work for companies that serve the public good, and lobbyists who serve companies that serve themselves. Lobbyists advocate to government bodies on behalf of businesses, causes, or individuals. Some lobbyists get paid and some don't. I prefer to get paid and get paid well. The common perception of the public is that lobbyists work on behalf of entities that seek to do things that benefit a very few people to the detriment of common good. Some do, but this is not always the case.

Lobbying is part of the free speech process in America. It has certain restraints placed on it, like limitations on whether lobbyists can give to a political organization or provide meals or other amenities, and those rules change as the laws governing lobbyists change. When I first started lobbying in North Carolina in 1985, the activities it was legal for us to engage in made the profession seem kind of like the Wild West compared to what is legal today. We could spend as much as we wanted to of the clients' money and buy politicians meals and booze at the finest restaurants in town. The only constraint was that the amount of money spent had to be reported. We would go to Sullivan's or 42nd Street Oyster Bar and spend $800 or $900 a night and not bat an eye. Most of my clients were happy to spend however much it took to be able to plead their case. The legislators were glad to have a great source of free meals and lobbyists were glad to have a setting in which to advocate their cause and earn their money.

Then the laws changed so that we had to pause to ponder whether or not we could even send an elected official a Christmas or condolence card. I have worked under the extremes of both conditions—where spending on entertainment was virtually unlimited and where it was almost completely prohibited. At any rate, I am pleased to inform you that the ethics committee drafted a policy stating that it is indeed permissible for a lobbyist to send a lawmaker or other official a Christmas card. Other questions abound: can a lobbyist send flowers to a deceased relative of a public official, or to the public official himself without violating lobby laws? Yes, he or she can, at the moment, according to ethics laws.

In the end, it has always seemed to me that you can pass all the laws you wish and if someone has nefarious intent, no threat of legal action can deter that person from doing wrong.

I hold to the principle that the vast majority of people elected to public office are decent, honest people who want to do something to better society, no matter what their crazy views might be. It's not the money I've made lobbying that means the most to me, though it sure has come in handy. It is advocating sound intellectual viewpoints and common sense. In this way, lobbying has been an extension of my public life. I have always liked to solve problems, and tried to put things together to make them work better. I enjoy finding ways my clients can get most of what they want. A good lobbyist will never push, cajole, or ask a public official to go against his or her conscience. A good lobbyist doesn't do everything a client demands, but instead will say, "I can get you to the table and then you have to sell yourself."

Listening is essential, to both clients and public officials. This is something I do naturally. Mama was known to say, "If you just listen a minute, there may be something to what they say." She taught me not to be too quick to judge. I've tried keeping my ethical bearings in my work. The work, done properly, is complicated and difficult. I do not accept every potential client. As a rule, I will not represent any organization or corporation that hurts animals and I refuse to represent polluters. My dear friend and star lobbyist Zeb Alley was called by the cockfighters' association to represent them and he referred them to me because he didn't want to do it. "Will you?" he asked. "Hell, no!" I replied.

People hire me because I have been around a long time and I have a lot of influential contacts, but also I think because I have intimate knowledge of how government works. Companies need this knowledge because they need to know how to stay out of trouble. The workings of government are complex. You can run afoul of laws and not even know it.

Over the years, I have represented an unbelievable array of clients from Fortune 500 giants to nonprofit organizations like Rare Disease Council. I probably spend more time lobbying for causes that don't pay than those that do pay. I am proud to say that I still work for my first client, Phillip Morris—now called Altria.

I've enjoyed the challenge of lobbying, and until they haul me out on a slab, I imagine that's what I will be doing, whether it's paid or not.

15

My Garden and
Our Four-Footed Friends

When I think of my garden, sometimes an old hymn from the Broadman Hymnal that I got to know so well at the Three Forks Baptist Church comes to mind. Often I hum "In The Garden" absent-mindedly, and sometimes I belt it out like Pavarotti. It goes like this:

> I come to the garden alone,
> while the dew is still on the roses;
> And the voice I hear, falling on my ear,
> the Son of God discloses.
> And He walks with me, and He talks with me,
> And He tells me I am His own,
> And the joy we share as we tarry there,
> None other has ever known.
> He speaks, and the sound of His voice is so sweet
> The birds hush their singing,
> And the melody that He gave to me,
> Within my heart is ringing.
> I'd stay in the garden with Him
> Though the night around me be falling,
> But He bids me go—through the voice of woe,
> His voice to me is calling.

It all began in a garden. Gardening of all sorts has always been an integral part of my life, beginning with the rich, albeit rocky soil on the farm where the New River caressed the bottomlands with loads of that wonderful topsoil washed down from somebody else's real estate upstream.

I learned mountain gardening at my mama's feet. Mama was the "flower lady" for the Three Forks Baptist Church, so she grew gladiolas, zinnias, and many kinds of perennial and seasonal flowers on the place. It was her job to have the flower arrangements sitting on the table in front of the altar, along with the label that said, in bold letters, "In Remembrance of Me."

Mama would start her gardening year in late January with the arrival of the seed catalogs. She spent many happy winter evening hours poring over those catalogs. The seeds arrived in the thick of the spring whirlwind of plowing and planting, baby calves and chickens, Easter at the church and spring graduations. No matter how hectic things got, Mama remained centered and calm. I often thought it was because she found so much peace in her gardens. I share that with her.

Mama gardened in between preparing meals three times a day, so she could always use some help. I figured out early that if I could stay with Mama and help her in her garden, I might avoid heading down to the bottomland to do the real heavy work of weeding and hoeing corn, tobacco, cabbage and other small row crops and grains we grew for the livestock. I also really loved being with my mama, so it was a genuine accomplishment if I could convince her to pick me to help her in the garden. I would try to tell her the other boys would mistake flowers for weeds and pull them up.

Working beside her is where I developed my love of flower gardening. I enjoy the feel of the soil crumbling through my fingers, cool and damp on my hands. (You don't work it when it's wet unless you like your flowers set in concrete.) Gardening is in my blood. When I was in Washington, D.C., I lived in an apartment so I couldn't garden. I had to be content with visiting the big Congressional Greenhouse at the base of the Capitol, and the National Arboretum.

After I settled in to our Raleigh home in 1979 I began gardening in earnest. It didn't take long to realize that not all of Mama's garden tricks worked so well in this part of the state. My mountain home had rich, beautiful, loamy soil—a gift the New River left behind. After a lot of trial and error (or as Linda would say, yelling and swearing) I began to become acclimated to the peculiarities of the piedmont. I had to learn how to cultivate the various plants I love, and some I didn't yet know I loved, in hard clay soil. Of course, I amended the soil.

My gardening has mostly been focused on raising the same flowers my mama grew in her flower garden, and ones that resemble the pretty pictures in the big picture Bible story book my grandmother read to me when I was small. This book had beautiful pictures and my favorite picture was the Garden of Eden, except for that horrible serpent. I have a thing about snakes. I don't advocate killing snakes for no reason. However, a sharp hoe is a good thing to leave in strategic places in the garden. Every dog we've had has been bitten multiple times by copperheads. Their heads swell up and it is painful for them and awful for us to see.

I love vegetables, but for almost forty years I have lived within a quarter mile of the North Carolina State Farmers Market so don't feel I have to grow bushels of stuff to give away to neighbors. Everyone knows, you can only give away so many zucchinis. So it's flowers and trees and flowering trees and shrubs in my garden—and of course, tomatoes. There can never be an Edmisten garden without those eye-popping, mouth-watering, juicy, perfect tomatoes.

Growing up, flower gardening meant making sure the soil was right and the manure was right. According to Mama the recipe for roses was horse manure at least two feet down and for some reason, Mama needed cow manure for gladiolas. I adhere to that to this day. The key to success is choosing the right plant for right amount of sun or shade and of course, growing what makes you happy.

I try to work with nature by cultivating as many native plants as I can, and using as many natural tools as I can. I amend and fertilize my garden soil with composted stall waste—or "MacNure" as we call it—from MacNair's Country Acres where Linda's horse boards. This is why my wife says her horse and my garden have a symbiotic relationship.

This manure mixture grows the best tomatoes in the world—particularly my favorite heritage tomato—there is absolutely nothing on this earth like a homegrown Cherokee Purple tomato picked right off the vine still warm from the son, sliced and smothered with Duke's mayonnaise between slices of what we used to call "light bread." If there were ever such a thing as backyard ambrosia, this is it.

My tomatoes occupy the sunniest, choicest quadrant in my garden, along with the ghost and tabasco pepper plants I sharecrop for my brother-in-law Robert, another lawyer who has made quite a name for himself as the creator of what must be the hottest pepper sauce on the planet. One of our inadvertent annual traditions is the frantic picking of the peppers before the frost bites them. After a couple of painful pickings, we learned to wear gloves, especially for the ghost peppers.

I have been fortunate for the past fifteen or more years to be a regular guest on the beloved "*Weekend Gardner* radio program on WPTF AM 680 on your radio dial," as the country announcers would say. To my knowledge this program is the longest running radio garden show in America. It began as a spin-off of *Tar Heel Gardener*, started forty years ago with North Carolina State professor John Harris. He had only fifteen minutes to answer write-in questions on gardening, and I am told by Anne Clapp and Mike Raley that the envelopes often contained funny looking critters and all sorts of vegetation that had disease or some kind of crud. He was supposed to analyze it on the spot and tell them what it was and how to cure it. Of course, it had probably sat in the sun or post office for days prior to being opened so was quite the science project by the time it got to Professor Harris. The show now runs three hours every Saturday morning from eight to eleven.

Mike Raley, one of the kindest, most decent individuals I have known, has been the host for over 40 years. Mike has worked at WPTF radio since 1975. He is from Rocky Mount and often talks about the small-town atmosphere where his father was the Chevrolet dealer and would race cars in the early days. I cannot recall a time when Mike has had an ill word to say about anyone. His sidekick for years, Anne Clapp, is a wizard with plants. She was a professor working in textiles at NC State for years and she is often asked about the connection between gardening and textiles. Like me, from early childhood she had developed a love of plants. She has an expertise that causes me to fall into an uncustomary silence when there is a complicated question from a caller. I always defer to Anne. She has great experience and knows her gardening from a practical and a technical standpoint. I enjoy that show so very much. It's like sitting around an old country store. I love it when people see me and say "I heard you on the *Weekend Gardener*! I love that show!" One thing I love about the show is that we do not engage in any religious, political or other controversial discussions. It's all about dirt, manure, and the stuff that comes out of the ground

My approach to growing plants is to experiment, experiment, experiment, and that's what I often advise other gardeners to do. I have a bad habit of doing most of the things landscape architects tell you not to do. I put tall plants in front of small plants, and plants that are said to need full sun in partial shade and they do just fine sometimes. And sometimes they don't. That's the way experiments go, and how we learn. When I see something I like, I will find a place for it.

I remember a funny thing that happened on the show one day. I was telling a caller about how my mother used to love to use manure in her garden, and after I had described the different kinds of manure this caller said, "Where can we get horse or cow manure?" Well, the smart aleck in me came out and I said, "Well, you get it from the south end of a northbound horse or cow." Anne looked aghast because that was probably the most risqué thing ever said on *Weekend Gardener*. The woman caller must have been from up north because she didn't get it. It's probably better she didn't.

Garden to enjoy it. Don't do it to please the garden book writers, landscape architects or neighbors. Do it to make you heal and feel good. I favor a lot of old-fashioned plants, like the Rose of Sharon, which appeared in my grandmother's storybook Bible. I have attempted to have something blooming in our yard all seasons of the year. When we bought the house there was a remnant of a garden and I could tell from a surviving semi-circle of stones that there had been a wonderful gazebo, too. I built upon that garden remnant. There were also ancient pecan trees—two in front of the house and two in back. I usually don't recommend growing them in the yard due to their brittle limbs that often break, but these are magnificent old trees.

Spring is announced by the blooming of the old-fashioned azaleas that were probably planted around the time the house was built in the 1920s. They, along with the camellia japonicas and narcissus, personify the joyful rebirth that is the hallmark of the Carolina spring. The most stately and grand of all the trees at our house are the fabulous old-fashioned crape myrtles. They bloom later than the newfangled hybrids but have the most interesting trunks. These trunks look like works of art. I love them just as much in the winter time as I do in full bloom in July and August because of the intricate artwork painted by nature in the bark. Every fall, as the temperatures drop, the magnificent crape myrtles begin to shed bark in layers of thin, papery sheets.

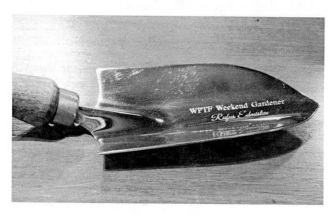

A commemorative trowel from the WPTF radio talk show *The Weekend Gardener.*

Linda has a ritual of peeling bark off the crepe myrtles. I think she could spend hours doing on it. We have developed a lovely habit of walking around the property most days. We do it to see what is happening, what is new, what is growing, what is dying. A garden has something new and different every day. The tulips waving at you when you forgot where you planted them, the narcissus that will laugh at you as you walk by—and then the winter favorites—like the little pansies with their funny faces bobbing in the breeze.

Daphne is a beautiful flowering shrub that I love but must hold at arm's length. Like a heroine in a Victorian novel, Daphne is as likely to swoon and fall into mortal peril as to delight. Daphne blooms in the gloom of the winter and has a heavenly scent. I don't know why someone in the perfume business doesn't come up with a scent with Daphne as the base note. They are strange, enticing beauties indeed. Though some are robust and long-lived, it is as though others have a death wish. I often say on the radio show, "Don't talk to them, don't pet them, and hold your breath when you water them. Only look at them once in a while out of the corner of your eye. If they catch you there's a fifty-fifty chance they will up and die on you. They will break your heart." I've had big ones with large blooms that seem to scent the entire neighborhood. Here is what I can tell you about Daphne: once you see a leaf droop, it has decided to die. If you want five good ones, plant twenty. Needless to say, I do have some expertise in rooting Daphne. I lose so many, I need the backups.

Every year a plethora of wonderful camellias blooms in our garden. Sasanqua in the fall, and regular japonica in winter and spring. If I had to pick a favorite shrub of all, it would be the camellias. I have over a hundred different species in the garden, but nowhere near as many as my friend Anne Clapp. I wouldn't even think of competing with her, because I would never win.

I don't use much fertilizer. I am a strong advocate of using little processed fertilizer.

We don't have to use it as often as the industry directs. Most people over-fertilize. I use cottonseed meal on camellias, and manure mixed in when I mulch. Then I'll use a little 10–10–10 here and there where needed. I have an even lighter hand when spraying for bugs and disease, because I really love the sight of a butterfly bush with 50 to 100 monarchs swarming around it. I try to use as little pesticide as possible. On plants that bugs and fungus find as delicious as I do I use a little slow-release, systemic mixture that protects the plants from insects and diseases and also feeds them. It soaks into the ground and protects the plant from the inside. I do want to point out that the overuse of any chemicals like this can not only harm *you,* but can also harm beneficial insects and the runoff can contaminate the water supply. So it is wisest to use these treatments with care and caution. A good way to avoid having to use a lot of chemicals is to grow native plants. North Carolina's mountains, piedmont, and coastal plains each have a treasure trove of beautiful things you can grow.

The beauty of gardening to me is the sense of inner peace it can give you even when you are in the depths of despair. Tranquil, green, blooming places have a beautiful, soothing neutrality that is as refreshing as a long cool drink. Despite what we have done to her the earth holds no ill will for us. My garden has comforted me in times of great stress. No therapy or any pill can take the place of a good walk through the garden or taking a shovel or hoe and digging into the earth.

As I stroll around the garden, I spot some grape leaf mahonias and remember that General Alexander Boyd Andrews let me take cuttings of these. Here's a Russian tea olive someone from Shelby, North Carolina, gave me. Throughout my long political career, I visited many homes and talked to a lot of people about gardening. I liked to see what was growing in their gardens. I would sometimes ask, "Do you mind if I take a cutting?" They were all only too happy to oblige. Of course I had gardening tools in my car at all times— garbage bags, paper towels, freezer bags, shovels, etc. Throughout my travels, I collected plants. Some lived and some didn't.

So many plants in my garden remind me of loved ones, some still with me and some long departed. Here is the Clyde Nolan shrub, the J.C. Raulston rose, my dear mother's peonies, and the Cecil Williams daffodil patch. Cecil Williams from Pittsboro, North Carolina, ran the L.C. Williams Oil Company. He had a floppy hat and a laugh you couldn't forget. He knew I loved plants and once he said he knew a place near Bonlee—an old home site with loads of daffodils. I said we would come dig them up, and put my shovel in the car. When I got to his business he said, "Jump in the truck." He had a backhoe on the trailer! He was not about to use a shovel when he had a backhoe. Cecil drove the backhoe, unloaded it and dug up what must have been 200 daffodils. We put them in sacks. I always remember that day and laugh when I see that particular patch of daffodils.

There is something in my garden from every diverse climate. Things sometimes grow in impossible places and things sometimes die in perfect growing conditions. Then there are the plants that thrive too well! Japanese knotweed is beautiful but so invasive. It has runners that could win marathons. I spent an entire summer trying to get rid of it. I have fought these invasive plants so many times.

A friend and a big name in the gardening community is Phil Campbell. I've known Phil and her husband, Carlton, for years. She has supplied the Capitol building with poinsettias every year at Christmas and gives generously to other good causes. She went with me to the Jim Valvano Kids Klassic golf tournament and after giving a talk to the spouses of the players, presented everyone with a coleus or begonia to take home.

Gardening has been an anchor for me. When I think about growing older I worry more about when I will be unable to garden than anything else. Other pleasures will pale long before gardening does.

I can't talk about my garden without including a little bit about our canine companions over the years. I got used to having dogs around back home on the farm. My first memory of "man's best friend" was a dog named Old Tip. He was sheepdog, according to my daddy. Of course, if Daddy said it, to me it was the Gospel truth. In those days farm dogs were not pampered. They were rarely petted, and never set foot in the house. If any dog or cat came within five feet of the front door, here would come Mama with a broom to shoo it away.

Like all of us, Old Tip had his regular chores, which included securing the farm from all intruders that were not invited guests. Occasionally a pack of stray dogs would attempt to harm newly born calves in the springtime. More often than not they were coming through chasing a bitch in heat and we had to make sure Old Tip didn't join in the chase. Tip's job was to secure the entire curtilage. (In old English law the curtilage was the dwelling house and all the buildings surrounding it: the wood shed, chicken house, spring house, smoke house, and yes, even the outhouse. Under English law if someone broke into any building in the curtilage it was legally the same as breaking into the house.) If you wanted to set Old Tip off just let some human or nonhuman creature try to breach the property within the curtilage.

I remember the sadness of the day that one of the neighbors came and said "Walter, your dog got hit out on the highway." It was so terrible, because Tip was my daddy's buddy. Daddy just said, "Go get me a hemp sack." I did and he told me to stay put, then walked slowly down the dirt road toward Highway 421 carrying the empty sack. After what seemed like hours he returned, cradling that sack like a baby, though he had probably never petted Old Tip in his life. I cried to myself. Daddy went to the tool shed, got a shovel, put that feed sack with Old Tip inside into the hole he dug, covered him up, and said, "These drivers drive too fast." That's all he said about it, ever. I didn't let him see me cry because that is not what farm boys did. Daddy was raised to consider animals simple beasts of burden that you surely didn't cry about. Still, I could tell Tip's death hurt my daddy. Later when Daddy was out of sight I went to the grave and said goodbye to Old Tip.

Linda and I have had some wonderful dogs. First there was the grand Moses, a stately English setter who thought he was some sort of prince. Our dear friends Sis and Buddy Cheshire gave Moses to us. In his younger days he'd leap ten feet through the air, land on the ground and as though his four feet were springs, make another, even higher leap. He loved to ride with me in the pickup, and if I had to leave the driver's seat to run an errand he'd replace me in the driver's seat as though he wanted to take the 1972 Chevy Cheyenne for a spin. Moses went to work with Linda every day when her office was in the old post office in Mordecai Historic Park. He was above all Linda's constant companion. When she gave tours of the historic site, Moses went along. Moses was a bird dog and a good pointer. Once when I was attorney general and Moses was with me over on the Capitol grounds he put a perfect point on Governor Jim Hunt. I got a big kick out of that and I could swear I caught a sheepish doggy smile on Moses' face too. Moses was a gentle dog with a sense of humor. We once had a parakeet that loved to ride on Moses' back. He was a bird dog, after all.

One of the hardest, saddest nights of my life was the night I realized that sweet old Moses, then age 17, was at the end of his life and must be humanely helped with the transition. I would never have considered such a thing if the night had not come when our fine old man could no longer lift his head and had soiled his sleeping chair. Linda was away at a preservation conference in Kentucky and would not get to say goodbye. I couldn't let him suffer, and though I could not bear to be in the room when they put Moses down, I took him in my arms afterward. I had such a hard time telling Linda when she came home, but when I did, she put her arms around me and told me I had done the right thing.

Fortunately we had Moses' daughter Lily, a beautiful pup who didn't point as much as Moses and was mostly interested in pointing squirrels. After many years Lily became ill and despite the best vet care, her quality of life deteriorated so terribly that we finally had to make the decision to say goodbye. Of course, I couldn't bear to take Lily to the vet that last time. Linda did, and as she left with Lily lying in the back of the car, I wept like a baby.

Sissy, a mixed breed, came to us after some friends found her in a ditch, abandoned and starving. She was about six months old, all legs and so skinny she looked like a scarecrow. When Sissy was about three years old, a friend gave us a beautiful Brittany spaniel we named Nellie, after my mama. Nellie and Sissy were fast friends, and partners in paroling the perimeter of the Edmisten curtilage. When Nellie went blind from diabetes, Sissy served as her guide.

As each dog has left us, my wife and I decided that we'd take their ashes and place them under our newly planted camellias. Moses has a bright red camellia that glistens in the sunlight, reminding me of the wonderful time with him. We chose an apple-blossom camellia for Lily, which reminds me of springtime in Boone. Then Sissy got a pure white camellia. So each fall, I have those magnificent blooms honoring Moses and Lily, and then as spring finally comes around, the aroma of that white camellia reminds me of Sissy. My camellias help me remember those warm feelings that all three of those close friends gave Linda and me.

The current Dog-In-Chief is Jasper, another feisty bird dog. I love the story of how we came by Jasper. Our dear, late friend Caroline MacNair had a dream that I, after a string of girl dogs, simply must have a boy dog. Her dream was so vivid that the next morning she came and picked up Linda and they drove somewhere deep into the wilds of Orange County where an ol' boy had a litter of bird dog pups for sale. While the women were talking to him, one pup grabbed Linda by the ankle and would not turn loose. What could Linda do but bring him home? It was meant to be. They brought him to my office, and there was this adorable puppy in Caroline's arms. We bonded immediately. Jasper is fanatically loyal and extremely helpful—or at least well meaning. He sometimes helps me in the garden by bringing me formerly potted plants he seems to think I've forgotten in his mouth. I hope Jasper will spend many more years with us.

Daddy and Mama at my swearing in as secretary of state in January 1985 (photo by Sheila S. Davis).

Our side garden, featuring caladium, ferns, pansies, impatiens, azaleas and English ivy. That's Virginia creeper on the trellis (photo by Susan Buchanan Woodson).

Oak leaf and limelight hydrangea in our formal mountain rock garden (courtesy Susan Buchanan Woodson).

C2

Linda's beloved Moses, the prince of dogs, who accompanied her to work every day at her job as a historic preservationist for the city of Raleigh.

With Nellie, Lily and Sissy among the clover I grow in lieu of a manicured lawn. It keeps the bees busy and the air smelling sweet.

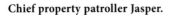

Chief property patroller Jasper.

16

The Grim Intruder
Guillain-Barré Syndrome

From the National Institute of Neurological Disorders and Stroke:

Guillain-Barré syndrome (GBS) is a disorder in which the body's immune system attacks part of the peripheral nervous system. The first symptoms of this disorder include varying degrees of weakness or tingling sensations in the legs. In many instances the symmetrical weakness and abnormal sensations spread to the arms and upper body. These symptoms can increase in intensity until certain muscles cannot be used at all and, when severe, the person is almost totally paralyzed. In these cases the disorder is life threatening—potentially interfering with breathing and, at times, with blood pressure or heart rate—and is considered a medical emergency. Such an individual is often put on a ventilator to assist with breathing and is watched closely for problems such as an abnormal heart beat, infections, blood clots, and high or low blood pressure. Most individuals, however, have good recovery from even the most severe cases of Guillain-Barré syndrome, although some continue to have a certain degree of weakness.

Guillain-Barré syndrome can affect anybody. It can strike at any age and both sexes are equally prone to the disorder. The syndrome is rare, however, afflicting only about one person in 100,000. Usually Guillain-Barré occurs a few days or weeks after the patient has had symptoms of a respiratory or gastrointestinal viral infection. Occasionally surgery will trigger the syndrome. In rare instances vaccinations may increase the risk of GBS. After the first clinical manifestations of the disease, the symptoms can progress over the course of hours, days, or weeks. Most people reach the stage of greatest weakness within the first two weeks after symptoms appear, and by the third week of the illness 90 percent of all patients are at their weakest.

On an August day in 2007 my law partner Thomas Moore and I had gone to the Research Triangle Park to meet with a client. It was one of those humid Raleigh days that wring me out like a rag and still leave me soaked. (It seems when I was born in the cool, cool mountains near Boone, North Carolina, my comfort-level temperature was permanently set between sixty and seventy degrees. Anything over that and I roast.)

Right around the middle of the meeting I felt a strange nausea and an achy feeling. I thought, "Oh no, I am getting a cold and there is nothing worse than a summer cold." When the meeting ended and we were walking down the stairs every bone in my body ached. I said, "Thomas, I feel like I drank too much last night and have an extreme hangover, but the thing is, I didn't drink last night." We went to eat at a barbecue place on the way back to Raleigh and I remember I could manage only a few bites. I was in extreme pain and flooded with nausea.

I walked into our building and tried to navigate the two sets of stairs, every ounce of my body aching. When I got to the mezzanine I had to sit and rest. Normally, I climb these stairs every day with no problems at all. This time, when I got to the last step, I collapsed onto the landing. Cheryl and I both thought I might be having the kind of acute attack you can get when you have a really bad case of the flu, especially in the summertime. She helped me to my feet and told me, "You need to go to the doctor. Something serious is wrong with you."

In the way of one of those proud mountain men who never needs help (though I'm not usually this way), I thought, I won't worry Linda, I'll just go see my old friend, Dr. Douglas C. Keith. Doug is a fine physician with excellent credentials, and something of a non-conformist. I call him the "Guerrilla Doctor." At that time, Doug had set up shop in an abandoned service station that he'd converted into a medical office, which he named Rapid Response Family Care. He is dedicated to the art and isn't afraid to give patients hell when they don't follow his instructions. Over time we became friends. I also did some work for him, so between our mutual professional nondisclosure requirements we could tell each other anything and neither one of us could ever make a peep about it.

I thought of stopping on the way to Doug's office to get Linda and take her with me but thought better of it. I didn't want to worry her and I knew she probably had things to do. By the time I arrived at his office I was starting to feel numb. Doug thought it best that I go home for the night and return at 7 a.m. when he could properly diagnose me, adding that if I felt any worse I should call an ambulance and head to the hospital. That would be easy, since I only lived three miles away from Doug's office.

When I went home, I told Linda what had happened. She said, "You look like all the blood has been drawn out of you. Get in the bed." I said, "No, that will only make me feel sicker. I'm afraid if I get down, I won't be able to get back up." I settled into a comfortable chair and dozed on and off during the night. I kept feeling numbness and strange, electrical tingling sensations.

I had not slept well when we went to meet the doctor at 7 the next morning. Linda had to help me get into the car and into the doctor's office. Doug asked me to stand on a stool, and when I tried I fell to the floor like a sack of flour. It was one of the most horribly memorable moments of my life. After he examined me, Doug said, "You have Guillain-Barré syndrome, and it is very serious." I knew a little about this syndrome so the diagnosis really scared me. I had an acquaintance in Tarboro, North Carolina—Martin Cromartie, a prominent lawyer and decorated war veteran—who came down with it. Martin was one of the friendliest people I have ever met and a dear, wonderful supporter. We often caught up on the telephone, and one of the last times I called him his secretary said, "He's on the couch. We'll have to carry the phone over and hold it for him because he is paralyzed. He can't hold the telephone himself." When he got on the phone, I said, "Martin, what is this terrible thing?" He went on to explain his symptoms and told me he had Guillain-Barré syndrome.

As I listened, all I could picture was my friend lying helpless on the couch while his secretary held his phone. I said, "Doug, are you sure?" He said, "Yes, I'm sure. I am calling Rex Hospital right now to send an ambulance for you." He laid a hand on my shoulder and said, "We don't want to fool around with this, Rufus. The sooner we get on it the sooner you can recover." While I have been prone to panic attacks in my life, sheer dread that set in after my diagnosis was the worst. It was a kind of slow-motion terror, almost like a suspenseful horror story unfolding, one awful detail at a time. I felt myself sinking deeper and deeper into a staggering sense of dread. I thought, "I've been through so much and overcome so many challenges with the help of so many wonderful friends, and now I'm going to end up like this—totally incapacitated, paralyzed, completely dependent—what people used to call 'a cripple.'"

In a stern voice, I yelled, "NO AMBULANCE!" I was not going to be hauled away like a slab of beef to Rex Hospital. I said, "Linda will take me there." Dr. Keith picked me up like a baby and got me into the car.

The ride to the hospital was like a long, strange dream from which I could not wake up. Linda, who has never been prone to breaking the speed limit, may have exceeded the speed limit by a whole eight miles per hour that morning. When we arrived attendants came out with a wheelchair and took me back to the emergency room. I struggled to call up the perfect hymn to sing that would give me solace and strength and wound up humming, "What a Friend We Have in Jesus." The emergency room was fully prepared for me, and the staff there, along with Dr. Keith, may have saved my life that morning. Nevertheless, I was not so bad off that I missed the fact that the neurologist on duty was an absolutely gorgeous woman.

By the time they wheeled me down the hall to run some tests, I wasn't able to stand up on my own. Numbness crept over me and I could feel the paralysis moving its way up my body. They wheeled me into a little room and hooked me up to several devices. The doctor said, "I am going to send some signals and I want you to tell me what you feel after each one." It seemed like some variation of electrotherapy, what they used to call "shock treatment." The machine hummed and swished and I could feel faint tingling despite my numbness. The strangest things go through the mind at such times, and at that time I thought of all the people electrocuted by North Carolina's penal system. The tests allowed the neurologist to confirm Dr. Keith's diagnosis. I had Guillain-Barré syndrome.

The week I was at Rex was a blur, just a cycle of being sedated and waking up to sheer panic and being sedated into calmness and sleep again. Waking up was the hard part. I was in a strange room, my sight was blurred, and I didn't really know what they were doing to me, I just knew I was gravely ill. My greatest comfort was Linda, who remained beside me. A minister named Rufus Massengill who was also once an employee of mine from the secretary of state office checked in on me and was a great comfort. Rufus prayed for me. I remember he came in and asked, "Can we pray together?" I said, "You bet we can!" I prayed loud and long and asked for forgiveness and absolution for every wrongdoing I had ever done. I cannot even begin to express how wonderful the people were at Rex. I am still grateful to every single person who cared for me and about me during this terrifying time.

My collapse and diagnosis presented a dilemma. I didn't want my clients to think I was permanently incapacitated, I didn't want my friends to worry, and I didn't want rumors to spread about my condition. I had to wonder, "What should we do with this news of my disease?" I didn't have to wonder for long. Linda took over. She had kept the initial events very hush-hush and told me that we were going to have a well-thought-out, methodical way of dealing with news of my illness. We could not have all my friends crowding into my hospital room, no matter how much I might love to see them. Linda knew that I needed to concentrate on getting well and did not need to worry about entertaining my friends. The truth is, I was too sick to see anybody and I didn't want my friends and loved ones to see me so helpless.

"You'll need all the energy you can find to heal," said my dear wife, who I came to call the Warden. Linda called my family and a few of my closest friends and told them I had a rare condition. She told them she knew they would love to come see me, but now was not the time and that she would keep them informed. I was not surprised when many of them did not want to hear this.

My brother David's oldest daughter, Claudia, is a successful real estate agent in Raleigh and somehow found out the time and day I would be transported from Rex Hospital to

Wake Medical Center for intensive rehabilitation. By this time, I was like a mold of jelly that slipped off a flat plate. I had no control over anything. They were wheeling me to an ambulance to transport me from Rex Hospital to Wake Medical Center and suddenly I heard Claudia exclaim, "Uncle Rufus, we found you!" Linda said, "Claudia, you need to go back and tell the family that he is going to be just fine. Rufus is going to rehab and if anyone finds out how sick he is, it will be in the paper and he could lose clients." Linda satisfied Claudia that I wasn't going to expire and Claudia went home with tears in her eyes.

I remember being lifted onto a gurney and wheeled into the emergency vehicle and hearing many clicks as they strapped me in to the gurney. To make matters even worse, being snugly strapped in triggered my lifelong claustrophobia. A good ol' North Carolina boy was driving, and he drove slowly, no lights or sirens. I heard him say, "That's Old Rufus. I sure hope he makes it." I spoke up to tell him that reports of my impending demise were highly exaggerated. While otherwise paralyzed and unable to feel any bodily function, I could still hear and speak. I managed to have a good conversation with the driver and the ambulance attendants, though it took every bit of energy I could muster. I gave it my all because I knew they would talk about it and word would get out. I didn't want my clients or friends to know how sick I had become,

When we got to Wake Medical Center, they didn't have a private room for me. Linda had already been on the case regarding my housing. She had been told there were no single rooms left and I would have to share with someone else. Well, Linda wasn't going to let that happen. Keeping my sudden illness quiet meant protecting my privacy. She called our friend Roddy Jones, knowing he would be there for me, and Roddy, in turn, called Brenda Chappell Gibson, who was on the Wake Medical Center Board of Governors. Brenda somehow secured a private room for me and it was a good thing, because that was my home for a couple of months. Once I was ensconced in my room, Linda said "I'm calling Rob Christensen from the *News and Observer* and we are going to get ahead of any rumors. We will tell them that you are undergoing rehabilitation and will be out in no time." She spoke to Rob and he kindly produced a sensitively done article for which I am still grateful. After the article was out everyone was blowing up Cheryl's phone and dropping by the office saying, "We just want to go by and say hello to Rufus." In addition to those people who just loved me, there were also many who were just curious. No one could find me and when folks called around to the hospitals, they would get, "There is no such person at Wake Medical Center—there is no Rufus Edmisten here." When he asked after me, my own doctor, Doug Keith, was told I wasn't there, and he literally walked the floors until he found me.

At this point, my body shut down and nothing was working. It took someone to help me do anything I needed to do in the way of personal hygiene or functions. That will certainly humble you quickly enough if nothing else will. I thought, "I've overcome all this adversity and now I want to overcome this more than anything else." This was by far the greatest crisis of my life. Much as my feelings were hurt and my world seemed to fall apart at past hardships, they were nothing compared to this. I wasn't convinced I was going to live. I could feel this tingling coming up my body and my hands were limp and useless. I could not lift my arms. I was at Wake Medical Center for about four days when they said, "You are about to go to rehabilitation." I thought, "What do they mean? I can't even pee."

I still have a giant tender spot and a river of gratitude in my heart for Deborah, the tremendously kind, funny medical technician who took such good care of me when I was most helpless. I wish I knew her last name. I'm not sure she even knew I had been attorney general, secretary of state or what I was. She just told me with a wink, "Somebody down the hall says you are a big shot." And I said, "Not right now." She said, "I've seen 'em in here a lot worse than you are." She was there every day. On the fifth day there, I kept wanting a shower and I told Deborah, thinking, "I would give up chocolate cake for life if I could just get some of this filth off of me." Ever creative, Deborah figured out a way to get me in the wheelchair and into the shower and clean me up. I was embarrassed and ashamed but so grateful just to get clean I could have cried.

The first day they rolled me down to physical therapy there were about ten or twelve people in there. Most of them struggled with horrible conditions. Several could not speak and some had problems so severe I felt sure they could never recover. Most of the folks in that room were stroke victims. Though they couldn't talk, I could talk to them and I got to know their relatives that visited. One lady was a teacher and she kept trying to recover her speech, to say something, anything. One day, all of a sudden, she bellowed "OH, SHIT!" and the biggest, most beatific smile came over her face, an expression of pure joy. It broke everyone up and it felt good to laugh. These were her first whole words. I feebly tried to clap my hands.

They started pushing me hard. I still could not walk, shave or feed myself at this point. They would say, "Do you want to lose that?" and urge me to keep trying. Every day I was able to do a little bit more. I started to see things improve.

When you get Guillain-Barré syndrome many functions are shut down and you can get constipated. One night this larger than life vivacious woman came down to my room. She must have been about 6'5" and was "big-boned," as Mama would have said. She rolled a contraption in there that was nothing but a cord and an enormous thing my mama would have used to baste a turkey. It was dangling off a cord and is the size of a basketball. She held it up, smiled a dazzling smile, and said, "Big Mama's come to help you! Okay, son, I'm going to roll you over. I need you on your side." I figured out what she was there for and started laughing before I could even feel embarrassed. She laughed with me and I heard that thing start to go "Kawush, kawush" and my belly was blowing up. I thought, "My God, what is going to happen to me?" She had to run that thing twice but it got the job done. When this funny lady who towered above me told me she was leaving, I laughed and asked wistfully, "Will I ever see you again?" She said, "I bet you don't want to." I said, "I do. I love you." To this day sometimes when I am feeling low, I think of her and how hard we laughed while she did this necessary but not exactly pleasant job to help me that day.

In physical therapy, every day, I had to work harder and harder to bring back even basic abilities and movements. I could never thank enough the people who worked with me patiently and did these deeply personal, certainly unpleasant things for me when I was helpless, making me smile and laugh as they helped me. When I had a chance, I let the president of Wake Medical Center know what a great job they all did.

The part of my treatment I dreaded the most was the infernal CAT scans. The trip down what seemed to me to be a torture chamber seemed to take forever. That gurney ride seemed like twenty miles and for some reason it was always in the middle of the night. I went trip after trip down there. I had about five doctors taking care of me. It seemed like every time one of them saw me, they ordered another test, which involved another trip down there. I felt like there must have been a lot of duplication. Sharing information on managed care might not be such a bad idea.

I woke up one day and my voice sounded like I had the beginnings of laryngitis. It was raspy and broken. I sounded like Bill Clinton with a chest cold. I really panicked. I had been in rehabilitation for three weeks and a day, and though I was still having panic attacks I had assumed I would just be getting better and better. Now this damnable plague was shutting down my vocal cords! They called in an eye, ear, nose and throat specialist. While they conducted an ultrasound scan, the doctor had me speak and I could see that one of my vocal cords was lying limp next to the healthy one that vibrated as I spoke. Guillain-Barré had done this! It was horrifying. Speaking was and is the way I engage people, and aside from the social aspects, my livelihood depended upon my being able to speak.

The mental anguish of Guillain-Barré syndrome is like sitting and staring at a rattlesnake that you know is going to strike, but you don't know where or when, and you can't run away or make it go away. It had attacked my vocal cords while I was sleeping. They continued treatment and I was relieved when the doctor told me I would probably be able to speak just fine in time.

I remember the day I walked a few feet on my own. I thought my heart would burst with joy. Though I had mastered baby steps with a walker, I had not yet walked on my own. One day my therapist decided I should try to walk by myself to the nurse's station. The rehab therapists affixed a rope-like support contraption to me. While two people flanked me, one stood in front of me and one stood behind me, spotting me with ropes. "We will not let you fall," they reassured me. My first lurching step wobbled to the right, and I felt the ropes correct my path. Everyone applauded. I was so pleased. Shaky as I was I just wanted to keep going, but my therapist told me "slow down, Rufus! Rome wasn't built in a day." Every day after that, we worked on getting me out of that contraption. To practice, I would creep around my room holding onto things.

When I was finally allowed to move about on my own in my wheelchair, I maneuvered that thing into every nook and cranny of the hospital. I was on the first floor one day and a man visiting someone in the hospital stopped dead in the hall, looked at me wide-eyed and said, "Rufus! We heard you lost both legs." I removed the blanket on my lap with a flourish. "Voila!" We both laughed and went on our way.

At around week twelve of rehabilitation, I received word that I might get a home leave for a couple of hours. I felt like an inmate who was getting out on good behavior. A delightfully sensitive and caring therapist named Elizabeth told me she was going to let me leave to visit my garden! I cannot describe the joy I felt just thinking about having my first ride out of that hospital in weeks. I was as happy as a child on his way to get ice cream on a summer day.

The technicians helped me into Elizabeth's car and she drove me home. It was the drought of the summer and the ever-demanding hydrangeas were browning up, as usual. Still, I was overjoyed to see even those pitiful plants because I had not been sure I would ever see my garden again. She said, "You have one hour." I must have made a face because she said, "And don't get sassy with me because you're not the only person in the world who wants to do things." She had to push me around in the wheelchair, which was no easy task over the grass and stepping stones. She didn't complain. That day I felt for the first time that there was a chance I might be well again.

At the end of the hall on my floor, there was a nice, carpeted, plush room for families to visit patients. On one occasion, Linda had arranged for her brother Robert and nephew Jack and Robert's wife Lisa to bring our little niece Lucy to do a ballet for me and play a little tune. It was the sweetest thing in the world. Lucy was about four years old at the time. She was in full ballerina regalia, all so beautiful, but the prettiest thing she wore was her smile. She was there for Uncle Rufus, full of love and concern because she knew something bad had happened to me.

Once my friends at the Cardinal Club sent us a lovely meal. That day Cheryl and a friend gave Linda and me a candlelight dinner in that same special room down the hall. It was such a sweet thing to do, and I will never forget their kindness.

Linda had dinner with me most days. She often brought special treats, messages and notes from my friends, news of the day, and anything else that might lift my spirits. Seeing this lovely creature that changed my world by agreeing to marry me, and delighted my heart every single day probably helped me heal faster. No-nonsense and an excellent enforcer of rules when I needed her to be, Linda soothed my heart. Crisis after crisis, Linda has been the strong one. She never seemed to lose her nerve, and no problem, no matter how bad, was ever going to get her down.

I must digress here a little and tell about one of the few times I have seen my wife show actual fear. We were on a campaign trip when a dangerous storm suddenly appeared in our flight path. The plane seemed like it would break apart. I have always had a fear of being on a plane that snapped in two. Our stomachs were up in our throats. I felt Linda's nails digging into my hand. I tried to comfort her, but the rougher the flight got the harder she gripped my hand, until finally a nail broke and my calloused hand began to bleed. It took fear of imminent death to ruffle Linda's feathers. I sound impressed because I truly am.

While I was in the hospital there were several dear friends from my public life who would come and take me on outings. Shelley Castleberry took me for drives, and George Parrott also dropped by and took me on outings. George used to say he was taking me to the book store at Quail Ridge for a latte, which was a joke because I was not then, am not now, and will certainly never be the latte type. George is just the best friend. Once the nurses said, "George Parrott is coming and he will meet you down in the flower garden." It was a Sunday afternoon and one of many things that made George a true character is that he always showed up in a limousine. It was one of his peculiarities. I was permitted to wheel my chair down to the garden on my own to meet him. I spotted him coming around the circle in his limousine. He came to a stop and I saw two dear little snowy white doggie heads pop up in the back seat. George brought Sissy and Lily! Linda was there too, right in the middle of them! Lilly was the English setter and Sissy was the Brittany spaniel. George went to the back seat, opened the door as any proper chauffeur would. And they bounded out and jumped all over me as if to say, "Daddy, where have you been?" This was the kind of tender-hearted, lovely person George Parrott is. He was always trying to do something nice for people.

I was discharged on September 20th. I had spent almost two months there. Though I got to go home, I had to continue physical therapy on an outpatient basis. I was still in very bad shape. I had this huge thing with hand rails to put over the toilet so I wouldn't fall, and I had to use a walker. Linda also had a plumber friend install handicap railings and a chair in the shower and bath tub. I did a lot of holding onto counters.

I didn't make any announcements that I was home. While in the hospital I was touched to learned that the folks back in Watauga County had started prayer groups for me and that more of these groups had popped up all over North Carolina. Hundreds of letters and cards came from friends and well-wishers. These kind people made me feel loved, which is always good medicine.

In time I got the go-ahead to go back to the office. I had my trusty walker and my little sack to carry my illegal contraband—snacks and sweets and special goodies people were always sneaking me, out of sight of Warden Linda, of course! Although still shaken by the ordeal, I remember feeling full of gratitude that it hadn't been worse, and full of hope that I might return to a normal life.

When illnesses like this strike us it is natural to wonder "WHY?" Why did this happen to me? What is the cause of this rare syndrome that only affects one out of a hundred thousand people? At first I felt sorry for myself. Sometimes, my hands and feet hurt like hell because the nerve endings have literally consumed one another and it just sparks a chain reaction throughout my whole system. After a little more self-pity, I looked around and realized how lucky I really was. The lingering symptoms were nothing, a small price to pay considering I might have wound up paralyzed or dead.

As we all have, I have lost many friends and family members to terrible diseases, and have many pals who have survived such things but are walking around with braces and crutches, or truly debilitating damage. Yet here I am, except for some chronic neuropathy and nerve pain, as my brother Joe says, "Fat and sassy," still smoking my cigars and enjoying a snort every now and then.

After reading up on this disorder, I think I have an idea about what may have caused me to contract Guillain-Barré syndrome. The literature suggests that a physical trauma may set it off. I had just had oral surgery in preparation for a dental implant, and had unforeseen side effects including massive swelling. I may have contributed to the damage by insisting on traveling to Asheville to participate in a special taping of *NC Spin* before a prominent North Carolina civic group. Ten days later I had my Guillain-Barré attack.

Now, a decade later, I still have lingering symptoms of the syndrome, but the most debilitating memory of all is that of feeling totally helpless and the sheer panic it caused. Guillain-Barré syndrome changed my fundamental outlook on life. Now I treasure the abundance of little pleasures in life more, and appreciate knowing that when the worst happens, there will always be wonderful people ready to help me.

17

Remembering Watergate

There aren't many key Watergate participants still standing. I recently got to spend some time with John Dean when he was in Raleigh for a book signing. Many people may remember Dean's wife, Maureen, from the hearings. His beautiful, serene wife, Maureen, "Mo" (Kane) Dean, riveted the nation. She unfailingly appeared with John during his testimony. In later years she wrote a delightful book about Watergate called *Mo: A Woman's View of Watergate*. In this book she described the first day she and John were escorted into the hearing room. She related how uncomfortable she felt when all eyes were upon them and wrote, "Soon a big man with white hair, bushy eyebrows, and jelly-like jowls took his seat at the center of a long table and gaveled the hearing to order. Unmistakably this was Senator Sam Ervin. My first impression of him was both harsh and untrue, and I was sorry for it later. I thought he was senile. His eyes had sort of a wild look, he had difficulty coming up with the right words when he talked, [and] he looked even older than he was. I had not enough exposure to his wit and wisdom to realize that he was very much in command of himself and of the committee."

For our parts, we were mesmerized by Maureen. When John Dean walked in and this elegant beauty walked in beside him, she softened and complemented the man. She was there for him in his time of trouble and they are still together to this day.

When Dean came to Raleigh in 2014 to introduce his latest book, *The Nixon Defense: What He Knew and When He Knew It*, the folks at Quail Ridge Books asked me to be his escort. John was staying at Renaissance Raleigh in North Hills. The front desk called his room when I arrived, and he said, "Give me a minute—I'm on a call with my publisher." He came off the elevator like an everyday person and no one seemed to know who he was. He greeted me warmly. I had promised John some authentic North Carolina food, and called Greg Hatem, the eminent Empire Foods restaurateur, who was thrilled that I was bringing Dean over to his Raleigh Times restaurant, one of my favorite eateries. When we got there we discovered that Greg had assembled a sampling of North Carolina dishes from all of his restaurants. We had invited a few people, including some Watergate buddies, like Gene Boyce and Mike Carpenter, who have remained my close friends for over fifty years. Greg also fed Woodward and Bernstein on their visit to the North Carolina Museum of History for a speaking engagement.

People were thrilled to see John. Before we went to eat we spent some time in my office looking at my collection of Watergate memorabilia. I had found the place in my albums that had pictures of his dear wife, Maureen. I had about five different pictures of her. In an unexpected, tender moment, John smiled with a tear in his eye and said, "Oh gosh, I've never seen some of these." I just had to give him a couple. He bloomed like a peony. You would have thought I had given him the most prized possession in the world. I said, "Well, John, she still looks about the same, doesn't she?" And he replied, "Prettier."

At the restaurant we all sampled the delicious fare, and of course somebody trotted out the "Rufus blasts barbecue" story. I said the moral of the story is, when you are running for governor of North Carolina, do not criticize barbecue. He said, "Well, I can assure I will not be running for any office. I am still, in many quarters, a marked man." And it was with great glee that he said that.

After dinner, my intern Meaghan Lewis drove us to the book signing at Quail Ridge Books. When we got there, the crowd was stuffed in the building. People were literally sitting on top of bookshelves. John walked in, his low-key, unassuming manner instantly familiar to me. He always gave me the impression of being shy. Asked to make the introduction, I said, "Standing before you is the man, who in my opinion, helped bring to closure one of the darkest chapters of American history, who fought assaults from the White House from every corner and was absolutely accurate in everything he said. I am very proud to have been a part of that experience that was Watergate. The man I hold dearest, Senator Sam Ervin, always believed John Dean was telling the truth."

With John Dean, left, in front of the Raleigh Times restaurant after his book signing at Quail Ridge Books.

Seeing John was a reminder that though our looks may change over the years, our mannerisms and patterns of speech rarely do, phony people notwithstanding. One thing I learned in political life is that if you try to fake it, people catch on right away. That is one thing about John Dean. He is no phony.

Senator Sam J. Ervin, Jr., donated his Watergate papers to the Southern Historical Collection at the University of North Carolina at Chapel Hill. Since I went to school there I have many fond memories of the Wilson Library that houses the Southern Historical Collection. Since I had the original subpoena, I decided to donate it, and some of my most important papers, to this collection. To be honest, I didn't take stock of everything in the boxes I donated so I was surprised when I recently reviewed them to find that there are many personal photos and childhood materials in there. The university was thrilled to have the materials and I felt relieved that the subpoena, in particular, was out of my hands. I often worried that it might get stolen or damaged in some way.

During the height of a scandal

involving athletes and academics at Chapel Hill, the library administrator suggested we have an official public ceremony to commemorate the Watergate subpoena, and that I do a little talk. I liked this idea. This ceremony was my chance to present the donations. Because of the athletic scandal there was the feeling of a heavy cloud over the university at that time. Chancellor Holden Thorp, one of the sharpest leaders ever at Carolina, was catching a lot of flak. This particular time may have been one of the worst in his life. On the day of the presentation, my administrative assistant Cheryl told me that Chancellor Thorp was on the phone for me. I knew why. He was going to try to cancel. I decided I was not going to let him do that. I knew what it felt like to not want to show my face in public. When he told me he couldn't make it I said, "I want you to know a couple of things. First of all, you are still the chancellor of this great university and *you* have done nothing wrong. Second, you promised me you'd be there and you need to be there." In the end he agreed to come. I spoke to Chancellor Thorp that way because I knew what he was feeling—I had been there. The intense, unrelenting public scrutiny had pushed at him until he wanted to turn inward and just hide away. It's a terrible feeling.

That night I was so happy to be sitting there on stage with all my wonderful friends in the audience. In my introduction, I said, "Here on stage with me is one of the finest men I know, Chancellor Holden Thorp." The audience gave him a standing ovation. I know it lifted his spirits at a time when he felt utter despair and just wanted to hide. When someone is going through something like this they need to be reminded that everything will be okay and they are not a bad person, no matter what is happening, and that people make mistakes. This outstanding, gracious man thanked me for inviting him and pressing him to attend. His wife also thanked me and told me he had been in a terrible state earlier that day. I felt proud of so many things that night, especially that Chancellor Thorp could be with us.

18

A Few of My Favorite Things

Saving the New River

I've mentioned that I grew up on South Fork of the New River, arguably one of the most beautiful places in this state, this country and maybe even on the whole planet. The New River is one of the oldest rivers in North America and among the oldest on earth, and distinctively runs from south to north. Our farm was bordered on one side by the south fork of this river. Its water grew our cabbages, tobacco and corn. We swam in it, fished in it, and it sustained our livestock. The New River sustained us for generations. It flows north from Western North Carolina.

In June 1968 Appalachian Power Company proposed a project that would have dammed the New River, drowning over 42,000 acres of land in Western North Carolina and Virginia, removing in excess of 27,000 people from their homes. Eight hundred and ninety-three dwellings would have been submerged, along with thirty summer cabins, thirty-three commercial and industrial facilities, fifteen churches, five post offices, twelve known cemeteries (and scores of poorly marked ancient burial grounds). Livestock and crop losses were estimated in excess of $13 million annually, and that was in 1973 dollars. This proposal was called different variations of "The Blue Ridge Project," and it would have allowed Appalachian Power to produce more electricity, most of it going to people well outside the immediate area.

In the fall of 1973, Senator Ervin and Congressman Wilmer "Vinegar Ben" Mizell each introduced a bill providing for the United States Department of the Interior to conduct a study on the New River to see if it could receive Wild and Scenic River status. This referred back to a 1968 law, the Wild and Scenic Rivers Act, which required studies of these rivers preceding any decision to develop things like hydroelectric power plants.

I was with Senator Ervin when he, together with Senator Jesse Helms, showing important bipartisan support for the protection of the New River, once again introduced a bill to the United States Congress to begin a study to see if the New River qualified as a Wild and Scenic River. This study would take a few years and buy some time for the New River. This resulted in a stalemate broken by Governor Holshouser when he convinced the United States Secretary of the Interior to back North Carolina in delaying the building of the dam. At the hearing where the full United States Senate debated the issue, Senator Ervin argued, among other things, that the Appalachian Power project would simply destroy the New River. Virginia Senators Harry F. Byrd and William L. Scott said the bill was just an attempt to stop a project that would benefit Virginia far more than it would North Carolina. They said the decision should be left to the Federal Power Commission. They noted that only twenty-four miles of this "stream" lay in North Carolina, with 254 miles lying in Virginia

and West Virginia. They also said that ordering the study would be an abuse of the
national Wild and Scenic Rivers law, and that
at a time when the American people were
concerned about energy, nothing should be
done to prevent the construction of a large
power plant that would provide needed electricity to many areas.

Nevertheless, in early March 1976 the
New River was designated a National Wild
and Scenic River. A lot of people worked hard
to make this happen. Senator Ervin and I
were there at the national level in the beginning, and Senator Helms joined us later and
remained a loyal supporter.

The day finally came for the United
States Secretary of the Interior to sign the
designation that made over twenty-six miles
of the New River a scenic waterway. I, as
attorney general of North Carolina, waited
all day long in his outer offices to remind him

This button relates to the most important thing
Rufus did for the planet—his successful campaign, waged with bipartisan colleagues, to save
the New River, the second oldest river in the
United States, from being dammed by a power
company. Jesse Helms was a key player in the
success of this campaign.

that we were waiting and expected him to be as good as his word. He signed it and also
told us that President Ford supported our efforts to save the New River. Governor Holshouser and I testified against the Appalachian Power plan to dam the river at the May 6,
1976, hearing on bill H.R. 13374, which recognized as a national scenic river "that segment
of the New River in North Carolina extending from its confluence with Dog Creek down-
stream approximately 26.5 miles to the Virginia State Line." This bill also prohibited anything like the dam from being built on or near the New River.

I was and still am so proud of my fellow North Carolinians for helping to make this
happen, and being part of this effort is one of the shining achievements of my life. The
New River is part of my home, and my home is the biggest part of my heart.

If Appalachian Power had damned up the New River, hundreds of acres of this lovely,
loamy-soiled, historic river valley would have been drowned. It meant so much to me and
to so many others that loved the river.

The Super Kids Foundation

One day in 1993 I was sitting in my big, beautiful office in the mundane Legislative
Office Building when my secretary said, "You have a phone call from Johnny Shepherd." I
would never have dreamed that this call would be the beginning of the Super Kids Foundation, the cause that is and will always be closest to my heart.

When I am asked what charitable effort I find most satisfying I say, "It is the Super
Kids program." We identify kids who have experienced hardship and overcome tremendous
obstacles in their lives and help them succeed in school by offering them scholarships and
other help. We give these young people an opportunity to attend college when otherwise
they might never have gotten the chance to go. There is an undefinable quality in some
children that makes them strive to achieve and overcome obstacles, sometimes in the worst

circumstances. We try to recognize this quality, and help these hardworking children find success and pursue their dreams.

Johnny Shepherd, the principal of an elementary school in Kinston, North Carolina, had called one day to tell me that his kids would not be coming for their scheduled tour of my office that day even though they were all loaded up in the buses. Unfortunately, they had just discovered that all of the money they needed for the trip, bus fare, lunch money, and all, had been stolen.

He said, "It is such a shame. This trip was supposed to be a reward for these kids who had a rough start but have worked hard and become great students and good people. You know our school is in a poor neighborhood, and these kids don't start out with a lot. But they have all done extraordinary things, like finding a ten-dollar bill in the hall and turning in it to the principal or giving up their own lunch money so that a another hungry child could eat." I said, "Well Johnny, as for the ten dollar bill, I am impressed! I'm not sure I would have done that when I was a kid." Johnny told me he called this outstanding group of children the Extra Special Super Kids.

My dear friend George McCotter and James "Bonecrusher" Smith were with me that day for some reason, and I said, "If you two can come up with a hundred dollars apiece, I can pitch in two hundred dollars." Well, George came through with the whole $400 dollars. I called Johnny and said "Can you get the kids together again tomorrow? There will be a fella coming down there this afternoon with the money you need plus some extra. His name is Galen Newsom." Then I called Galen, explained the situation and said, "When you

With Super Kids executive director and board member Tara Britt, left, and outstanding program participant Ashley Crosby, a UNC graduate who is now enrolled at the medical school. Ashley's brother Lawrence Crosby was also a Super Kid, did his undergraduate work at Stanford Unversity and earned a PhD in materials science and engineering from Northwestern University.

get down to Kinston, have Johnny send you back the full names of all the kids, I want to do something special for them." There was a lady in my office who was good with calligraphy and I asked her to work up "Honorary Secretary of State" certificates for each kid, all bedecked with ribbons and seals.

When the children arrived I met them at the Capitol and we did a little practice exercise, then formally awarded them the certificates. They loved it, and looking at those children, many of them in worn hand-me-downs but every one of them clean and pressed and well-behaved, I saw what Johnny saw in them. I thought what Johnny was doing was great—inspiring, really—and that is why I decided to go statewide with his idea, and that is how the Superkids began.

A number of old, dear friends helped me create Super Kids. As mentioned earlier, my birthday bashes eventually turned into fund-raisers for this foundation. We continued this even after I left public office. My birthday party was the perfect way to keep up with old friends and make new friends—and it was the perfect way to raise money for the Superkids.

Over the twenty-three-year period we have been up and running we have had thirty-three college graduates, some from community colleges, some from state universities, and some from more prestigious private schools. We have a dentist, a pharmacist, and now a student in medical school at the University of North Carolina at Chapel Hill. It never ceases to amaze me what children from challenging backgrounds can do with just a little help and a pat on the back.

Past Executive Director Lloyd Hunter was by my side from the beginning. I met Lloyd when I was attorney general. We have had a wonderful board of directors from day one, people I care about who I know care about kids. Roddy Jones, from a prominent family that has built many of the buildings that make the city of Raleigh great, Crockett Long, Jerry McLaurin, Sarah Belk Gambrell, Frank Douglas, Keith Whitfield, Dick Carlton, Newton Fowler, and others over the years. These generous and enduring friends have played such a pivotal role in keeping the Super Kids Foundation alive. Friends on the board like Shelley Castleberry, Louis Dworsky, Melissa Essick, Fred Mills, George Parrott, Donna More, Casey Lovas, Michael Steele, Sr., and my law partner, William W. "Woody" Webb, keep the aspirations of these deserving children afloat. Our present executive director, Tara Britt, our executive vice president, the fantastic attorney Anna Smith Felts, and Cheryl Mattingly, our secretary and treasurer, have all made the foundation successful. In addition to the board members, supporters like Melissa Fender mean the world to me.

And then there is our long-serving executive director, Lloyd Hunter, who only recently retired. He has been the wellspring and the guiding light of our foundation, with tough love and genuine affection for every single Super Kid. He may have been known sometimes known as "Stern Lloyd" but the kids knew Mr. Hunter was a good man who cared about them. Lloyd has been a tremendous steward for the foundation and nurtured many kids through the program. Tara Britt assumed his role. I know that she, like Lloyd, will support my wishes and keep Super Kids going long after my death.

NC Spin

Some years ago, I was approached by my longtime friend Tom Campbell, who is well known in broadcast circles and is a member of the Broadcast Hall of Fame. Tom is a brilliant man with whom I travelled on various industry-recruiting missions when he was deputy treasurer to Harlan Boyles. I always thought Tom would have made a wonderful treasurer but he would often say, "I don't think I am willing to take all the abuse of running for public office." Wise man.

Tom said to me, "I am going to try to form a company that will produce a thirty-minute current events talk show. It's going to be called *NC Spin*. I would like for you to be a panelist on the show." Of course my love of North Carolina politics merged with my love of having a camera pointed at me and I was in! I said "Great! Just tell me when."

The show is the longest running television and radio statewide talk show in North Carolina history. The idea of the show arose when Tom and John Hood, the CEO of the John Locke Foundation, were talking one day and decided it would be a good idea. I was on the first show, which aired in September 1998. We still enjoy our relationship with UNC Television. Tom and the cast of characters feel this is a great fit. I like to try to make people laugh, and Tom has also pointed out that I can be "a little windy in the process" so that he has learned how to speed me up, or if that fails, to cut me off. That's show business!

Tom tries to stick to what he calls "Journalism 101—the who, what, when, where, why and how." His aim is return to in-depth discussions with those who have historical knowledge of North Carolina history and politics and get away from what Tom terms "gotcha" reporting. He also thinks that many people are tired of "sound bite" television news that flashes on and off, shocks or soothes with a "feel-good" story, but doesn't provoke thought or enhance understanding of the issues of the day. We don't have twenty-four-hour cable-style screaming matches, either, in which the objective seems to be who can be the loudest and the rudest. We just try to present all the sides of a given issue that we can. Different perspectives help people learn where they truly stand. Tom loves when people tell him they can't tell what side he's on because he is aiming to present an unbiased view. The motto of the show is "Balanced debate for the Old North State."

The North Carolina State Fair

From when I first became attorney general in 1974 one of the high points of my year has been attending the North Carolina State Fair. The livestock reminds me of growing up, and the Village of Yesteryear brings my childhood memories back to life. I think one reason why I loved it so much when I first lived in Raleigh is because I found so many people from Watauga County there! There was Mrs. Trivett, the fantastic quilter, who always said, "Honey, I'm so glad you came"; a Cherokee craftsman I'd met through Senator Ervin; James Moretz, a knife craftsman who lived down the road from our house on the river; and others who attended the Three Forks Baptist Church with me. Then there was the inimitable Willard Watson, one of the truest characters ever to be born in the mountains of North Carolina, and a cousin to musician Doc Watson. He was truly one of a kind. Willard wore a hat that was something like a cowboy hat crossed with a stovepipe hat. He had beady eyes so dark brown they looked black. Willard was one of those people who named you whatever he wanted to name you. I knew he was as aware of my name as he was of his own, but as soon as he saw me he said, "Here comes Walt's boy Luke!" Then he started in on the stories, wild tales I might have heard ten times before that got better every single time he told them. As I noted earlier, my daddy was featured in many a chase story where Willard usually outsmarted the "possum sheriff." One time I reminded Willard that Daddy had once caught him in his own hen house. Willard winked and said, "Maybe I was layin' eggs." While he's always a lot of fun, Willard and his wife, Ora Watson, were respected and accomplished traditional mountain artists, and famous for their crafts. Ora's quilts could not be beat and Willard cut a neat tune on a banjo when he wasn't telling tales. He also carved fascinating items mountaineers called geehaw whimmy diddles. These are wooden sticks about eight inches long and about a half an inch thick carved with notches. When the notches on the stick with a propeller on the end are struck with another stick the propeller spins to the right (gee in mountain language) or to the left (haw in mountain speak). These terms came from the directions mountain farmers would use to direct their horses.

Once I went to see Willard and Ora and Willard said "Oray, go get that pitcher of when we went to Arizoney that time." Ora came back with a postcard of a desert scene and told me, "This was where they faked the moon landing." Willard and Ora are gone now, but they will always be remembered as the gems of mountain culture that they were. I miss Willard and Ora Watson to this day.

The Wake County Chitlin Club

> Chitterling—(sometimes spelled/pronounced chitlins or chitlings) is an economical dish, usually made from the small intestines of a pig.
> —Frank Stephenson, Jr., *105 Handy Uses for Chitlins*

One of the most *distinctive* honors I have ever had in my life was being elected head of the Wake County Chitlin Club. This club has a storied history. Long ago, Governor Kerr Scott, always known for championing the common man and not well versed in the ways of high society, decided that good ol' Raleigh boys needed to have a club where they could get together, tell jokes, and enrich their culinary experience by eating chitlins. For those of you of gentle birth, the chitlin is a southern delicacy prepared from hog guts. It is an unjustly maligned food which merely requires a trained palate and an appreciation of southern culture. Fancy people in Scotland have a similar dish called haggis, which is also made of parts of an animal widely regarded as offal, but the animal in the case of haggis is a sheep. The Scots must share our southern practice of using everything and not throwing away part of the animal, including the guts. Which reminds me—no matter how you decide to prepare them, you must get chitlins perfectly clean. Occasionally gentle souls, upon discovering a grain of corn in a chitlin' dish, have been known to develop the vapors.

One of the anchors of the club was G. Wesley Williams, a true gem and a perfect southern gentleman. He is presently director of the Chitlin Investigative Agency, or CIA, as we call it. One of the cherished responsibilities of club members is the ritual shaming of any members who flaunt high culture. There are certainly extenuating circumstances, or subtle nuances that affect the rules. For example, a member might attend his daughter's ballet recital without rebuke, but if he is caught in a smoking jacket eating caviar and we get wind of it, he will be summoned before the Chitlin High Tribunal. As director, Wesley Williams's duty was to keep an eagle eye on the public social activities of Chitlin Club members so that he might identify any who flaunt high culture and haul them before the Tribunal. The Tribunal is made up of members with years of experience and finely honed interrogation skills. Nevertheless, it is not unusual to find Tribunal interrogators in the hot seat, felled by their own lapse into social pretense. Damning evidence often features photos of the offenders in tuxedos as well as eyewitness or media accounts of such egregious things as reciting Shakespeare in public.

My introduction to the Wake County Chitlin Club was by invitation when I was attorney general. (You have to be invited to join the club. The two most important rules are that you don't flaunt high culture, and you never disparage chitlins.) I had never had a chitlin in my life. All around me were pillars of society—some of the most accomplished men of the county—judges, doctors, legislators, lawyers and other highfalutin people. Everyone stared at me as I stared at the contents of the pot. I took a bite, to great applause. Beside me was my long-time sidekick, SBI agent Harry Knight, who once told me he had eaten so many chitlins in his life he was sometimes known to oink in his sleep. Harry cleaned his own plate as I picked at mine. As the meeting went on, I began to feel a little queasy. Under cover

In 2017 with Wesley Williams, right, long-time head of the Raleigh Merchants Bureau, the Raleigh Good Old Boy's Club, and most importantly, tsar of the Chitlin Investigative Agency (CIA), whose job was to ferret out those members of the club who might disparage chitlins or flaunt high society ways. At that time Wesley was 97; he died two years later.

of the spirited proceedings, I whispered to Harry, "Why don't you switch plates with me?" Harry said he'd be pleased to and switched his empty plate with my nearly full one. All the other members saw was me beaming over my empty plate. Or so I thought.

Once I had been busted down and hauled before the tribunal for the egregious violation of being photographed at a highbrow social event wearing a tuxedo and holding a martini glass with my pinkie out. (It wasn't me, I protested! I was framed, I cried!) While being interrogated someone ratted me out for sliding my chitlins over to Harry instead of into my gizzard for years. All I could do was throw myself on the mercy of the tribunal and beg for mercy. I remember when former Governor Kerr Scott was brought before the tribunal. He also received probation. At the same time I was tried, Governor Bob Scott was also tried. Our trial was held at Green's Garner Grill in Garner, North Carolina, just down the road from the Toot and Tell Restaurant, our current meeting location.

Ninety-eight years old at this writing, Wesley Williams is wise and wonderful, and definitely one of the funniest people I have known. Wesley deserves a whole book of his own. He was born on a farm in Wake County near Poole and Rock Quarry roads, which he remembers as "eighty-five beautiful acres." His family lost everything during the Great Depression. Wesley went on to prosper and to do many good things for Wake County. He helped desegregate Raleigh restaurants in 1963. He is responsible for persuading the city to build its first parking garage, and has organized the Raleigh Christmas parade for many years. All this from a man who recalls that he knew Raleigh when it was little more than a cow pasture. He is the head of the Raleigh Good Ol' Boys Club that meets once a week at the Carolina Country Club, and is "justifiably proud of his seventy years of working with myriad merchants organizations and civic groups in Raleigh" as Raleigh *News and Observer* columnist Barry Saunders put it. One of these groups is the Raleigh Merchants Association. Wesley's work has contributed to building some of the best parts of the Raleigh we know today.

In addition to protecting our members from high culture and chitlins from culinary insults, we often shared recipes with one another. Chitlin Tetrazzini is one example. Then there is Chitlin Parmesan, Chitlin Coq Au Vin, and Chitlin Alfredo. We of the Wake County Chitlin Club are dedicated to both preserving our beloved dishes past, and keeping our chitlins up with current culinary trends.

The North Carolina Advisory Council on Rare Diseases

My friend Tara Britt was working in gene therapy at UNC when she met Sharon King from Charlotte. Sharon's lovely little daughter Taylor had been stricken at the age of seven years by the rare and fatal infantile Batten disease, and this experience moved Sharon to become an advocate for people with rare diseases. On March 25, 2015, Tara and Sharon coordinated a legislative briefing breakfast for proposed legislation to study rare diseases in North Carolina. Tara had talked to me about this idea, and I of course was interested in becoming a member of the council because of my life-changing experience with Guillain-Barré syndrome.

Sharon's local representative, Becky Carney, attended the breakfast, along with Senator Louis Pate and others. Together they created the legislation, passed in August 2015, supporting the creation of the North Carolina Advisory Council on Rare Diseases which was later named Taylor's Law in honor of Sharon King's daughter.

Dr. Bruce Cairns, the director of the Jaycee Burn Center at UNC, chairs the council and under his tutelage the rare disease initiative continues to grow. Dr. Cairns and Dr. Michael Knowles work together to provide clinical leadership. Their dedication and support of the rare disease initiative is unsurpassable.

The Preservation North Carolina and the Ruth Coltrane Cannon Cup

This award holds a special place in my heart because it was presented to me and my wife, Linda.

Throughout my job as attorney general and a member of the council of state, I regularly questioned the state about tearing down buildings of historic value. I had always had an interest in history and historic preservation. When I met Linda, who was then preservation planner for the City of Raleigh, I became even more involved. I remember one year while we were courting, we attended meetings of the Committee to Preserve Estey Hall, the oldest surviving building at historic Shaw University in Raleigh—the first African American college in the United States with a four-year medical school. The illustrious Dr. George Debnam led the meetings, which were held at 7 a.m. Even back then Linda knew I liked to work in my garden early in the morning, so I thought I could get some courtship "brownie points" by attending those meetings.

In 2012 Linda and I received the coveted Ruth Coltrane Cannon Cup. This is the highest award presented by the nationally known Preservation North Carolina, the outstanding preservation organization headed by Myrick Howard that has done a world of good across the state in protecting our historical gems. I was particularly proud of this because we were one of the few couples to receive this award. Having held several preservation jobs in her career and having volunteered many hours to the cause, Linda did the lion's share of the work, but I was happy they let me tag along and receive the award with her. I had suspected she would get the award, but when they called my name, too, I was touched and honored. Linda has been a great inspiration, and over our years together we have remained active in the preservation community.

The Henry Clay Oak Award

The Henry Clay Oak Award was created in 2014 when the lieutenant governor of North Carolina, Dan Forrest, and his staff wanted to honor Henry Clay, for whom a magnificent oak tree that had stood near the northeast corner of North and Blount streets in Raleigh. (The tree became diseased and had to be taken down in 1991.) This tree was famous because it is said that 1844 presidential candidate Henry Clay sat under it when he wrote his famous "Raleigh Letter." In this letter, and in an election year in which he was running for president of the United States, Clay opposed a popular proposal to annex Texas to the United States without the consent of Mexico because he knew that this would mean war with Mexico. Standing by his principles probably cost Clay his third and final run for president. He said in his letter, "I'd rather be right than be president," and whether or not he was right he didn't get to be president. Known as the Great Compromiser, Clay had often reached across the aisle throughout his career to bring about peace between warring political factions, which is what I have liked to do when I have the opportunity.

The founders wanted to establish an award called the Order of Henry Clay Oak to honor those who have done the most to create harmony and understanding between political parties and reach over to the other side of the aisle and build bridges for understanding. This award means a lot to me.

The Order of the Long Leaf Pine

I have received this award three times: twice from Governor James B. Hunt, Jr., (1984, 1995) and once from Governor Beverly Perdue (2012). This award is given to those who have been of exemplary service to the state or to their communities, above and beyond the call of duty. I'm grateful to have been recognized in this way and appreciative of all who are responsible

The Nellie Mae Daylily

One hot, humid summer day I received a cell phone call from my friend and host of *Weekend Gardner* on WPTF, Mike Raley. "You won!" he cried. I replied, "Won what?" "You won a blue ribbon and an additional major award for your Daylily," he announced. I thought Mike was kidding. You could have heard me yelling with joy probably all the way to my hometown of Boone. I had rarely been as excited as I was at the news of this award, and with the help of lots of wonderful folks, I have won a few in my life time.

Here is the back story: Early in the morning before the *Weekend Gardner* show, almost as an afterthought, I cut my favorite daylily, a gorgeous orange double bloom with the intention of asking Anne Clapp to help me identify its proper name, if it even had one. This special daylily is one I had harvested from my dear mother's garden some thirty years ago. Yes, I have always been a mama's boy.

We were broadcasting that day at the Crabtree Valley Shopping Mall where the Raleigh Hemerocallis Club was holding its annual daylily show. Our booth was right next to the judging area where all the daylily enthusiasts were busy like bees doing all kinds of maneuvers and tricks of the trade to put their entry in the best possible light. I was fascinated to watch the scurrying around and the TLC they exhibited toward their potential prize-winning babies.

One of the organizers of the show, Dr. Linda Sue Barnes, came over to the radio table and I made inquiry of her about the Nellie Mae (my mama's name) daylily. She told me she thought it was a daylily called *Flore Pleno*, smiled at me and said, "Why don't we just enter your mama's daylily in the show?" I thought, oh, why not? It can't hurt. Dr. Barnes took my Nellie Mae daylily, put it in the proper show container, and placed it among the other entrants. I continued with the show and thought nothing more about my first foray into the flower show business.

After we wound up the show, I bought five daylily species from show official Steve Edwards, and headed home to plant them. I never dreamed I would get that 3 p.m. call from Mike. The next morning, Dr. Barnes called my office with official news of the award, and later that day my friend, Donna Shields, the first female police officer in Zebulon, came by the office with the official ribbons. It just goes to show you that fate and the little things in life make a difference and create joy.

Education Partnership Award

In 2012 the school board in my home county of Watauga rewarded me for supporting them over the years by giving me their Education Partnership Award. It was wonderful to be recognized for doing something good for the kids in my home county.

The Boxing Hall of Fame Award

In the spring of 2017 I was inducted into the Carolinas Boxing Hall of Fame! As hard as this may be to believe, it was not for my prowess in the ring. This fine group of people honored me for work I did many years ago with the help of my friends Mike Bivens, Bill Clancy, Bill McInnis and former heavyweight champion James "Bonecrusher" Smith. Together we lobbied the legislature to form the first North Carolina Boxing Commission in 1996. Our mission was to protect boxers and promote public confidence in the industry by making sure provisions for safety and fairness are followed. We created regulations requiring a contract spelling out the terms of an event, such as compensation for the boxers, licensing requirements for managers, weight restrictions, and rules regarding promoters. We also wanted to be sure that only healthy and capable people were recruited for fights.

The commission defined the terms "amateur" and "professional," restricted unlicensed people from participating in organizing boxing matches, required medical examination of boxers prior to matches, and allowed for both civil and criminal penalties for those who broke the rules. I'm thankful for this award and to my friends for helping me create a safer and fair environment for the boxing industry. Not to mention, the awards party was fantastic. We had so much fun. To top it off I received a giant bejeweled gentleman's ring replete with a golden boxing glove, the name of the award, my name and the year. This ring has caused some people to say to me, "I didn't know you played in the NFL." I admit to enjoying a short pause before I disabuse them of the notion.

The Mule Skinner Award

For years I was a judge at the time-honored Mule Days Parade and Festival in Benson, North Carolina. Recently, I was honored with the coveted Mule Skinner Award. When my Carolina classmates got wind of this, although understandably envious, they were kind enough to make sure this prestigious award was featured in the alumni magazine listed along with the accomplishments of my peers—who were honored for less glamorous achievements such as discovering new planets or being elected to the board of the New York Metropolitan Museum of Art.

I later discovered that one of my "friends" who had graciously opted to remain anonymous had submitted the award for inclusion in the magazine. It was a pretty good joke, and it still makes me laugh.

With former Governor James Martin, right, and his wife, Dottie, at a Capitol Society gala. I always respected him a great deal even though be beat me in the governor's race.

At the Grand Ole Opry with veteran Las Vegas performer Wayne Newton.

With Michael Jordan at a Carolina Mudcats game when he played for the Birmingham Barons. I was secretary of state at the time.

With Madeleine Albright, secretary of state under President Clinton, at the dedication of the Clinton library.

A 1999 party in the famous Senate Caucus Room on the twentieth anniversary of the Watergate break-in. With Senators Jesse Helms, left, and Strom Thurmond, center (courtesy Nick Crettier).

With my wife Linda and President Jimmy Carter at Elon College, where he was honored for his work with Habitat for Humanity.

With Senator Ted Kennedy.

In the early 1990s I hosted the association of secretaries of state at the Flat Rock Playhouse (the State Theater of North Carolina) and got the chance to meet Burt Reynolds.

P6

When I was a member of the North Carolina Film Commission I enjoyed a few lively discussions with the funny and talented Whoopi Goldberg.

With news anchor Connie Chung.

With the late, great North Carolina Commissioner of Agriculture Jim Graham, center, and the legendary former Secretary of State Thad Eure, right.

With President Bill Clinton.

As a frequent visitor at the Grand Ole Opry during my early years as secretary of state, I had the opportunity to meet comedian Bob Hope.

19

Thoughts on a Life Fully Lived

My Uncle Abe Edmisten was a Democratic sheriff. My Uncle Bynum and Uncle John were fierce Republicans. There were hard-fought battles but everybody forgot all about them after the elections. Daddy joked that Republicans were scallywags. I was accustomed to having Republicans around, and noticed that other than at election time, there did not seem to be much difference in the way people thought. At church, half the congregation was Republican and half were Democrat, but we didn't become grim over the beliefs of others or go into a morbid trance and envision the end of the world if the other side won an election.

There was nothing remotely like the vicious, personal attacks we see now under the name "politics." There were no vituperative radio or television shows, and of course we didn't have the primary tool with which people now savage one another: the Internet. Heaven knows the newspapers got nasty enough but even they knew where to draw the line between decency and needless savagery. Politics have become deeply personal. Your party defines not only what your thoughts are on policies, but who and what you are, and apparently you aren't doing it right unless you're always at each other's throats. The idea of diverse groups compromising for the good of everyone has been lost in the rancor, and altruistic ideals have been lost as those in power try to run government as a business. This never works for a simple reason: a business is designed to make a profit, while politics is designed to bring order, and civility, and create the opportunity for an abundant life. A large part of governing is to learn how to listen effectively and often. Someone once said that politics is the art of humanizing people.

In 1988 when I became North Carolina Secretary of State, I served with the man who beat me in the gubernatorial election: Governor Jim Martin. I had wanted the governorship more than any political position I had ever wanted in my life. I got over it and had a wonderful relationship with Governor Martin. This might not happen in today's fractious environment. The rancor runs too deep and is too deeply personal. I have been shocked at how polarized North Carolina—and for that matter, the entire United States—has become. This is fueled by the media whose ratings rise the more outrageous their content becomes. Today if your beliefs are different from those of someone else, you are their enemy and they are yours. This was not always the case.

There are still those things we can agree upon. Imbalances of power have existed forever politically, but the pendulum always swings back. We have had tyrants that meant to rule (their way or highway). They come and they go and they come again. North Carolina will always change, and most of us will hope the changes are not too radical.

There was a time I call the golden age of politics in North Carolina. When we had Republicans like Senator Ham Horton of Winston-Salem, who was a great senator and not

201

afraid to say that he was an environmentalist. That golden age is gone now. So much of this factionalizing talk is simply a mechanism by which to hold on to power. That's the foremost aim of political power—once you get it, keep it. Politicians can get as greedy as Wall Street and think they have to have more and more power. All of this bothers me about my state but I can still happily sing James Taylor's "Carolina in My Mind" with pride. I'm not ashamed of a state that still has good basic instincts.

While change is the only constant in life, this particular change in the character and tone of discourse seems to be a symptom of a deeper problem in our society. This is not mine to diagnose, though I have my ideas.

The idea of reaching across the aisle to find common ground through compromise is one that is not only worthy of serious consideration today—it is the way out of the increasingly difficult impasse we have created by "standing our ground" and squaring off bitterly against one another. I've worked to find satisfying compromises my entire career, and I've seen a lot of others in public office do it too. Does anyone really want to be at war with their fellow citizens all the time? To hate their neighbor because his ideas are different from yours? Of course not.

We can begin to build a bridge to peaceful coexistence simply by listening. As my mama used to say, "You never know. They might have a point. If you're talking you're not listening." People are not out to get you with their politics, more often than not, they are afraid and trying to preserve something they hold dear or protect those they love. I don't know what the answer is to all this division and ugly strife, but I do know that listening to one another is a good place to start. And for goodness sake, people, *calm down.*

That said, I do think it is the minority extremists on both sides (and sometimes apparently way out in space) that make the most noise and the most trouble. For what it's worth, I still believe that an overwhelming majority of people in this country are kind, decent people who would stretch forth a saving hand if somebody really needed it, regardless of political party. I've seen it.

The need for empathy, kindness, and good will goes double for politicians. Public officials have to remember that their constituents are real people with real needs. When I was in public office I tried to cut through the red tape, delays, and bureaucratic nonsense that frustrates so many citizens and makes them feel like they have no voice in things and nobody to fight for them. I made sure that people who reached out for help got to talk to a live person. For decades it has too often been nearly impossible for people to reach a real person in government. It started with answering machines and has continued with automated telephone systems and their litany of numbers to press that lead to more impersonal recordings. Email and texting remove tone and important nuances from our daily communications and contribute to the depersonalization. Many government agencies put up websites where they appear to cover everything anybody needs to know just so they don't have to bother talking to anyone.

I just don't think this is why government or government servants are there. While it is true that plenty of people in government (and other occupations) are overworked and underpaid, we still need to be responsive to people who are in need. Sometimes just referring people to the right person to help them is all they need to get their problem solved.

I've also had many people go out of their way for me and am so grateful for other people's help. Especially in the down times of my life, I've had a lot given to me and I want and need to give back. We are put on earth to help one another. Folks in the mountains will sometimes ask companions, when climbing uphill, "Are you give out?" I try not to be "give out" when people need my help.

Empathy might come naturally to some but it can also be instilled by an upbringing that teaches you to always find the good in people. Most people are good, but nobody is perfect. People do make mistakes and get wrong-headed and sometimes even hard-hearted, but from all my experience in life, I truly believe that most people are decent. As for the other people, as my grandmother used to say, you can always *try* to find something good in everyone. Sometimes it is hard. Sometimes it is buried in a lightless corner of a hard little heart, but it is there.

I have had the opportunity to be around some of the finest people in the world and some who were not so fine and didn't treat me well. If I had gone through life burning bridges, I wouldn't have gotten very far. It seems to be so hard for some people to give others credit and to simply say, "Thank you." Second only to the pitfall of hubris is vanity, in that you fail to recognize that if you've done anything of significance anywhere, a heck of a lot of hands reached down to help you get where you are. It is a pitiful individual who never says, "Thank you." Some of us fail to do that often enough.

Even though I have stumbled myself, I've always tried to say "thank you." I do fear we are seeing a lot of children today who have been blanketed with such privilege and exposed to so little hardship that now they are fundamentally incapable of empathy or seeing the world through the eye of another. When one is living on Social Security benefits, $5 is a lot of money and for many kids, the question is not how wide your television screen is, and how many you have, it's whether or not you have anything to eat when you're hungry. I'm not as pessimistic as most people. There are a tremendous number of really, dedicated young people who truly care about the world they live in, and they warm my heart and give me hope for the future.

Another important part of day-to-day empathy is to be aware of how people feel when they fall on hard times or find themselves the target of public criticism. When someone I know gets caught up in a tough spot I like to call and remind him that he is still the same good person he was, and that this too shall pass. Even good people can make bad decisions and it is rarely the end of the world when they do so. A kind word can be like light in the darkness to those having hard times. A little empathy might help convince someone who is in pain that better days will come.

Index

Numbers in *bold italics* indicate pages with illustrations

205